How Armies Respond to Revolutions and Why

How Armies Respond to Revolutions and Why

Zoltan Barany

PRINCETON UNIVERSITY PRESS

PRINCETON AND OXFORD

Published by Princeton University Press, 41 William Street,
Princeton, New Jersey 08540
In the United Kingdom: Princeton University Press, 6 Oxford Street,
Woodstock, Oxfordshire OX20 1TW
press.princeton.edu

Cover photograph: Chinese man stands before a tank during a student-led
demonstration in Tiananmen Square, 1989. AP Photo / Jeff Widener

Library of Congress Cataloging-in-Publication Data

Names: Barany, Zoltan D., author.
Title: How armies respond to revolutions and why / Zoltan Barany.
Description: Princeton : Princeton University Press, 2016. | Includes
bibliographical references and index.
Identifiers: LCCN 2015035501 | ISBN 9780691157368 (hardback)
Subjects: LCSH: Military policy—Decision making—Case studies. | Revolutions—
History—21st century—Case studies. | World politics—1989– | Comparative
government. | BISAC: POLITICAL SCIENCE / Political Freedom & Security /
International Security. | POLITICAL SCIENCE / Government / Comparative.
| POLITICAL SCIENCE / Government / International. | POLITICAL SCIENCE /
International Relations / General. | POLITICAL SCIENCE / Civics & Citizenship.
Classification: LCC UA11 .B29 2016 | DDC 355.02/18—dc23 LC record
available at http://lccn.loc.gov/2015035501

British Library Cataloging-in-Publication Data is available

This book has been composed in Sabon LT Std

Printed on acid-free paper. ∞

Printed in the United States of America

1 3 5 7 9 10 8 6 4 2

Once again, for Patti

Contents

Tables

Acknowledgments

One of the many pleasures of writing a book is to arrive at the stage when one registers one's gratitude to those who made the intellectual journey—which started with an idea and ended with the submission of the final manuscript—more interesting, rewarding, and enjoyable. First and foremost, I want to thank Kurt Weyland, whose comments and criticisms were immensely helpful. We discussed the project at the beginning, as I prepared my response to the proposal reviews commissioned by Princeton University Press. About two-and-a-half years later, Kurt read the first draft and returned it with a six-page (single-spaced!) critique, complete with editorial markings. It is a privilege to have a colleague as smart and candid as Kurt, who is willing to seriously reflect on one's work. This time around, I was not going to ask my old friend Daniel Chirot to read another one of my manuscripts. Still, during a July 2014 family visit to the Chirots, I noticed that Dan was reading novels, something he seldom does when he is deeply engaged in writing projects. So I ventured to suggest that perhaps he might read my draft instead. He happily (it seemed) acquiesced and suggested several changes that improved the book. I also received splendid advice for tweaking the manuscript from two anonymous reviewers. I deeply appreciate their insights and criticisms; even those that contradicted each other prompted me to think things through again as I was revising the manuscript.

I am fortunate indeed that some of the world's foremost experts on my case study countries were kind enough to read critically the appropriate chapters: Mehran Kamrava (Iran), Andrew Selth and Min Zin (Burma), Andrew Scobell (China), Vladimir Tismaneanu (Romania), and Philippe Droz-Vincent and Yezid Sayigh (the Arab world). In addition, Valerie Bunce, Zsuzsa Csergő, F. Gregory Gause III, Jack Goldstone, Ellen Lust, Sidney Tarrow, and Harrison Wagner suggested ways to think about some of the key issues differently, tinker with the methodology, or reconsider the case selection. Kenneth Roberts inquired if I would share the manuscript in progress with his Spring 2014 graduate seminar on social movements at Cornell University. I agreed and asked for the participants' merciless comments in return. I don't know about the students, but I certainly benefited from this exchange, given their (and Ken's) valuable feedback. Thank you all!

I am happy to register my gratitude to those who made introductions, helped with interviews, invited me to give talks, spoke with me about their areas of expertise, and responded to queries: Denzil Abel, Holger Albrecht, Mansoor Al-Jamri, Omar Ahmad Alubaydli, Habib Azzabi, Matt Buehler, Val Bunce, Philippe Droz-Vincent, Badra Gaaloul, Greg Gause, Richard Hirschman, Hind Kabaj, Jack Kalpakian, Stanisław Koziej, Wolfram Lacher, Jack F. Matlock Jr., Nizar Messari, Min Zin, Jiři Pehe, Jeffrey Robinson, Stephan Roll, Abdallah Saaf, Sławomir Szczepański, Prokop Tomek, Werner von Scheven, and Jerzy Wiatr. As in my last book project, my friend Ian Murray helped me out whenever I asked him to activate his network of contacts. For a variety reasons, I should not or am not allowed to thank by name the many helpful Burmese, Iranian, and Arab-world experts, as well as the intelligence analysts in Washington, DC, and their colleagues at US embassies, whom I was fortunate to interview.

I am thankful also for the opportunities to present the argument and/ or specific case studies and for the many probing questions and comments I received from audiences at Al-Akhawayn University in Ifrane (Morocco), the Al-Urdun Al-Jadid Research Center in Amman, the American University in Cairo, Cornell University, the Danish Royal Defense College, Derasat in Bahrain, the Doha Institute in Qatar, ELIAMEP (the Hellenic Foundation for European and Foreign Policy) in Athens, the International Studies Association's annual meeting in Toronto, the University of Malaya in Kuala Lumpur, the National Defense University in Washington, DC, Paññāsāstra University of Cambodia in Phnom Penh, Queen's University in Ontario, Southern Methodist University, the University of Tunis, the US Naval War College, and the Yangon School of Political Science (Burma).

Chuck Myers, the editor of my two previous books with Princeton University Press, was an enthusiastic early supporter of this project as well. His successor, Eric Crahan, was a sure-handed pilot of the manuscript through the review and publication process, commissioned reports from expert referees, and was always available to discuss my concerns. In addition, he made a number of smart suggestions that improved the book. Working with him was a pleasure, as it was with other staff members at the Press.

My very excellent friends—Dan Fitzgerald, George Mulder, Doug Phelan, Randy Sarosdy, and Bill Swann—have been great company through many adventures and distractions. My daughter, Catherine, once cheekily speculated that what I did in the little house at the back of the yard was "listen to Bob Dylan and check soccer scores." I offer this volume as evidence that I occasionally engage in pursuits other than those (enormously worthwhile) activities. Finally, this book is dedicated to Patti Maclachlan, my wonderful wife of eighteen happy years, who has endured—mostly patiently—my travels, odd work schedule, and absentmindedness. She understands the importance of knowing people, places, cultures, and histories for social scientists.

How Armies Respond to Revolutions and Why

Introduction

President Barack Obama's censure of the US intelligence community for its failure to foresee the spreading unrest in the Arab world sparked this book. Obama voiced his displeasure that analysts misjudged the Tunisian military's actions and the speedy collapse of President Zine el-Abidine Ben Ali's regime in early 2011.[1] A sitting president's public criticism of America's spy agencies is a rare event, and it caught my attention. I started to read whatever I could find on Tunisian politics and military affairs and came to the conclusion that Obama was right. For a number of reasons it seemed quite likely that the Tunisian army would not come to Ben Ali's rescue. For starters, he was an astonishingly corrupt and widely detested dictator who marginalized the army while showering funds and privileges on the interior ministry troops instead. The Tunisian military's highly cohesive officer corps had no history of political involvement. The demonstrations they were asked to suppress were large, peaceful, and representative of all Tunisian society, which, given that the armed forces' manpower was based on mandatory conscription, was where the soldiers came from. In light of these and other factors, then, it did not seem all that surprising that Tunisian commanders decided to protect rather than shoot the protesters and, consequently, precipitated Ben Ali's exit from the country.

To be sure, virtually all experts were surprised by the Arab uprisings even though, as two prominent journalists argued a year later, "There is much to suggest that the Arab Spring should have been predictable."[2] Prior to the upheavals many observers believed that these regimes were so well entrenched and their armed forces so dedicated that, as one expert put it slightly over a decade before the revolts, "Even the most professional militaries of the region would not hesitate to intervene in politics to try to maintain the status quo."[3] In the winter of 2012–13, I visited Washington to meet with a number of intelligence analysts specializing in the Arab world to find out what went wrong.[4] Not surprisingly, they were all fluent Arabic speakers and extraordinarily knowledgeable both about the countries of their specialization and about the Middle East and North Africa more generally. One thing several of them said that struck me was that while they were well aware of the underlying political and socioeconomic problems in the region—"Egypt was on the verge of revolution," a recent analysis contends, "as it had been for as long as modern history had been recorded"[5]—they were less appreciative of just how close to the surface societal dissatisfaction was simmering. But most revelatory was the admission of a veteran Middle East specialist who told me, "We kept asking the wrong question, which was 'Why now?' when the question we should have asked all along was 'What's taking so long?'"

As I watched the subsequent revolts of the "Arab Spring" unfold, I could not help noticing the armed forces' pivotal role. The military's stance, certainly at first glance, seemed to be the key to many of the puzzles regarding the uprisings. Why were the demonstrators at Cairo's Tahrir Square ultimately more successful than their counterparts at Manama's Pearl Roundabout? Why were the young rebels able to oust Ben Ali so swiftly, while the Syrian opposition failed to do more than loosen Bashar al-Assad's grip on the reins of power? The results of these upheavals, more often than not, hinged on each military's reaction to them. But how could one explain the behavior of the troops themselves and their varying responses to the revolts? Why did soldiers in Tunisia and Egypt back the uprising that culminated in the fall of Ben Ali's regime and the overthrow of Mubarak? Conversely, why did the troops in Bahrain support the state and turn against the demonstrators? And why did the divisions within the armed forces in Libya and Yemen result in civil wars?

The military, the institution that, by definition, plays a critical role in revolutions, frequently does not receive sufficient attention from experts. In the case of the recent Arab revolts, the academic community seems to have assumed that the generals would stand by the authoritarian regimes in a potential upheaval because during the preceding decades they had regularly confirmed their loyalties—which, to be sure, were seldom tested.[6] Few scholars studied the Arab armies, and no one, to my knowledge, speculated in writing about their generals' probable responses to mass demonstrations because few experts believed that mass protests were likely to occur. For two decades prior to 2011, I had taught comparative military politics, but my colleagues studying the Arab world were unable to assist me when I asked for their recommendations for up-to-date readings to assign my students: "You are asking for what does not exist," as Robert Springborg, one of the most knowledgeable American experts on the Egyptian military told me.[7] The reason certainly was not ignorance of the literature; they could not help me because, as a recent article concluded, the Arab armed forces were an issue that had

> received inadequate scholarly attention in recent years, and the (very few) available works on this topic are only rarely informed by significant

theoretical and comparative advances in the study of the security sector in general and the military in particular.[8]

The Arab armies were difficult to study given that the entire Arab world was composed of authoritarian states that did their best to control information and shroud their security sectors in secrecy. Learning about the armies of other repressive regimes—such as those of the communist states during the Cold War—was similarly challenging owing to the lack of transparency in their public affairs.

Lest we be unduly critical of scholars and intelligence analysts focusing on the Arab world, it is useful to remind ourselves that their inability to foresee the Arab Spring was hardly unique. Iran's Islamic revolution in 1979 and the collapse of communism in Eastern Europe a decade later equally confounded area studies experts and spy agencies in the United States and abroad.[9] The failure to foresee the fall of East European regimes like so many dominoes is particularly perplexing considering the extensive resources devoted to studying them. Researchers scrutinizing communist regimes perfectly well understood their profound economic vulnerability, their lack of legitimacy, and the corruptness of their political elites, yet they did not anticipate their downfalls. I worked at an American research institute at the end of the Cold War in Munich, West Germany, and I will not forget my colleague, a noted expert on Romania, who, in early December 1989, publicly contended that Romania was different from the other states of the region and Nicolae Ceaușescu's regime was in no serious danger. (Within three weeks Romanian communism, along with Ceaușescu, was dead.)

Why do the vast majority of experts time and time again miss the warning signs of coming mass uprisings and fail to forecast these momentous events?[10] Rebellions nearly always overthrow authoritarian regimes of one hue or another. Two defining characteristics of modern autocracies are directly relevant here. First, they suppress information, particularly information regarding political and socioeconomic matters they consider sensitive. Second, they tend to be relatively stable and propped up by a coercive apparatus whose main function is regime preservation. Studying these regimes presents special obstacles to researchers, owing to the dearth of reliable information and the ostensible political stagnation that, at times, obscure noteworthy changes underneath the surface. Therefore, many experts focus on explaining the reasons for the persistence of authoritarian rule rather than the challenges—however modest they may be—to it. Another reason is that in most institutional environments questioning the conventional wisdom—in our case, the stability and durability of this or that authoritarian regime—is seldom a good career move, and intelligence analysts tend to withstand the temptation to express whatever doubts they might entertain.[11] The ideological orientations of analysts might also be a contributing factor to their failure to recognize significant trends. For instance, the left-liberal political stance of many Soviet and East European affairs researchers "undermined their capacity to accept the view that economic statism, planning, socialist incentives, would not work."[12] Others have claimed that many analysts' excessive reliance on various social science methodologies, statistics, and pseudoscientific models caused them to "[lose] contact with the subject of their inquiries—the messy, contradictory, unpredictable *homo sapiens*."[13]

Revolutions and popular uprisings tend to surprise just about all of us.[14] After all, they "break out" and "erupt," not "develop" or "evolve." At the same time, politicians, policy makers, and foreign-, defense-, and security-policy elites are perfectly reasonable in expecting from analysts careful assessments of revolutionary environments, appraisals of the probable outcome of uprisings, and a range of potential alternative responses to the situation. Given the decisive role military establishments play in uprisings, the ability to understand and anticipate what an army is likely to do in a specific popular upheaval is invaluable. My hope is to offer a framework—that will permit us to intelligently and knowledgeably speculate about the generals' role in revolutions—as an improvement over the informal methods of forecasting on which researchers and policy makers have tended to base their judgments.

ARGUMENTS, DEFINITION, LITERATURE

What role does the state's coercive apparatus—more specifically, its regular armed forces—play in uprisings that threaten the regime? In other words, how do militaries react to revolutions and why? Under what circumstances do they remain loyal to the regime? When do they side with the rebels? What factors cause them to split their support and end up fighting one another? What compels them to sit on the fence and not take sides at all? What are the main concerns that influence the army's behavior? These questions are essential to the understanding of revolutions, and yet they are surprisingly under-studied. I seek to set forth a comprehensive explanation for these fundamental problems.

No institution matters more to a state's survival than its military, and no major uprising within a state can succeed without the support or at least the acquiescence of the armed forces. This is not to say that the army's backing is *sufficient* to make a successful revolution; indeed, revolutions require so many political, social, and economic forces to line up just right, and at just the right moment, that revolutions rarely succeed. But support from a preponderance of the armed forces is a *necessary* condition for revolutionary success.

I make two central arguments. The first is that *the response of the regime's regular armed forces to an uprising is critical to the success or failure of that uprising.* This is a contention that is by now largely, but not universally, accepted as one of the cardinal tenets of revolutions: they cannot succeed without the support of the regime's coercive apparatus, most particularly the regular army. Lenin remarked, "No revolution of the masses can triumph without the help of a portion of the armed forces that sustained the old regime."[15] The sociologist Stanislaw Andrzejewski was similarly categorical in his contention, "So long as the government retains the loyalty of the armed forces, no revolt can succeed."[16] There is no full consensus on this key point, though. Dissenters—prominent "practitioners" such as Mao Tse-tung and Che Guevara, and scholars like Eric Hobsbawm and C. Wright Mills—held that guerrilla bands "led by determined men, with peasants alongside them, and a mountain nearby, can defeat organized battalions of the tyrants equipped with everything up to the atom bomb."[17] I disagree with them for the reasons Diana Russell, Charles Tilly, James Rule, and others did: they advanced inconsistent and illogical arguments, ignored contradictory evidence (all), discounted outside powers (Hobsbawm), and were hampered by ideological bias (all): as Tilly noted, their theorizing was "remarkably weak."[18] Perhaps Katherine Chorley put it best: "No revolution will be won against a modern army when that army is *putting out its full strength* against the insurrection."[19] My contribution here is to offer additional evidence to confirm this contention.

Once we recognize that without the army's support uprisings cannot succeed, we must turn our attention to figuring out *how* and *why* militaries respond the way they do to popular upheavals challenging regime survival. The second major argument of this book, one that has not been made before, is that *we can make a highly educated guess about—and in some cases even confidently predict—the army's response to a revolution or popular uprising* if we have in-depth knowledge about a particular army, its relationship to state and society, and the external environment.

The crucial question is, then, what factors influence the military's stance in times of upheaval? Put differently, if the army is *not* "putting out its full strength against the insurrection," why is it not? In this book, I hope to convince the reader that familiarity with political and military elites, the armed forces, and some key information regarding the state, society, and the external environment will both help explain the military's behavior in response to past upheavals and anticipate its response to future revolutions. Once we are able to forecast the position of the armed forces vis-à-vis the revolutionary upheaval, we ought to be able to speculate with increased assurance about the likely fate of the revolution, as well.

I aim to explain a set of three possible principal outcomes in which the military either (1) supports the revolution, (2) opposes the rebellion, or (3) is divided, meaning that some parts of the armed forces support the uprising while others oppose it. As we will see, even when the army backs or suppresses an uprising, the entire organization seldom does so without the hesitation, disagreement, and occasionally, defection of some of its members. Therefore, I will also discuss how generals endeavor to minimize and root out various forms of dissent in ways that range from personal persuasion and institutional indoctrination to imprisonment and summary execution. The central institution in this book is the regular military that, for stylistic convenience, I also call the armed forces, or more simply, the army. In my usage the military includes all services: the army, air force, and navy; in cases where I specifically refer to the army as a land-based force, I make that clear.

Before proceeding further, I ought to say a few words about how I think of revolutions, the other main subject of this study. Even though it is one of the most elementary concepts of social science, scholars have not agreed on what "revolution" actually means, let alone accepted a general theory of revolutions. In fact, academics have thought of revolutions in starkly different terms. Barrington Moore, Jr., the eminent political sociologist, recognized only four revolutions—the English (1640), the French (1789), the Russian (1917), and the Chinese (1949)—while his colleague and the founder of Harvard's Department of Sociology, Pitirim Sorokin, counted over one thousand.[20] The English historian Lawrence Stone defined revolution as "the seizure of power that leads to a major restructuring of government or society and the replacement of the former elite by a new one" or "a coup d'état involving no more than a change of ruling personnel by violence or threat of violence."[21] For Samuel P. Huntington, it was "a rapid, fundamental, and violent domestic change in the dominant values and myths of society, in its political institutions, social structure, leadership and government activity," in other words events that others have called "great revolutions, grand revolutions, or social revolutions."[22] Theda Skocpol thinks of social revolutions as "rapid, basic transformations of a society's state and class structures; and they are accompanied and in part carried through by class-based revolts from below."[23] Stephen Walt considers revolution as "the destruction of an existing state by members of its own society, followed by the creation of a new political order."[24]

Any definition of revolution is likely to be contested, so I want to lay out, up front, how I use the concept. I define revolution simply as *a bottom-up mass popular challenge to the established political regime and/or its ruler(s)*. My main concern here is not the origins of or reasons for the revolution but the armed forces' response to what they perceive as a threat to the stability and survival of the regime and its leadership. That threat is usually manifested by large demonstrations, violent or not, mobilizing thousands of protesters in settings where such events have no or few precedents. This expansive definition allows me to use the concept of revolution precisely as I intend to for the purposes of this study: as synonymous with "uprising," "rebellion," "revolt," and "upheaval."

What is most interesting about societies and their political lives is how and why they change, and, of course, there is no more spectacular change than a revolution. So it is hardly surprising that the literature on revolutions and mass uprisings is remarkably wide and deep; indeed, thousands of books have been written on the subject, and many of them are profoundly thoughtful and full of insight about the causes, courses, participants, motivations, and outcomes of mass upheavals. It would take a hefty tome just to summarize this massive body of work with its evolving theoretical sophistication, trenchant debates, and myriad case studies, not to mention the fact that several scholars have already accomplished this task.[25] What I want to do here is merely to call attention to a shortcoming of that literature: in many studies on the subject, authors discount or disregard the role of the armed forces.[26]

As others before me have noted, although military affairs should be a central concern for those studying revolutions, it has been a largely and consistently overlooked subject.[27] This point is even more germane for theoretically inclined scholars: "For the most part the army, despite its massive size and manifest power, is an institution that is regularly omitted from discussions of macro theory."[28] But why is this the case? How could such a seemingly obvious part of the resolution of uprisings be largely ignored? Most social scientists, including Karl Marx and Max Weber, were

primarily interested in understanding the forces propelling revolutionary change in their studies of political and societal upheavals. They put
little emphasis on studying the ancien régime's coercive apparatus, although Marx was certainly concerned with Bonapartism—that is, military
counterrevolution—and understood why and how the Paris Commune, in
which he had invested such high hopes, was put down.[29] The voluminous
literature on social movements and contentious politics has remarkably
little to say about the potential or expected behavior of the armed forces
as well, even though the military is usually *the* key institution demonstrators face and, optimally, should win over to their cause.[30] More generally, as social scientists working on various aspects of the armed forces
have long noticed, military-related variables are quite unpopular with
historians and sociologists who study rebellions, revolutions, and social
change.[31] Furthermore, many intellectuals and academics harbor an an-
timilitary bias, a predisposition that is manifested through their neglect
of the subject matter. As one prominent international relations scholar
noticed, even though the "literature on revolution is enormous, virtually
all of it focuses either on the *causes* of revolution or on the *domestic* consequences of revolutionary change."[32]

In sum, though the outcome of a rebellion is nearly always determined
by the state's coercive agencies—whether they defend the state or support the rebels—few writers on revolutions give the military its due and
treat its part in this or that revolution with the attention and sensitivity
to nuance it deserves. The main exceptions to this rule are, perhaps not
surprisingly, the most prominent contributors to the literature. Let me
first mention Vincenzo Cuoco (1770–1823), one of the great eighteenth-
and nineteenth-century political theorists, whose recently republished
principal work, *Historical Essay on the Neapolitan Revolution of 1799*
(1801), reminds us that some of the insightful treatments of this subject originated long ago. Cuoco synthesized what Niccolò Machiavelli
(1469–1527) and Giambattista Vico (1668–1744) thought about uprisings, carefully considered the French Revolution, and also showed keen
awareness of the importance of and different roles played by various
types of forces (army, militias, national guard, navy, etc.) maintained by
the state.[33] Among more contemporary writers, Tilly recognized the fundamental role of the armed forces in a number of major works on revolutions. He demonstrated a close understanding of the internal workings
of the military; in this respect, his writings on European revolutions are
particularly insightful.[34] Skocpol's classic study, *States and Social Revolutions*, is also a discerning comparative analysis of the armed forces of

the old regimes and of the rebels in the French, Russian, and Chinese revolutions. She argues that there is no institution more important for a regime's survival than its armed forces and, therefore, maintaining the unquestioned loyalty of those forces ought to be a priority of ruling elites. In his *No Other Way Out*, Jeff Goodwin exhibits his nuanced knowledge of the various types of armed groups—insurgents, guerrillas, paramilitary organizations, death squads, regular armies—that played such key roles in the outcomes of popular uprisings in Southeast Asia and Central America.[35] And Jack Goldstone is one of the few scholars whose writings on the subject—including his essays on the Arab uprisings—are consistently mindful of the military's position.[36]

The primary focus of an important recent book, Erica Chenoweth and Maria Stephan's *Why Civil Resistance Works*, is the societal side of revolutionary upheavals, but it is informed by a keen understanding of the military's behavior.[37] The Chenoweth/Stephan volume's key interest is collective *action*, but it emphasizes military *reaction*. In contrast, my study's main focus is the generals' *reactions* to uprisings (i.e., collective actions), but I will also explain how the army integrates societal factors into their decision-making process and how different types of revolts tend to elicit different types of military response. Thus, my book's approach might be considered as the reverse side of or a counterpart to Chenoweth and Stephan's volume.

Several students of international relations have examined revolutions from the perspective of the wars that often follow them. The most important recent contribution to this literature is Walt's *Revolution and War*, in which he convincingly argues that states affected by revolutionary regime change are far more likely to be involved in a war than states that emerge from a more evolutionary political process.[38] The reason, Walt contends, is that revolutions encourage states to view their external environment in ways that intensify their security competition and make war appear as an attractive option. An earlier book, Jonathan Adelman's *Revolution, Armies, and War*, is a political history primarily concerned with revolutions spurring social change and impacting state power.[39] Nevertheless, neither Walt nor Adelman deals with the question of the military's behavior during revolutionary upheaval, let alone what explains that behavior. Because of its title, I was excited to find John Ellis's *Armies in Revolution*, but it is essentially a series of well-informed but entirely descriptive case studies of revolutionary war, focusing on the rebel forces in the American, French, and Russian revolutions, concluding with a case study on the Chinese Civil War (1926–49).[40] Ellis's emphasis is on the social and political factors that influence military affairs. He is refreshingly aware of the importance of geography in revolutionary wars and of the impact of technology on the adoption of different modes of armed struggle and in helping to explain the performance of the warring sides. Ellis does not, however, question the status quo armies' response to revolts, let alone the motivations behind it.

Only two English-language books are devoted specifically to the role of armed forces in revolutions. Chorley's 1943 classic, *Armies and the Art of Revolution*, convincingly shows that a successful revolution must involve winning over at least part of the military.[41] Chorley analyzes several major revolutions—the English (1688), the French (1789), the Irish (1916–21), and two in Russia (1905 and 1917), among others—and distills pertinent lessons from them. Russell's *Rebellion, Revolution, and Armed Force* is a very different book. She focuses primarily on her native South Africa with complementary vignettes on numerous other cases, Cuba (1959) being the most recent.[42] Both of these books are seminal contributions to the study of revolutions, and the decades since their publication have not dulled their insights. Chorley's work is rich in historical detail and calls attention to a number of critical factors—such as the effect of defeat in war, fraternization, and discontent within the armed forces—that explain the armies' behavior during revolutions. Russell's book features a brief but valuable conceptual component, and it is filled with perceptive observations regarding the causes of mass rebellions. Although it does not explain the reasons why armies react to revolutions the way they do, she does list a number of possible factors that might be responsible and need to be investigated.[43] Russell, and especially Chorley, understood and brilliantly explained the critical importance of the armies' reactions to rebellions, but they did not seek to systematically analyze the variables that explain those responses. That is the task I strive to accomplish in this study.

CASE SELECTION AND PURPOSE

This book centers on the question "Why do armies respond to revolutions the way they do?" As we will see, the generals' decisions regarding their reactions to any given revolution are driven by a large number of factors. Moreover, some factors—for instance, ethnic or sectarian division within the armed forces—might be of decisive importance in some cases but trivial or irrelevant in others. Determining the comparative weight of factors is a methodological challenge, particularly when one studies relatively few cases. Because the number of cases is too small for statistical analysis and the number of factors (the independent variables) that affect what I want to explain is too large, assigning values and weights to each of the predictor variables is somewhere between extraordinarily daunting and impossible. Therefore, I will use the process-tracing method to identify causal mechanisms. More specifically, I will offer detailed narratives of the cases to illuminate how formative decisions were made.[44]

The contrasting of cases will follow the method and logic of structured-focused comparison: in each case, the same questions are asked, and the narrative will focus on the main concern of the study, the military's re-action to revolutions.[45] Consequently, I will not investigate the cause of the revolution in question, how it came about, or what happens after the revolution, but restrict the analysis to my core concern. The task of chapter 1 is to propose the key variables and suggest a way to rank order them in terms of their power to affect the armies' responses to revolutions (the dependent variable). At the end of each of the four case study chapters, a table summarizes the relevance and, as far as can be determined, significance of individual factors and deals with the question of how difficult it would have been to forecast the generals' behavior vis-à-vis the upheaval. In addition, the conclusion will feature integrated tables assembling the data from all case study chapters.

The four case study chapters that illustrate the arguments make up the bulk of this book. When I selected the cases, my guiding principle was to pick cases that allow me to say something directly relevant to contemporary audiences and to construct a tool for those who wish to conjecture about the military's likely reaction to uprisings in the future. A number of issues then, affect the choice of cases. First and foremost, my central concern is, strictly speaking, the military's response to uprisings. While all revolutions want to alter the status quo and overturn the prevailing regime, they can be quite different as to their desired outcomes. Some revolutionaries seek to establish democracies, others Islamic republics, communist dictatorships, or constitutional monarchies. The question of what kind of regime rebels aspire to create, however, is beyond the scope of this endeavor. Another weighty issue is the role of the armed forces following the revolt. Will the army move back to the barracks, establish military rule, or become a trusted servant of the emerging postrevolution-ary state? It is an intriguing problem but, it too lies outside the param-eters of my inquiry. In other words, my case studies terminate with the fall of the old ruler and/or the ancien régime.

Second, I am interested in the reaction of the armed forces to uprisings directed against the prevailing *local* rulers. Therefore, the revolutions of 1848 in the Italian states or the 1991 Baltic revolutions do not satisfy my selection criteria because they set out to gain independence from foreign/ imperial powers. Third, the army whose response I want to learn about must be a domestic army maintained by and serving the ruling regime and not that of an invading power. So England's Glorious Revolution (1688–89), in which King James II was overthrown by a union of English Parliamentarians with an *invading* army led by the Dutch William of Orange, does not satisfy the condition that both the army and the revolutionaries must be based domestically. Fourth, the armed forces must play a significant role in the events; smooth transitions of power—such as those that occurred in Poland and Hungary in 1988–89—do not qualify. Fifth, the military cannot be the institution that starts the revolution (as in Ethiopia in 1974, for instance) as, again, the matter I want to study is its *reaction* to the revolution. Sixth, the state must have a regular military force; consequently, the 1964 Zanzibar Revolution in which the insurgents fought against the Sultan's mostly untrained police detachments does not fit the bill. Seventh, the uprisings I am interested in studying must have a direct impact upon the entire state and society; in other words, they have to be *national* revolutions. Consequently, the 1932 Constitutionalist Revolution in the Brazilian state of São Paulo, triggered by federal policies that diminished state autonomy, does not meet this condition.

Moreover, as I noted above, relevance to the contemporary world is an overriding concern of this book. For this reason, I decided to consider uprisings from the post–World War II era. At the end of the day, from the available pool of cases that satisfy these criteria, I wanted to select a manageable number that were drawn from different world regions, were relatively well known, and also included clusters of revolutions. These are the reasons for my choice of the 1978–79 Islamic Revolution in Iran, the Burmese "People Power Uprising" of 1988 (with a complementary section on the 2007 "Saffron Revolution"), the revolutions of 1989 in China and Eastern Europe, and the "Arab Spring" upheavals of 2011.[46] The latter two case study chapters examine groups of upheavals providing an appealing opportunity to assess the generals' reactions to the spread or diffusion of the revolutionary spirit from abroad. Although many observers, analysts, and writers describe or refer to all of these cases as "revolutions," only Iran's Islamic Revolution and perhaps the Romanian Revolution would satisfy the most exacting definitions of the concept.[47] The other cases could be described as "revolutions" only in a more broad sense, that is, as massive popular challenges to the established political regime and its ruling elites.

Successful vis-à-vis failed uprisings is one way to distinguish between the cases. I view the cases from the revolutionary side because most up-heavals are directed against autocrats, even if they do not necessarily result in the eventual establishment of democracies or, indeed, in better regimes than they replaced. Therefore, the Iranian, Romanian, Tunisian, and Egyptian uprisings may be thought of as "positive cases," given that the revolts succeeded both in overthrowing the regimes or their ruling elites and obtaining the support of the armed forces. Believing that noth-ing teaches lessons as well as failure does, I will also analyze a number of unsuccessful revolts—they might be called "negative cases"—to explain why they came up short: what did the armed forces "do right" to repel the protesters' challenge, and what did their opponents do or not do that prevented them from overthrowing the regime. This notion lies behind the decision to study the uprisings in Burma and China, as well as in Bahrain and Syria.

I strongly believe that social science should seek to engage, inform, and, if possible, propose suggestions, answers, and solutions to real-world questions.[48] My intent is far more modest than to endeavor to offer some grand theory of armies and revolutions; I have always been deeply suspicious of grand theories and their real-life usefulness. If Albert O. Hirschman, one of the few authentic giants of twentieth-century social science, "never trusted himself sufficiently to indulge in grand theoriz-ing," how could I?[49] My ambition is merely to pursue what Hirschman called the *petite idée*, an attempt "to come to an understanding of reality in portions, admitting that the angle may be subjective."[50]

My aim here could not be more practical: to offer a concise, policy-relevant book devoid of social science jargon that asks a simple but fun-damental question and advances a straightforward argument illustrated by a manageable number of targeted case studies. I do not aspire to offer a treatise on the causes of revolutionary upheavals or to recount the ori-gins of this revolution or that, let alone to retell the stories of the revolu-tions themselves in intricate detail. Neither do I wish to present compre-hensive analyses of social movements and contentious politics in various contexts. What I want to show political and military experts, area studies scholars, and others interested in public affairs is that familiarity with the political and military elites, the armed forces at large, and some key social data will help them make an educated guess, and, in some cases, perhaps even a confident prediction regarding the action the army is likely to take in a popular uprising. If the analytical framework I set out will enhance their ability to make that guess, then I will have succeeded.

A Roadmap of the Book

Chapter 1 is the conceptual "meat" of the book, where I lay out the analytical framework and outline in detail the internal and external variables that, I argue, affect the armed forces' responses to revolutions. In the remaining four chapters, I will demonstrate how these factors actually operate; how they influence the behavior of generals, officers, and soldiers in a variety of contexts; and how individual factors assume greater or lesser importance in different historical, political, and societal settings. Chapters 2 and 3 focus on single case studies, those of the Islamic Revolution of Iran (1979) and Burma's 1988 "Four Eight Uprising," complemented by a shorter section on the 2007 "Saffron Revolution." Chapter 2 will explain why Mohammad Reza Shah Pahlavi's Imperial Armed Forces (IAF) were unwilling or unable—the distinction itself is significant—to prop up the crumbling edifice of his regime. At first glance, the outcome would have been difficult to have anticipated; after all, the Shah built a large and modern army and treated his officers extremely well. In chapter 3, we will see the generals' responses to the attempt to depose a different kind of regime, a military dictatorship, in the case of Burma. Military regimes are very difficult to unseat unless their rulers evidence some willingness to give up power. In Burma they did not, either in response to the student-led revolution in 1988, or, nearly two decades later, in the series of large demonstrations led by Buddhist monks that is now customarily referred to as the "Saffron Revolution." Looking at Burma could not be more timely, given its ongoing but still nascent, still hesitant, and still easily reversible democratization process that began in late 2010.

In chapters 4 and 5, the focus shifts to two clusters of revolutions that occurred in 1989 and 2011. I made the decision to trade some nuance about the militaries in question for comprehensiveness and the chance to compare cases, particularly in chapter 5. I am confident that we have much to learn from contrasting the military's role in and general approach toward the distinct revolutions in China and Romania and the Arab uprisings, and the insights yielded by these comparison are an acceptable trade-off for the detail we have to sacrifice in order to keep the length of these sections manageable. In chapter 4, I explain why politicians and generals in the six East European Warsaw Pact member states (i.e., Bulgaria, Czechoslovakia, East Germany, Hungary, Poland, Romania) and in China reacted to the upheavals and revolutions so differently. In particular, I will briefly explain why senior officers in Poland and Hungary remained inactive during the transitions there, why the Bulgarian army leadership supported the "elite transfer" in Sofia, and how the top brass in Czechoslovakia and East Germany reacted to the mass demonstrations in their principal cities. I will devote the bulk of the chapter to China and Romania, however, where bona fide uprisings—one failed, one successful—took place, and the armed forces did turn their guns against the people, albeit reluctantly and in very different circumstances.

In chapter 5, I analyze the armies' roles in the 2011 upheavals in the Middle East and North Africa, concentrating on the six countries where considerable bloodshed occurred: Bahrain, Egypt, Libya, Syria, Tunisia, and Yemen. As we shall see, the regular military forces assumed roles that followed one of three distinctive patterns: they either supported or opposed the uprising or split because they disagreed about how to respond to it. I will explain that once one is reasonably familiar with these countries' political dynamics, societies, and civil-military relations, the reactions of the armed forces to the revolts should not have been all that unexpected. Looking only at cases where the military did play an important role constitutes something of a selection bias, so I will also briefly survey two Arab kingdoms, Morocco and Oman, where the armed forces' involvement in controlling the unrest was far more subdued. In the conclusion, I sum up what we learned with the help of tables that comparatively evaluate the usefulness of the different factors I follow throughout the study to explain the behavior of the armed forces in various political settings.

In sum, my ambition is no more than to satisfactorily answer the deceptively simple questions implicit on the cover of this volume. No subtitle was needed because its title could not reflect more accurately what it is about. That said, I vacillated about using the subtitle, "A Framework for Analysis," to underscore my commitment to make this study valuable in a very practical sense to professionals whose job it is to think about rapid political change and to try to anticipate its result. The military's behavior is not a perfect indicator of how revolutions will play out. Nevertheless, I hope that with our improved ability to intelligently speculate about that behavior we might also increase our capacity to anticipate revolutionary outcomes.

1

What Determines the Army's Reaction to an Uprising?

The recent uprisings in the Middle East and North Africa confirmed, yet again, that neither social scientists nor politicians and intelligence analysts are good at predicting revolutions. We may be able to observe that a country or region is "pregnant with revolution," to use Lenin's memorable phrase,[1] but we have no idea when, if ever, a revolution might actually break out. Indeed, it is amazing how autocracy may persist for decade after decade, only to have a seemingly trivial event trigger a massive upheaval that, on rare occasions, might span an entire region: in January 1848, students in Sicily distributed leaflets that criticized the monarch, in reaction to the closing of their university or, in December 2010, the humiliation of a fruit vendor in Tunisia by a low-level municipal official.

Although we might continue to puzzle over what sparks revolutions, we do know one critically important thing about them: once they start, they can seldom succeed without the support of the regime's coercive apparatus, most particularly, the regular army. One of the main arguments of this book is that military responses to uprisings, in fact, largely decide their outcomes. Social scientists generally dislike monocausal explanations with broad applicability; however, I am not suggesting that the military's response to a revolution is the *only* predictor of whether it will succeed in supplanting the status quo regime or not. Rather, I argue that the military's disposition toward the revolution is the most important predictor of its outcome, and the army's support is certainly a *necessary*, if not sufficient, condition for a revolution to succeed. Consequently, if we want to contemplate the fate of revolutions, then we must take the next logical step and answer the fundamental question of why armies react to revolutions the way they do? What factors sway their actions? Is it possible to predict a military's reaction to a revolution in a specific context?

Consider the following scenario: you are an analyst at an intelligence agency and your assignment is to advise the president on the action the armed forces are expected to take in Country X, which is experiencing a revolutionary upheaval. (Let's just assume that the president is a bright person who already knows that the way the military will go will probably decide the fate of the uprising.) Where will you start looking for answers? The rest of this chapter will give you the tools—in the form of questions you must ask—that you will need to produce a coherent and logical analysis and provide the most informed report possible.

WHICH FACTORS MATTER, HOW MUCH, WHY, AND WHEN?

Political science is not a predictive discipline and most, though certainly not all, social scientists would shudder to forecast political events and societal processes given the plethora of factors that would need to be considered.[2] Nevertheless, I believe that we might be able to anticipate—or, at the very least, make a highly educated guess about— the army's response to a revolution *if* we know enough about that army, the state it serves, the society it comes from, and the international environment in which it exists. If we possess this knowledge, then we ought to be able to suggest—with, to be sure, a degree of accuracy that would vary according to the given context—how the armed forces are going to behave. Given that the army's response to a revolution is critical to determining the revolution's fate, we should also be in an excellent position to offer conjecture about the revolution's outcome.

So, the sixty-four-thousand-dollar question is "How will the generals respond to the uprising?" Will they support the old regime or the rebels, or will they split their support between the two? Deciding which factors best explain the generals' responses to revolutions is a formidable intellectual challenge. One must analyze a potentially large number of variables that interact in complex ways, and all explanatory factors are not created equal: some go much farther in explaining the armed forces' reactions to revolutions than others. The relative significance of these variables can and will differ from case to case. One country's generals might have to take into consideration the prospect of foreign intervention as they decide how to react to an uprising, while in another country, meddling from abroad may not be a factor at all. Similarly, ethnoreligious differences within the armed forces may be critical in shaping one army's response to a revolution in one setting, but in an army that is composed of personnel of the same ethnic origin and faith as the rebels, those issues will have no significance whatsoever. Moreover, these factors might be reinforced or weakened by circumstances that have a bearing on revolutionary outcomes in some states but not in others.

To be able to make an educated guess regarding an army's response to an uprising, one must be familiar with the given context. There is no clever model that can tell us, once we "plug in" all the appropriate variables, what a military will do in a crisis. Ultimately, there is no way around the sobering reality that the weight of each factor is determined by its individual context. There is no shortcut, no substitute for having an in-depth knowledge of the individual case. That said, it is possible to identify some useful generalizations that allow us to distinguish variables that are more important in most cases from those that usually have less impact on the generals' decision-making.

Several scholars have attempted to explain considerations that might enter into the military's decision to respond to a revolution, either listing germane factors or privileging one variable or another in their analyses.[3] In her classic study, Chorley favored military attributes, such as professionalism, political leanings, the latent disaffection of the officers, and the conscripts' willingness to fight as well as their propensity to fraternize with the enemy. Her selection of these criteria was rather haphazard, and her attention was basically limited to military characteristics. Russell, although clearly aware of the importance of identifying which impulses drive the generals' decisions to shoot or not, only lists some potential variables—social-class composition of the armed forces, the proportion of officers to men, recruitment criteria, promotion opportunities—but leaves a more thorough examination to future researchers.[4]

In articles published in the October 2011 and April 2013 issues of the *Journal of Democracy*, I outlined my initial thoughts about the generals' responses to revolutions: the first concerned the "Arab Spring" specifically with regard to the settings in the Middle East and North Africa, and the second tackled the subject more generally, though discussed the independent variables in far more detail.[5] My work was informed by the important contributions of Chorley, Russell, and a few others and has continued to develop as I have become ever more convinced that only a more comprehensive—if necessarily more difficult and labor intensive—approach allows the would-be analyst to make confident predictions. Nevertheless, I have found the work of scholars who emphasize individual factors, as opposed to a more inclusive argument, quite useful as a test of my framework. The crucial variable for Eva Bellin, and for many military sociologists, is the "professionalization" of the armed forces—in other words, the level of the military's institutionalization. She argues that a highly institutionalized/professional army—that is, one that is rule-bound, in which promotion is based on merit, where there is a

clear separation between private and public realms to discourage corruption and predatory behavior, and that has no allegiance other than to
the constitution and the national interest—is going to be more likely to
support reform and less likely to defend a corrupt regime against widespread popular revolt.[6] The opposite of institutionalization, what Bellin
calls "patrimonialism," depicts a military marked by favoritism, corruption, and politicoideological loyalties that negate institutional rules and
undermine meritocracy. This patrimonial army would be more likely to
oppose reform movements, as it will remain loyal to its benefactor and
the status quo regime.[7]

The problem with this explanation is that many highly institutionalized armies tend to exist in democratic polities, where few revolts ever
target overthrowing democratic rule. The very appropriateness of the
"institutionalized-patrimonial" dichotomy to help explain the high command's loyalties might also be questioned. There are many examples of
exceedingly professional militaries that have defended corrupt and fundamentally unjust political regimes—examples can be found in some of
the armies of the communist world. What the professional/institutional-
versus-personalistic/patrimonial contrast addresses is better explained by
the military decision-makers' views of the regime in power or, put differently, their appraisal of the regime's legitimacy. If authoritarian regimes
can persuade—a better phase might be "successfully indoctrinate"—their
professional officers to view them as legitimate, they are likely to defend
those regimes.

Furthermore, as Derek Lutterbeck correctly notes, Bellin's
institutionalization-patrimonialism scale also possesses little explanatory
power to illuminate cases where low institutionalization might lead to
a fracturing of the armed forces. He suggests that another factor—the
distinction between armies based on mandatory conscription as opposed
to volunteers—is more critical to explaining military loyalties during uprisings.[8] Drafted soldiers, after all, have far more in common with the
citizens in revolt than with the professional armed forces that is called
upon to suppress them. As Chorley remarks, "Soldiers are under arms
for a short period only, and regard their military duty merely as an incident in their lives rather than the exclusive purpose of their working
years."[9] Conscripts are less likely to shoot at crowds that might include
their friends and relatives than are volunteers. "Inhibitions to the use
of coercion," as Tilly put it, "are likely to increase when the coercive
forces are drawn from (or otherwise attached to) the population to be
controlled."[10] Nevertheless, while the question of whether an army is

made up of conscripts or enlisted soldiers is an important factor, it does not offer an infallible method for anticipating a military's reaction to an uprising. No individual factor does, but the conscript-professional dichotomy is undoubtedly a key explanatory variable in many contexts.

Social scientists have long recognized the cohesion of the officer corps and especially the unity among senior officers—the bonding and integration between officers, the length of their military service—as another critically important variable that helps illuminate the generals' responses to rebellions.[11] Cohesion and esprit de corps are the most important parts of what we think of as a military culture that is also composed of discipline, professional ethos, and ceremonial displays and etiquette. Cohesion generally refers to relationships between soldiers on the unit level, while esprit de corps denotes the commitment to and pride in the larger military force to which that unit belongs.[12] A recent study hypothesized that military cohesion depends on two essential factors: the degree of control the regime holds over its citizens and the level of organizational autonomy armies possess that allows them to focus on training and warfighting.[13] Most experts differentiate between social cohesion, which denotes personal bonding between members of a group, and task cohesion, which sets and imposes behavioral standards, "sustains the individual in the face of stress," and promises to diminish that stress through the assistance, cooperation, or collaboration of other group members.[14] The armed forces' internal cohesion is directly relevant for those studying a military's response to an uprising.

When an army is tasked to put down a rebellion, its soldiers must be prevented from defecting to the enemy. Theodore McLauchlin distinguished between two basic strategies for maintaining the troops' loyalty: individual incentives—that is, rewards and punishments—that are vulnerable to a "cascade" of defections across the army when uprisings erupt, and group-based strategies, such as ethnic preferences that might produce out-group defection but generally make in-group defection less likely.[15] In an individualized incentive system, soldiers' beliefs in the regime's chances of survival—a belief that is largely based on other soldiers' behavior—would either result in their loyalty or, if they thought the regime would collapse, provoke mass defection, "bringing about the very collapse it predicts."[16] In a group-based strategy, on the other hand,

the belief that in-group members have a proregime preference and that out-groups are opposed to the regime helps generate precisely those preferences. Thus preferences can become public by matching public prejudice.

The result is a durable cleavage between in-group and out-group, where out-group soldiers are likely to defect but in-group soldiers are likely to remain loyal.[17]

Although McLauchlin might be right that these self-fulfilling prophecies might explain some experts' erroneous assumptions about the expected resilience of regimes under stress, his is, as he concedes, a unidimensional approach that cannot explain the diversity and complexity of the large variety of cases. In many uprisings, different ethnic or even ethnoreligious identities of the soldiers—a key issue in McLauchlin's scheme—is simply not an issue at all. More fundamentally, his reliance on soldiers' beliefs— something that is rather difficult to correctly and reliably ascertain— limits the usefulness of this approach. My hope is that the comprehensive framework I outline below will allow us to more accurately anticipate the army's behavior in domestic conflicts.

To be sure, cohesion is one of the essential explanatory variables, but it, too, has significant shortcomings, and it is certainly not an "omnipotent" variable. First, there are numerous different disruptions that could affect the cohesion of the officer corps, from officers' educational backgrounds to the more common "senior officer vs. junior officer" divide. These splits within the officer corps might be minor, or they might be quite significant, depending on the setting and the particular source of schism. Second, ascertaining the true level of the officer corps' unity often requires a great deal of field research and personal access to military personnel. Taking all this into consideration is necessary because the credibility of official information regarding this particular issue is seldom beyond suspicion: few governments affected by revolutionary upheaval would concede that their armed forces are fraught with internal divisions, lest they should aid their opponents.

Contemplating officer corps cohesion brings up another crucially important issue. Most authors who write on the military's behavior in revolutionary environments restrict their analyses to only one segment of the military, the officer corps. For example, a recent essay by David Pion-Berlin and his coauthors on why armies might or might not stay quartered during civilian uprisings fails to mention the nonofficer component of the armed forces at all.[18] This is a mistake. Elite-centered analyses overemphasize the significance of the officer class while ignoring a major dimension of the armed forces. If officers cannot persuade noncommissioned officers (NCOs) and the enlisted/conscripted soldiers to follow their orders, even the army with the most unified officer corps will fail to reach its objectives.

In other words, we must assess the cohesion and integration among *all* uniformed military personnel, not just those within the officer corps. Just as those who write on tactics, training, combat readiness, and social origins of the armed forces cannot overlook the NCOs and ordinary soldiers of an army; those who write on armies and revolutions ignore them at their peril, as well. We cannot make an accurate prediction of the army's response to a revolution if we do not give due consideration to those whose job it is to carry out the decisions of the officers or, put differently, to the question of whether soldiers be willing to turn their guns on peaceful protesters or not. Aside from institutional cohesion, the aforementioned article by Pion-Berlin and his colleagues identified several potential causes that might account for military disobedience during civilian crises, such as the army's material interests, professional identity, and what they call "legalities." Some of the problems of this otherwise very useful study are that it is overly deterministic in identifying the causes of the military's behavior and misses some of the important nuances of its numerous cases.[19] Most importantly, the essay overemphasizes military-centric factors at the expense of state-related, societal, and external variables that often have a decisive impact on the generals' decisions and are nearly always seriously considered by them.

So is there a helpful way of ordering the many independently moving pieces, as it were, the variables that affect the generals' decision-making, and assign some weight to them that would indicate their relative importance? Qualitative Comparative Analysis (QCA) is a research tool for analyzing datasets by listing and counting all possible combinations of factors and is designed to work well with and reward in-depth empirical knowledge of a small number of cases.[20] I realized, however, that it oversimplified the very complex issue of weighting the variables we need to work with, and the results of the QCA did not do justice to real world experiences.[21] I found the most useful way of arranging the key variables of a comprehensive empirical analysis that assessed the evidence collected from dozens of past uprisings is to consider the sources of information that influence the generals' behavior vis-à-vis the revolts. There are four such spheres: the military, the state, the encompassing society, and the external environment. Within these four categories, I group the individual factors hierarchically, clearly identifying those that tend to be most influential, most of the time.

The first challenge of the additional methodological matters is the temporal issue. Clearly, the closer we get to the time of the event—the point at which the generals make their decisions about how to respond to the revolutions they face—the easier it will be to come up with an accurate prediction, given that the situation evolves and a number of relevant dynamic factors become facts rather than variables. At the same time, we must accept the frustrating reality that no analyst can possibly know every issue that pertains to decision makers and how they reach their rulings. Although former US Defense Secretary Donald Rumsfeld's now well-known statement was widely derided at the time, it had a great deal of truth to it:[22]

> Reports that say that something hasn't happened are always interesting to me, because as we know, there are known knowns; there are things we know we know. We also know there are known unknowns; that is to say we know there are some things we do not know. But there are also unknown unknowns—the ones we don't know we don't know.[23]

There is no complete knowledge, and few predictions about issues as complex as the ones we are discussing here can be made with one hundred percent confidence or accuracy.

Another, potentially major, difficulty is the availability and reliability of the information accessible to analysts. Conducting research—especially field research and interviews—about subjects as sensitive and possibly risky to one's well-being as an army's internal politics, political linkages, and connections to societal groups is often fraught with difficulties. The multifaceted institutional and personal rifts that might exist within the top brass and the larger officer corps, as well as the web of interests through which generals and politicians might be linked, are at times nearly impossible to disentangle. Only a seasoned analyst can confidently and judiciously evaluate the credibility of the information culled from the media and the available literature. If field research could be conducted safely and would promise to be useful, information could be obtained from academics, journalists, nongovernmental organization (NGO) personnel, and foreign diplomats even if politicians and generals would not agree to be interviewed or were not assumed to be truthful. And, of course, it must be recognized that even if we assume that generals and their troops are rational decision makers, their rationality is bounded rationality: they must make decisions in a restricted time frame with limited, and potentially inaccurate, information. In sum, there might be many challenges and obstacles to acquiring the knowledge we need before we can confidently report on the likely response of military leaders to a revolution. At the end of the day, the only thing a conscientious analyst can do is to learn as much as possible about the setting in question.

Previous contributions have explained the army's role in past revolutions. My purpose is to try to *anticipate* the military's behavior in future revolutions. I contend that a more comprehensive approach, one that takes into account where the army obtains its information, will not only lead to a more accurate prognosis of its likely reaction to a revolution but will also have broad applicability to disparate settings. The structure of the rest of this chapter corresponds to the four principal spheres of information that influence the military's response to revolutions. I will begin by outlining the key variables, discussing them in declining sequence of general importance, that is, list the variables from most to least significance *in most contexts*.

SPHERES OF INFORMATION

The army draws on four separate domains of input as it formulates its response to a revolution. In descending order of importance these are (1) the military establishment, (2) the state, (3) society, and (4) the external environment. Most critically, the generals must consider the attributes, conditions, and composition of the armed forces. The army's decision-making process is also influenced by the state, its treatment of the armed forces, record of governance, and directions to the military during the revolution. The third sphere of information military leaders take into account is society, in particular, its relations with the armed forces and the key characteristics of the protests or rebellion. Finally, the army's response to a revolution is often influenced by the international setting, which includes issues such as the threat of foreign intervention and relations with those states providing military aid. These spheres do not exist in isolation but often influence one another.

I. Military Factors

Considerations specific to the armed forces are the most important determinants of how generals respond to uprisings. The most critical is usually the military's internal cohesion, but the others might also play a decisive role given the "right" conditions. Let us look at these explanatory variables more closely.

I. I. THE ARMED FORCES' INTERNAL COHESION
The most important attribute to judging the armed forces' response to a revolution is its internal cohesion. An internally unified military will

likely act in unison—it will either support the regime or not—and it is unlikely to be much affected by defections. Being able to measure the extent and scope of cohesion within the armed is, therefore, essential and, as Terence Lee suggests, a reliable method of doing so is to assess "whether cliques or groups exist within the organization, possess goals, and hold beliefs that are inimical or contrary to the prevailing military organizational culture."[24] That is precisely what my framework sets out to do by identifying and exploring factors that could compromise the army's cohesiveness. The military's internal cohesion is, in fact, a composite of several factors. What are the markers of a cohesive military or, put differently, what potential divisions can affect the army's unity? What sort of rifts should we be attentive to?

I. 1. A. *Ethnic, Religious, Tribal, and Regional Splits* Armies, particularly conscript armies, in many cases represent a cross section of a country's population. In multiethnic and multireligious states, the armed forces are often affected by the sectarian and ethnic rifts that exist in society at large. An individual's sect or ethnicity can often trump other identities—elbowing aside military professionalism, formal citizenship, or ideological adherence—even in settings where the army has tried hard to build a common identity among its troops.[25] In such environments, the key rift may be an ethnoreligious split in the officer corps and/or among the enlisted men. If the revolution touches upon especially sensitive ethnic or sectarian matters—deep-seated grievances, fears, or resentments of an ethnic or religious nature, for instance—one might especially benefit from understanding those issues when trying to anticipate where the officers will stand. Tribal and regional identification usually go together in some more traditional societies where tribal membership tends to be a more important marker of one's identity than others. They are particularly pertinent in the Middle East, North Africa, Southeast Asia, as well as some Latin American countries with large indigenous populations, such as Bolivia and Guatemala.

Multiethnic and multireligious states have tried different methods to stop ethnoreligious factions within their armies from taking organized form. In the vast USSR, for instance, conscripts served, as a rule, in mixed units far from home. Certain troops—often including Central Asian Muslims—were kept unarmed and placed in labor battalions dedicated to nonmilitary tasks.[26] In countries where intergroup relations are particularly fraught, entire ethnic or religious groups might be shut out of military service and, indeed, the whole security establishment. In Bahrain and Jordan, respectively, Shia Muslims and Jordanians of Palestinian origin are effectively barred from serving in the armed forces. One of the main challenges for countries where tribal affiliation is a significant social trait is to build national armies in which the soldiers' identification with the *national* supersedes the tribal. Only relatively strong states can accomplish this extraordinarily difficult objective, and, even for them, it tends to take generations.

I. 1. B. *Generational Divisions: Senior vs. Junior Officers*   As in many other contexts, the varying perspectives of young people and those of their elders are often in conflict. This is especially so in the armed forces, a highly hierarchical organization where length of service—and thus, age— translates into higher rank, more pay, more perquisites, and more responsibility. Junior officers in many cases tend to be more prone to radicalism, and thus more liable to support revolutionary action. Furthermore, because of their shorter service in the military, they also tend to be less invested in the current regime and are thus more likely to side with rebellions than their more senior colleagues.

I. 1. C. *Divisions between Officers and NCOs/Privates*   As I noted above, nearly all writers on this subject ignore the key point that what is ultimately important is not just cohesion within the officer corps but cohesion within the *entire* armed forces.[27] NCOs and soldiers tend to come from different socioeconomic backgrounds, have less education, and receive lower salaries and fewer benefits than officers. In some authoritarian states, soldiers are treated very poorly; consequently, their loyalty to the regime in revolutionary environments is likely to be questionable. Officers *need* soldiers to carry out their orders, and if those soldiers, whether enlisted or conscripted, are reluctant to do so, the decisions generals reach vis-à-vis their revolutionary opponents will not be implemented. Deep divides between the NCO corps and regular soldiers, however, are comparatively rare. Another important factor is the type and amount of information about the uprising that officers share with the soldiers. In many cases, commanders will try to control and manipulate the information reaching the troops—which might mean keeping their men in the barracks and isolating them from independent news sources— spreading falsehoods about the protesters' identities and intentions, which can boost soldiers' willingness to turn their weapons against them.

I. 1. D. *Divisions between Elite vs. Regular Units*   Many authoritarian regimes set up elite units or even entire special branches of service to complement—and maintain control of—the ordinary armed forces. Whether formally located within the military establishment or held entirely apart from it, these units provide the regular army with a constant source of professional competition. The presence of such units is a signal that the rulers distrust the army and want to counterbalance it with a more reliable force. Usually given higher pay, more perquisites, and better equipment than the regular army, elite units easily become the army's envied and resented rivals. In the event of an upheaval, the security establishment might fracture as the regular army or a large part of it embraces the revolution, while the privileged special units stay loyal to the regime that has long been their benefactor. For example, in 1960—three years after becoming the first president of newly independent Ghana—Kwame Nkrumah created a company-sized Presidential Guard. Within six years, it grew to a strength of 1,200 and was renamed the President's Own Guard Regiment. The privileged parallel force posed a direct threat to the regular army's professional autonomy and self-image, which intensified the officer corps' already deep resentment of Nkrumah, whom they eventually overthrew in a February 1966 coup.[28] Iraq's elite Republican Guard, formed in 1969 under President Ahmed Hassan al-Bakr, began as a presidential bodyguard. It fought reliably in Iraq's wars and, during Saddam Hussein's dictatorship, operated under the direct command of his younger son, Qusay.[29] However, not all examples support the hypothesis that elite units will have greater allegiance to their regime, just think of Ethiopia's experience. After World War II, Emperor Haile Selassie developed a crack Imperial Guard with troops who swore personal loyalty to him. In December 1960, however, it was the Imperial Guard and not the regular army that took advantage of his absence from the country, staged a putsch, and briefly seized control of the capital, Addis Ababa.[30]

I. 1. E. Splits between Army, Other Branches, and Security Sector Entities In militaries around the world, interservice rivalries are a fact of life. Armies, navies, and air forces typically cultivate strong internal loyalties as a way of building the camaraderie and esprit de corps that are essential to military success. Individual branches often secure different levels of state funding and are frequently stereotyped within the military establishments: the navy is elitist, and the air force is technologically advanced but overly accustomed to comfortable surroundings. Interservice antagonisms may come into play when one branch—usually the army—becomes involved in politics, while others are content to remain on the sidelines. For example, in Greece between 1967 and 1974, the so-called colonels' regime was entirely an army affair. The air force and the navy played only minor roles in government, had no officers on the twelve-person junta that ran the country, and showed notably less enthusiasm for military rule. In May 1973, a group of Greek naval officers was even implicated in a failed countercoup against the army.[31]

In many authoritarian states, the regular armed forces have institutional rivals, not inside the military proper (as under I.1.D) but outside of its organizational confines. Police or secret- police agencies can become powerful and might be favored by the regime, as did Tunisia's national police under Zine el-Abidine Ben Ali and the Romanian *Securitate* under Nicolae Ceauşescu. The motive behind elevating distinct security organizations may be to give command positions to members of a ruling family, as was the case in Muammar Qadhafi's Libya and Ali Abdullah Saleh's Yemen. Like elite military units, such organizations also serve as counterweights to the regular armed forces, which will typically view them with suspicion, as political watchdogs and snoops for the status quo regime.

I. 1. F. Sociopolitical Divisions between Military Elites   High-ranking officers might be divided by political orientation, professional outlook, or educational background. Some might support the current regime, while others might be more sympathetic to the goals of the opposition. They might disagree on doctrinal matters, armament programs, and training methods. Officers who were trained at elite military academies might nurture a bias against colleagues who were educated at less prestigious institutions. In some armies—such as those of El Salvador, Indonesia, South Korea, and Thailand—there have been officers' cliques, distinguished by the year they graduated from the national military academy. Year after year, those in each academy class would band together and follow a career-long custom of looking out for one another's interests.

An army might feature an officer corps bifurcated by class, in which some officers hail from elite circles and families where military service is a long and valued tradition, while others come from poorer backgrounds and households that view the military as a vehicle for upward mobility. The former, one might expect, will be more likely to look askance at revolution. Having said that, this is the least common type of split within the officer corps. Most armies strive to form a common bond among their officers and employ techniques of institutional persuasion or indoctrination so that officers internalize the regime's values as their own. So, while some divides—such as ethnic and religious identity—are difficult for regimes to bridge, bringing political views closer is a more attainable goal. Similarly, while an individual's social background obviously cannot be eradicated, its impact is likely to lessen the longer a soldier spends in military service.

I. 2. PROFESSIONAL SOLDIERS VS. CONSCRIPTS

One of the army's key characteristics is whether it is a conscripted or volunteer force, or some mixture of the two—and in that case, the question becomes what is the ratio of draftees and enlisted soldiers. An army made up of those who have willingly enlisted is a force of self-selected young men and women who tend to embrace the military's ethos, hierarchical nature, discipline, regimented life, and conservative values. Draftees, on the other hand, are supposed to represent—assuming conscription is imposed fairly—a wide cross section of society. Conscripts will be more likely to sympathize with a broad-based revolutionary movement, while volunteers will probably favor the stance held by their senior officers. If a revolution comes down to street-level showdowns between troops and protestors, the ruling regime will normally regard soldiers who have volunteered for military service as more reliable than draftees, who might pose a risk not only by refusing to shoot when ordered but even siding with the revolutionaries.

Virtually all major rebellions in the twenty-first century bear out this hypothesis. Revolts in countries where soldiers were conscripted from the general population tended to succeed: Serbia and Montenegro (2000), Georgia (2003), Ukraine (2005), Lebanon (2005), Kyrgyzstan (2005), Tunisia (2011), Egypt (2011). Conversely, uprisings that faced volunteer armies (sometimes filled by targeted recruitment) failed: Burma (2007), Zimbabwe (2008), Iran (2009), Bahrain (2011).[32] There are notable exceptions, however, when conscripts did fire upon their fellow citizens, such as the Chinese army in 1989 and Egypt's Central Security Forces (CSF) in 2011.[33]

I. 3. THE GENERALS' PERCEPTIONS OF REGIME LEGITIMACY

What do officers in the senior echelons of the military think of the political rulers? Are they legitimate in military eyes? Do the generals believe that the regime is supported by society at large, or do they think that the majority would like to see it replaced? Not surprisingly, military elites are more likely to back a regime they believe to be robust and popular (even if a small radical rebel group opposes it) than one that looks weak and unpopular. Legitimacy is a highly germane concept for this study—revolutions are usually staged because the status quo regime is widely regarded as illegitimate by its subjects—yet it is notoriously difficult to define, let alone to operationalize.[34] Legitimacy is dependent upon several indispensable components: level of trust among the people, their attitudes toward authority, their beliefs regarding the effectiveness of political institutions, and their willingness to engage in cooperative behavior. According to Andrew Janos, legitimacy is "the ability to evoke compliance short of coercion;"[35] I prefer to think of it as the popular acceptance of authority. Authority, on the other hand, to cite Janos again, "usually involves monopoly of the functionally specific instruments of force (armies, police) but not a *complete* monopoly of force."[36] The latter would be hardly conceivable because even an unarmed crowd of people represents a certain coercive potential.

What we must realize is that citizens' assessments of governing elites are important factors that military elites take into consideration when they decide how to respond to rebellions. The generals' unfavorable appraisal of regime legitimacy was certainly an important reason for their support of the revolutions in Romania (1989), Tunisia (2011), and Egypt (2011). Conversely, the Chinese officer corps' belief in the communist regime in 1989 was, likewise, a key reason behind its suppression of the student democracy movement.

I. 4. THE ARMY'S PAST CONDUCT TOWARD SOCIETY

A military establishment is not just part of the state but also belongs to the society from which its members spring. When a revolution is afoot, the armed forces' stance toward the revolt is influenced by the past history of those forces in terms of their behavior toward civilian society. An army that has brutally suppressed demonstrations, disregarded the law, violated human rights, become mired in corruption, and generally treated people poorly is more likely to follow the ruling regime than to support a change that might hold those soldiers responsible for their past misdeeds.

With the ever-growing instances of retrospective judgments and retributions for past human rights abuses, as well as the growing influence of institutions like the International Criminal Court, generals will want to limit their legal vulnerability and maintain an awareness of the prevailing attitudes held by opposition groups toward the military. It is hardly surprising that when military regimes decide to give up power, one of their main conditions is usually to be granted immunity from prosecution for their past human rights abuses.[37]

II. State Factors

The influence of state-related factors are second only to the military variables in affecting the generals' responses to revolutions. How has the status quo regime treated the army? How does the regime want the army to confront the uprising? The answers to these questions can be decisive in determining how the armed forces will react to a revolt.

II. I. THE REGIME'S TREATMENT OF THE MILITARY

This, I contend, is ordinarily the most important state factor to consider. All things being equal, if the regime treats the armed forces well, the generals are likely to remain loyal during a revolution. Conversely, a regime that treats its soldiers poorly is asking for trouble. This question of "treatment" comprises several components.

II. 1. A. Taking Care of the Personnel's Material Welfare Does the state provide its soldiers—especially its professional officers, NCOs, and career enlistees—with decent salaries and perquisites? Military personnel who believe that they receive pay and incentives commensurate with their education, skills, and experience—and proportionate to those of civilians of similar qualifications—are more likely to support the regime when called upon than those who believe to be remunerated poorly in the given economic context.

II. 1. B. Taking Care of the Army Does the state equip the armed forces adequately with bases, weapons, fuel, spare parts, and other supplies necessary for the execution of their mission? All things being equal, if the regime makes a genuine effort to supply the military with the facilities and equipment that it needs, the top brass are likely to stand by their rulers. Budgetary constraints often prevent the generals from getting *everything* they need—let alone everything they want—but a clear indication that the regime is trying to accommodate them goes a long way in securing military loyalty. In many countries, especially authoritarian and developing states— Egypt, Pakistan, Thailand, Turkey, Yemen, for instance—the state allows the military, explicitly or implicitly, to participate in the national economy through various profit-making ventures. In most cases at least some of the earnings benefit individual military officers—therefore this factor could also be considered as a part of II.1.A.—but the income from these enterprises is just as often used to make up for the inadequacy of state defense expenditures. This is certainly the case in Indonesia, for instance, where part of the profits from military enterprises are used to purchase fuel, food, uniforms, and even weapons for the armed forces.[38]

Only two of the six components of regime treatment have anything to do with "material interests." The army lives "not by bread alone"; its well-being is also determined by factors that include their professionalism, prestige, and the like.

II. 1. C. Appropriateness of Missions Does the state involve the military in unwise, unnecessary, and unpopular (among the personnel) missions? Defending the nation from its foreign enemies is the raison d'être of armies, it is what officers and soldiers consider their professional roles. Regimes that habitually order the military to discharge functions more often associated with a civilian police force (e.g., control crowds, provide security at large events, suppress minor protests of unarmed civilians) or execute orders of questionable legality tend to quickly lose their generals' respect and loyalty. Other missions usually despised by the officers and soldiers are those that take advantage of the army as a source of cheap labor for the state, which might be facing a lack of unskilled workers. Especially in countries where labor is scarce, conscripts are customarily used as seasonal farm workers or laborers on infrastructure maintenance and construction projects. As a rule, the government should ask the army to fulfill only two missions in a domestic scenario: first, to provide help following natural disasters, a mission that the armed forces' equipment and logistical capabilities make them uniquely qualified for; second, to serve as the *last* line of the regime's defense against its domestic enemies—that is, a revolutionary upheaval—once it was ascertained that the other agencies that comprise the regime's coercive apparatus (police, security forces) are not equal to the task.

Another dimension of this issue is the *kind* of war the regime asks the army to fight. Involving the military in avoidable, unnecessary, and unwinnable conflicts usually serves to erode the generals' confidence in and loyalty to the ruling regime. Defeat, in particular, nearly always decreases the army's confidence in the government and elevates the chances of revolution.[39] This is true, of course, for the entire army, including the lower ranks, who tend to become more politically aware and more receptive to radical political messages the longer a war lasts.[40] Revolutions following a losing war frequently enjoy the army's backing because the generals tend to blame political elites for policies that forced the country into war to begin with and for poor leadership during the war effort. Moreover, a long, exhausting, and losing campaign can cause an army to disintegrate—often with part of it heading straight into the arms of insurrectionists. This happened in the case of the Paris Commune of 1871: the Franco-Prussian War was brief, it is true, but France's defeat was exceptionally humiliating. Other classic examples are found in the later stages of the First World War, when uprisings—with the participation of soldiers still on active duty as well as those already demobilized—swept away the German, Austro-Hungarian, Ottoman, and Czarist empires and saw new regimes, some of them communist, strive to install themselves from St. Petersburg and Munich to the banks of the Danube and the Bosporus. In his classic study, Ted Gurr asserts,

> The most common solvent of the bonds of military loyalty, however, is defeat in war, which alienates the officer corps to the extent that they believe the regime responsible for defeat, and which may signal the populace that the military is too weak to maintain internal order.[41]

II. 1. D. The Generals' Professional Autonomy and Decision-Making Authority Does the state meddle in professional military matters, such as training and routine promotions, or otherwise try to control the minutia of military life? Are generals straightjacketed by their civilian masters, or are they left at liberty to make independent, professional choices in relation to the forces they command? These questions are rooted in the differences between what Huntington called a system of objective control (in which the army leadership enjoys significant autonomy in professional military matters) and subjective control (where generals are closely watched and allowed to make few decisions on their own).[42] In some countries, the state holds the military under tight control, owing to its past political involvement (e.g., Argentina) or fears that giving the military wide professional autonomy might set the stage for generals to meddle in politics (e.g., India and Japan).

The result is that military elites who are not used to making important professional decisions and whose civilian masters are always looking over their shoulders might be hesitant or unwilling to take decisive action. In some cases, they are virtually paralyzed by the great responsibility facing them: should they back the regime or should they turn against it? An excellent example of this is discussed in the next chapter—Iran's military leadership during the 1978–79 Islamic Revolution, which unseated Mohammad Reza Shah Pahlavi.

II. 1. E. Fairness in Top Appointments Does the regime follow the principles of seniority and merit in filling top military posts? While in democracies and even in some semiauthoritarian regimes civilian government leaders appoint top generals, it is important that they consider recommendations from the armed forces—or clearly justify their choice if it differs from that of the military elites—and that the process takes more of a consultative form rather than a unilateral resolution that the military is forced to accept. Tactless and undiplomatic decision-making often sharpens factionalism and, ultimately, can lead to a split in the military leadership's loyalties.

II. 1. F. The Military's Prestige and Public Esteem Does the regime encourage the public to hold the military in high esteem? The regime can strengthen the army's loyalty by fostering its institutional prestige and respect in the eyes of society, as well as by promoting the military occupation as an appealing career alternative to young men and women. The state can increase awareness of the army's historical role and sacrifices it has made for the nation; it can also stage celebrations and public events when conferring medals on outstanding officers and soldiers. Creating a general atmosphere in which the military is a highly valued part of the state is a usually a cost-effective way for the regime to cement the army's allegiance.

As we have seen, the regime's treatment of the military is a multifaceted variable that involves material and nonmaterial factors—and, in the given context, the latter might be far more important than the former. An army that receives good pay and equipment and that is allowed to dominate a portion of the national economy might still turn against its regime if its other needs—social prestige or political influence—are ignored or threatened. Many authors ascribe far too much weight to the military's "material interests," designating it as the main impulse motivating its actions. While those interests are certainly important, they are occasionally trumped by others.[43] A fitting example is the Egyptian military in the recent upheaval: even though the army was financially well taken care of—both in terms of salaries and its license to run a substantial part of the Egyptian economy—it had three major grievances, none of them material: its diminishing political influence, particularly vis-à-vis the internal security establishment; its intense disdain of Mubarak's powerful son, Gamal, who was being groomed to succeed his father; and the regime's poor record resolving issues of youth unemployment and Islamic radicalism.

II. 2. REGIME DIRECTIONS TO THE MILITARY

During mass uprisings, the armed forces need unambiguous orders from their civilian masters. At what point should the military get involved and in what manner? Should it use heavy weapons and live ammunition against demonstrators or restrict itself to nonlethal police tactics? Political leaders must make these decisions and communicate them plainly to the military leadership. Generals who receive clear goals and directives from resolute political leaders will respond to a revolution differently than generals who get conflicting orders, uncertain objectives, or no direction at all. The differences between clear and confused leadership are obvious when we contrast, for example, the direction the Russian Imperial Army received during the foiled 1905 Revolution as compared to the February Revolution of 1917, which successfully toppled the Czarist regime.[44]

III. Societal Factors

The third major source of information the armed forces will consider when facing a revolution is the society at large. Society spawns the revolution, usually beginning with public demonstrations of some sort. The military's reaction will be heavily influenced by the characteristics of these demonstrations. Additional societal factors include the generals' *perceptions* of the extent of popular support and the degree of threat the revolution presents to the regime as well as the rebels' fraternization efforts with armed forces personnel.

III. I. THE SIZE, COMPOSITION, AND NATURE OF DEMONSTRATIONS

Just how large a protest is makes a significant difference in the army's response. Small demonstrations usually can be handled by the police, security agencies, or paramilitary forces. If army units are dispatched to deal with minor protests—and especially if troops arrive in large, intimidating armored vehicles—it is usually a sign that the regime is committed to crushing the unrest quickly. The larger the demonstration, the more likely it is that the regular army will appear. Mass demonstrations, in which tens of thousands of people participate, will generally lead regimes to deploy the armed forces. Nonetheless, there is no clear correlation between the size of the crowd and the army's likelihood of opening fire. The military's decision to shoot at protesters will probably hinge on two additional factors: the composition and the nature of the demonstrations that are taking place.

One of a demonstration's most important attributes is who shows up for them. Are the protesters drawn from a wide societal spectrum or just from a particular section of the population? A crowd of radical young men is far more likely to be met with bullets than one that includes children as well as adults or one representing a variety of political views. During Ukraine's 2004 Orange Revolution, protest leaders reduced the chances of a shooting incident by astutely placing rows of young women on the edges of the crowd nearest to the government troops.[45] Another important factor is the ethnoreligious identity of the demonstrators, particularly if it differs from the predominant identity within army ranks. The most important reason Bahrain's army supported King Hamad's regime in the recent uprising was the difference between the religious identity of the military and the ruling elites (Sunni Muslim) and that of the protesters (mostly members of the marginalized Shia Muslim majority).

In any revolutionary situation, protests might remain peaceful or take a turn toward turbulence or even violence, especially when demonstrators physically confront security forces, counterdemonstrators, or bystanders. How the protests unfold will affect the military's reaction to them. Generally speaking, the more violent the protests are, the more likely the soldiers are to respond to them with violence. In fact, it is rare for heavily armed troops to be deployed against peaceful and orderly demonstrations, and even more rare for such deployments to end in violence. If the military does fire upon peaceful marchers—as President Bashar al-Assad's did at Daraa, Syria, on 18 March 2011—it is typically a sign that the regime has chosen the path of no compromise and believes it has troops loyal enough to enforce total suppression.

III. 2. THE POPULARITY OF THE UPRISING

Another factor that enters into the army's calculations is the top brass' perception of the popular support behind the revolution. Military leaders are more likely to back a revolution that enjoys broad-based societal support. Conversely, a revolution that does not have a wide segment of the population behind it is unlikely to obtain the army's backing. Nevertheless, it is always important to be aware of the particular setting the army encounters. Military leaders who might lose much if a broadly popular revolution succeeded—fearing anything from rights-abuse charges to defense budget cuts—can be expected to turn against the insurrectionists. During the last phases of the Cuban Revolution, for instance, there were few defections from the army of the dictator, Fulgencio Batista, given its reputation for brutality toward the rebels. Those who continued to back Batista knew that they had two options left: either remain loyal to the dictator until the end, or leave the island. His supporters' fears were confirmed during the immediate aftermath of the revolution when Fidel Castro's new regime executed hundreds of Batista loyalists.[46]

III. 3. FRATERNIZATION

A recurring image of many revolutions is that of dissidents placing flowers in rifle barrels or the muzzles of tank guns. Those who take part in uprisings often realize just how crucial the military's support is to their success. History is replete with rebels appealing to the soldiers through fraternization, information campaigns, attempts to exploit the disaffection and flagging morale in the ranks, and promises of policies favorable to the military, should the revolution triumph. In most cases, common soldiers along with low- or middle-ranking officers and NCOs are most likely to listen to such entreaties. They are paid less, may be mistreated, and have less invested in the regime's survival than do their seniors. Fraternization has been a widely used tactic in many revolutions—for instance, France (1789, 1848, 1871), Russia (1917), Hungary (1956), Iran (1979), and all of the recent Arab revolts with the exception of Bahrain.[47]

IV. External Factors

The factors discussed thus far are internal, in the sense that they originate within the armed forces, the state, or society. Nevertheless, the external environment may also influence and, under the right circumstances, even alter the military establishment's response to a revolution.

IV. I. THE POTENTIAL FOR FOREIGN INTERVENTION

In most contexts, the key external variable is foreign involvement. This factor comprises two fundamental (and obvious) questions: first, is there a realistic potential for foreign intervention? Second, on which side are forces from abroad expected to intervene: the regime's or the rebellion's?

In many revolutions, foreign intervention is not a consideration. In some, however, its importance would be difficult to overstate. In the recent upheaval in Libya, the expected NATO bombing impelled even more of Muammar Qadhafi's officers to defect and, in many cases, to join rebel militias.[48] In Bahrain, the decision of the Gulf Cooperation Council (GCC) to intervene on the side of the ruling regime probably made little difference to the country's military leaders, since they were already solidly loyal to the king—it only made the suppression of the opposition easier.

Some armies acquire a reputation of not putting up a fight against invaders. For instance, the well-trained and well-equipped Czechoslovak military—equipped by the vast Škoda Works, one of the world's leading arms manufacturers—stood by as Hitler ordered his *Wehrmacht* into the Sudetenland in 1938. Thirty years later, when the Soviet Union and several

Warsaw Pact states sent tanks to put down the reformist Prague Spring, the Czechoslovak People's Army once again did nothing. Such a tradition of passivism—no one who has read Czech novelist Jaroslav Hašek's First World War satire *The Good Soldier Švejk* (1923) is likely to ignore it—should also inform expert analysis regarding the army's potential response to domestic unrest. One needs not to go far to find a counterexample. Polish armies, throughout history, have fought valiantly against aggressors, no matter how poor their odds.[49] In a popular contemporary joke during the Solidarity movement of 1980–81, a journalist asks a Polish officer who his army will engage in battle first once the East German and the Soviet armies begin their invasion of Poland. The officer crisply responds: "First the Germans, then the Russians. Business before pleasure."

IV. 2. FOREIGN AFFAIRS

The ruling regime's relations with foreign states that provide economic and military aid might well influence the army's response to a revolution. In particular, the senior officers are likely to pay attention to the position their uniformed colleagues abroad and foreign aid administrators might develop regarding the revolution and the stance they desire the military to take. A recent example is the Egyptian army elites' concern regarding the continuation of US military assistance during the "Arab Spring" and their interest in attracting other potential benefactors among the oil-rich Arab monarchies.[50] International military-security organizations like NATO or the Peninsula Shield Force (the military side of the GCC) that enjoy an influence over the generals—for instance, the power to withhold or grant membership privileges or extend benefits like training programs or invitations to joint exercises—might also affect the generals' responses to the revolution.

IV. 3. REVOLUTIONARY DIFFUSION

On rare occasions, multiple revolutions happen in quick succession as revolutionary fervor "infects" a series of countries in the same region. This phenomenon, known as revolutionary diffusion, took place—in rather different forms—in 1989 in Eastern Europe, from 1990–2008 in the former Soviet republics, and in 2011 in the Middle East and North Africa.[51] On even more rare occasions, revolutions actually spread from one continent to another, as the events of 1848–49 in Europe and then Latin America can attest.[52] How might the process of revolutionary diffusion shape generals' calculations? Officers who have just watched a nearby regime topple will be more inclined to support the revolution in their own country rather than risk ending up on the losing side. Conversely, seeing dictators elsewhere fall, taking their supporters with them, might redouble generals' efforts to stay in power and crush any uprising. The Burmese generals who suppressed their country's "Saffron Revolution" in 2007 were well aware that Nicolae Ceauşescu and his wife had been lined up against a wall and shot almost two decades earlier (footage of their execution had been shown over and over again on worldwide television).[53] And there can be little doubt that Muammar Qadhafi's demise is on Bashar Assad's mind as the civil war in Syria rages.

IV. 4. FOREIGN EXPOSURE OF OFFICERS

An analyst attempting to predict how senior military officers will behave in a revolutionary crisis will want to know whether these senior officials have exposure to foreign military advice or training on their service records. An implicit—and often explicit—goal of countries that provide instruction to foreign officers in their military educational institutions is not only to provide professional training but also to imbue the participants with certain political values. This was especially apparent during the Cold War, when foreign officers studying in the Soviet Union, the United States, or the United Kingdom were expected to become supporters of the host nation.

In recent years, foreign officers studying in the military institutions of democratic states have received instruction in the principles and practices of democratic civil-military relations. To the extent that such education takes hold, it should make these officers more sympathetic to revolutions advocating democracy than they might otherwise be. In some cases, however, it appears that study abroad has actually turned some officers against the host nation. One example is Mengistu Haile Mariam. As a promising young Ethiopian army officer, he spent half of 1967 training in the United States. While there, he developed anti-American sentiments, and a decade later became the head of a communist military junta that unleashed a genocidal campaign on his homeland.[54]

RANKING THE FACTORS: THE TOP SIX

Let us briefly discuss the weight given to each of these individual variables. I listed the four spheres that provide the military the information they need to decide how to respond to a revolution in descending order of importance—that is, the military factors tend to be the most important, followed by state factors, societal factors, and external factors, and so on. Within those four domains, I also listed additional factors according to the same principle. All of these variables might influence the top brass' decision-making but, if pressed to decide, there are six factors that should help the hurried analyst come up with a cohesive and concise report with the correct prediction *most of the time*. Having studied dozens of modern uprisings, I hypothesize that these variables are the most important, and I list them here, again, in descending order of significance:

1 the military's internal cohesion;

2 volunteer or conscript army;

3 the regime's treatment of the military;

4 the generals' view of the regime legitimacy;

5 the size, composition, and nature of protests; and

6 the potential for foreign intervention.

In the conclusion, we will be able to assess whether the evidence I present in each of the following case studies confirms or refutes the relative importance of the factors I outlined above.

At the end of the four case study chapters I will rank the degree of influence these factors had on the generals' response to the uprising in question on a 0–6 scale where 0 = irrelevant or not a factor, 1 = of trivial importance, 2 = of little importance, 3 = somewhat important, 4 = quite important, 5 = very important, and 6 = critical or decisive. I will also rate the relative ease or difficulty of accurately predicting an army's response on a 0–4 scale where 0 = "no brainer" or very easy, 1 = relatively easy, 2 = somewhat challenging, 3 = challenging, and 4 = very difficult. Moreover, I will do so in reference to three chronological junctures: T1 = 3 months before the first mobilization event of the crisis, T2 = on the day of the first major demonstration, and T3 = three weeks into the crisis.

KNOWNS AND UNKNOWNS

In the discussion above, I attempted to give a sense of just how difficult it may be to offer an accurate prediction of an army's response to a revolution given, the number of potential factors that impact on that decision. Still, some of those decisions could have been predicted using research collected even months before the uprising occurred, given that some of the weightiest variables that influenced the military's decisions *were known* prior to the revolt! In other words, there are factors we know and factors we cannot *know* but that, depending on the context, we might be able to anticipate with a measure of confidence.

Indeed, we can already answer a number of the key questions before the revolution begins. Let us play our hypothetical game. We are sitting in some office building in suburban Washington, D.C., and need to come up with a confident prediction of how the army of Country X—for the sake of argument and for no ulterior reason, I will pick Thailand—would respond to an uprising that threatens to erupt but has not yet happened. There are a number of key variables we already know.

Known Knowns

Depending on the availability of information about a country and its armed forces, there might be quite a few important pieces of the puzzle we can come up with prior to the hypothetical revolution. Let us survey our main variables in the case of a relatively open semi-authoritarian state like Thailand. Let us also hypothesize that Royal Thai Armed Forces (RTAF) are *not* currently in power and some years removed from the last coup they mounted. What do we *know* for sure?

The Military: The Thai armed forces are an overwhelmingly cohesive force. There are no ethnoreligious splits in the military because the vast majority of its officers and soldiers share a common ethnoreligious identity. Experts of the Thai army will know that while the Thai military has been highly prone to factionalism, it has become united for the sake of a larger purpose, such as trumping civilian authority to gain political or economic concessions.[55] A main basis of these factions is the officers' loyalty to their military academy classmates, which usually lasts for the rest of their careers. It manifests itself mainly in gaining assignments and postings.

There are no major divisions between elite and regular units or branches of service, although there are some minor differences that could be of interests between the army and the police. Nonetheless, their grievances are not sufficient to seriously affect the army's deliberations. The RTAF is based on enlisted soldiers, and there is no mandatory conscription. The generals' decision-making authority is very high—in a potential crisis situation they would be likely to obey civilian authority only if doing so promoted their own interests. (Generals might listen to the king but historically the monarch has seldom interfered with the military and occasionally even supported their coups.[56]) The RTAF contradicts customary arguments about institutionalized vs. patrimonial armies: it is very professional, but its allegiance is to its own corporate interests.

The State: We do know that the state treats the armed forces very well. Numerous outspoken Thai military leaders have made clear they have little confidence in the crisis-management capacity of the current regime and generally believe the prime minister and her cabinet to be incompetent in dealing with social and economic pressures.

Society: The RTAF's history with society—information on its sociopolitical affairs—is readily available. We do know which opposition groups have had antagonistic relations with the armed forces, and we also know that the generals would not allow political forces that are hostile to the military to replace the government.

External Environment: Foreign intervention into Thai domestic affairs is highly unlikely. Thailand is surrounded by far weaker countries—with the exception of Malaysia, which might conceivably interfere only if the uprising were launched by the Malay Pattani ethnic minority in the four southern provinces of Thailand.[57] But even then, Malaysia might only "conceivably" become involved, because the many problems—drug trafficking, jihadism, and so on—associated with that minority make it such that the government in Kuala Lumpur would be hard pressed to support it.[58] We also know whether revolutionary diffusion would be an issue to consider, and we would also have a fairly good understanding of the political views of at least some of the leading Thai military officers, given their training in and with Western military institutions and personnel.

Known Unknowns

There are also things that we do not know. Still, we should recognize that as time passes, and we keep our focus on the country, additional information would undoubtedly increase our familiarity with the situation and our confidence in being able to provide an accurate prediction. So, staying with Thailand as our hypothetical case, what do we *not* know?

Military: It appears that we can be quite confident that we have appraised the military side of the equation well, there seem to be no major gaps in our knowledge.

State: We cannot possibly *know* what directions the government would give to the armed forces. Will they ask the generals to provide crowd control and get involved in policing operations, or have government officials learned from the past and choose not to burden the military with such tasks? The history of recent political upheavals in Thailand is well known, and an enterprising analyst would learn as much as possible of the past behavior and political proclivities of key personalities in political crises. There might well be revelatory facts or helpful indications an analyst could glean from the Thai media and from potential field research.

Society: We cannot *know* how many people will demonstrate, what societal segments they will represent, and how they will behave, but past protests and opposition activities—and in the Thai case, there have been many to learn from—will aid the analyst in reaching a confident prediction. Prior to the events actually taking place, we also cannot know how popular the revolution would be, but again, studying the recent past would be a good way to arrive at a solid forecast.

Unknown Unknowns

This is the realm where surprises come from because, by definition, we just do not know—we *cannot* know—what we do not know. Major political actors could fall ill or die, previously undiscovered political relationships might be revealed between leading generals and politicians, natural disasters could occur, unusually harmful intelligence operations might come to light, and all of these, as well as a plethora of other unforeseen circumstances, could change political dynamics. We cannot know every factor that might have a bearing on the generals' decisions, and we cannot in good conscience offer predictions with one hundred percent confidence. Nevertheless, in our hypothetical scenario it is fair to say that it would be relatively easy to predict that the Thai army would support any government it considers legitimate, in the case of a revolution.

One could easily think of much more difficult cases. The less information is available about a country—and the more complex its military establishment, civil-military relations, societal dynamics, and external environment—the harder the analyst's job will be. Of all these challenges, the most difficult to conquer is the absence of reliable data. Thus, for instance, predicting with confidence how the North Korean army would respond to an uprising would seem to be an unusually complicated task, given the dearth of information one can trust about that country, but even this case should not intimidate a bright analyst.[59] In recent years the academic, policy, and intelligence communities have made major contributions to our understanding of the North Korean regime, enabling experts to find answers to the questions my framework poses.[60] A dedicated researcher should certainly be able to make an educated guess, even if that means presenting a forecast with less confidence and a lower "percentage count" than her colleague down the corridor who was tasked with assessing the Thai scenario.

CONCLUSION

By examining the factors above, analysts will be well equipped to predict with some confidence, or, in the more difficult cases, offer informed guesses regarding the military's position on future revolutions and, consequently, about the ultimate fates of those revolutions. Because so many variables can potentially influence how military decision-makers decide to respond to uprisings, the would-be analyst's explanation has to be multidimensional and heavily contextualized. In some cases, as we shall see in the case study chapters, anticipating whether the army will side with the regime does not seem to be—particularly with the benefit of hindsight—problematic. In other cases, one is required to draw out fully one's knowledge of the given setting. Still, I believe that approaching this crucial question in the holistic and systematic manner I suggest will provide a useful tool for those interested in the generals' likely responses to revolutions in the future. In the balance of the book, we are going to assess these factors through the analyses of several modern revolutions. The task of the conclusion is to evaluate, based on the evidence of the case study chapters, which variables are indispensable—in other words, are the ones I proposed as the "top six" really the most essential?—which are merely useful, and which are those that analysts can perhaps do without.

2

Iran, 1979

Iran's Islamic Revolution was one of the most momentous political events of the twentieth century. For the uninitiated, the revolution must have appeared as wildly improbable just a year or two before it occurred. After all, Iran's ruler, Mohammad Reza Shah Pahlavi (or the Shah), seemed like an enlightened king who implemented political and economic reforms to Westernize and modernize his domain, created a large and well-equipped military, and was supported by most major foreign powers. Furthermore, the opposition that eventually coalesced around a 76-year-old cleric, Ayatollah Ruhollah Khomeini, was overwhelmingly unarmed and commanded meager obvious material resources. And yet, in early 1979, the rebels swept away a two-thousand-year tradition of monarchy with relative ease in what was, until that point, the most popular revolution in modern history. A far larger proportion of the population participated in the Iranian revolution (over ten percent) than in other major upheavals until that time, such as the French Revolution of 1789 (two percent) and the 1917 Bolshevik Revolution (less than one percent).[1] But this is just one of the several reasons why social scientists attribute to the Iranian revolution a level of historical importance and influence similar to the other two, where the monarchy was followed by republican and communist regimes. In Iran, however, under the leadership of a marginalized cleric, the monarchy was destroyed and replaced by a new type of dictatorship, one based on conservative religious tenets.

For political analysts, the most exciting questions to pursue are rather more specific and center on the behavior and the relationships between the state, the armed forces, and society, particularly as the Shah's regime came to its end. The key question is why the Iranian army—a 440,000-strong force led by highly trained generals who were loyal to and closely controlled by the Shah—failed to intervene and essentially stood by, more or less restrained, as the rebels destroyed the state.

In the first section of this chapter, I draw the main contours of the political and socioeconomic setting of Iran in the late 1970s, followed by a more detailed outline of the conditions of the Iranian military and its relationship to the Shah as well as to the population. Subsequently,

I focus on the main events of the January 1978–February 1979 period that led to the regime's collapse and then consider the role of the armed forces during the revolutionary period, explaining the reasons behind their actions or lack thereof. Finally, I sum up the reasons for the success of the uprising and ponder whether experts should have been able to foresee the military's response to the revolution and, if so, at what point? Table 1 more formally presents an assessment of the relative influence of the independent variables on the generals' responses to the revolution.

THE CONTEXT

Mohammad Reza Pahlavi's father, Colonel Reza Khan, was an ordinary army officer who deposed the last ruler of the 140-year-old Qajar dynasty and crowned himself the new shah in 1925. In a deeply religious society, Reza Shah, an admirer of Mustafa Kemal Atatürk's modernization efforts in Turkey, was staunchly secular. His time in power was characterized by ill-conceived and inefficient reforms that concentrated a growing share of wealth in ever fewer hands, intense reliance on the armed forces, and such heavy-handed suppression of dissent that, in 1934, a visiting American official likened Iran to Soviet-Russia's most repressive period.[2] Reza Shah's leanings toward Nazi Germany resulted in a joint Soviet-British invasion of his domain in August 1941. His soldiers laid down their weapons without noteworthy resistance, enraging much of the population, which had made major economic sacrifices for the sake of strengthening the military. A month later, the British asked Reza Shah to abdicate in favor of his son, Mohammad Reza Pahlavi, and then sent him into exile in South Africa where he died three years later.[3]

In order to gain and cement their loyalty, the not-quite-22-year-old new monarch aggressively rehabilitated the army by attending its ceremonies, retaining the old chain of command, and appeasing the officer corps with rapid promotions and perquisites. Consequently, when the government attempted to take control of the armed forces in 1942, the officers were more than willing to side with the young Shah. In the first decade of his tenure his most important goal was to strengthen Iran's alliance with the West, particularly the United States. During this period the Shah still lacked political gravitas, and older, more established figures were able to either influence his decisions or to thwart the implementation of those they opposed.

The coup engineered by both the British and the Americans in 1953 against the progressive, democratically elected, and nationalist Prime Minister Muhammad Mossadegh—the CIA operation, code-named "Ajax," was coordinated by Kermit Roosevelt Jr., Teddy's grandson—was an important watershed both in the Washington-Tehran nexus and in the Shah's relationship to his citizens.[4] Mossadegh, a genuine modernizer with real democratic inclinations, demanded to name his own war minister and chief of staff, which was until this time the prerogative of the Shah. Even more importantly, he nationalized Iran's previously British-controlled oil industry in a move that did not fail to provoke London's ire. The Shah actively encouraged Mossadegh's overthrow—though he spent the heady days of the conflict in self-imposed exile in Baghdad and Rome—and when he returned to Tehran he instructed that the name of the fallen prime minister, under house arrest for the rest of his life, was not to be publicly uttered. From this point on—and it is important to underscore that "this point" was a quarter century prior to the Shah's overthrow—the opposition viewed the Shah as a servant of American interests, and his already shaky legitimacy continued to diminish. This view of the Shah was hardly unjustified: soon after returning to Tehran, he volunteered to the principal CIA agent there that he owed his throne to Washington.[5]

The Shah took nearly a decade after the 1953 coup to expand and consolidate his control over Iran's political life. He succeeded in this effort and became the dominant actor in Iranian politics for the last fifteen years of his rule—so much so that he developed the quintessential sultanistic regime: tremendous power concentrated in the hands of the monarch, narrow social base supporting his reign, and increasing political and socioeconomic distance between the ever-shrinking ruling class and the middle class, let alone the vast rural and urban proletariat.[6] He developed a large domestic security police, the State Security and Intelligence Organization (SAVAK), which brutally suppressed any opposition forces—whether Marxist, nationalist, or religious—that the regime was unable to co-opt. SAVAK effectively intimidated most of the population as it routinely engaged in both physical and psychological torture as well as a wide range of human rights abuses. When that did not work, SAVAK assassinated "undesirables," including Ayatollah Khomeini's oldest son, Mustafa, who was one of the ten thousand people the Shah's regime killed during the thirty years of its reign, according to Western estimates.[7] The UN-affiliated International League of Human Rights reported that in November 1978 there were "thousands" of political prisoners held in Iran who had been prosecuted not by civilian courts but by military tribunals.[8]

By the end of the 1970s, the religious establishment was the only autonomous social institution, with the partial exception of the Bazaaris (the merchant class) that managed to escape government control.[9] This was partly due to the nature of the Shia Islamist establishment and an unintended result of the regime's antireligious policies. The Shah had closed down numerous religious publishing houses, disbanded religious student organizations on university campuses, attempted to infiltrate mosques using SAVAK personnel, and detained and tortured influential clerics—some of whom became leaders of the upcoming revolution.[10] The regime's assault on Shiism actually helped produce a sort of religious revival among the middle and lower classes and opened many people's eyes to the appeals of traditional religious values.

After 1973, following the major increase in the price of oil—Iran's principal export—the Tehran treasury became flush with funds, and the Shah embarked on a modernization campaign at break-neck speed that included—aside from a massive military build-up—rapid industrialization. His explicit goal was to "have the same living standard that you Germans, French, and English have now" in a decade.[11] Although the economy expanded quickly, misguided political considerations drove the economic reforms and resulted in the growing alienation of the monarchy's traditional supporters, particularly landowners and the rural clergy. The fierce suppression of the 1963 uprising, which protested the Shah's land reform program, exacerbated this process and drove these societal segments into the arms of the regime's opponents. Nevertheless, the impressive economic growth continued throughout Reza Pahlavi's reign.[12] The Shah was convinced that he had written his name in his country's history with indelible, golden ink: "I have done more for Iran than any Shah for 2,000 years," he was fond of saying;[13] however, most of his countrymen had rather different views of his accomplishments.

The vast majority of Iran's population, approximately 35 million in the late 1970s, were disgusted with the pervasive corruption and the conspicuous consumption of the country's rich. Public offices, like governorships, were for sale to the highest bidder.[14] Broad segments of Iranian society were upset by the regime's sale of oil to Israel, the discriminatory treatment or exile of religious leaders, the growing reliance on foreign advisors, and the ostentatious lifestyle, provocative behavior, and immodest manners of many foreigners and "modern" rich who were often defiantly inconsiderate of the mostly poor and devout locals. As the fateful year of 1978 began, the circle of the regime's domestic supporters had narrowed to the officer corps, the high-level bureaucracy, and the business elites—in other words, the narrow societal segments that were direct beneficiaries of its largesse.

In the meantime, the Shah's regime had become more closely allied with Washington, even as the anti-Americanism felt by the majority of Iranians had steadily increased along with the size of the American colony that, by the end of the 1970s, numbered in the tens of thousands. One of the main principles of the Nixon-Kissinger Doctrine, introduced in July 1969, was to reduce American commitments abroad while keeping up with its treaty obligations. In the Middle East and the larger Arab world, the administration endeavored to construct a new security structure, one based on the "twin pillars" of Iran and Saudi Arabia. The United States, which needed strong allies in the Middle East and receptive markets for its sophisticated weapons, ignored the repressive nature of these regimes. The Shah's 1973 boast, "We can get anything non-atomic that the US has," seemed entirely justified.[15] Many experts considered Iran under Reza Pahlavi as "a military client state of the United States."[16]

The causes of the revolution were political, economic, and sociocultural. In the Shah's Iran, dissonant political voices were silenced, and the authorities met all opposition activities with merciless suppression. To many ordinary and devout Iranians, the state's modernization campaign signified Westernization, secularization, the destruction of village communal and religious life, and ever-increasing disparities between a small group of well-connected and improbably rich people and the large and still-growing majority of those crushed by poverty. Most Iranians held not just the deeply corrupt and insufficiently religious police state in contempt; they also despised the Shah personally. Reza Pahlavi, apparently unbeknownst to himself, was widely viewed as a puppet of Western—and especially American—interests and blamed for being more interested in posturing on the international stage than governing his country. Even his supporters—who were quickly dwindling in number—criticized his aversion to cultivating moderate religious leaders in order to counter the growing influence of Ayatollah Khomeini.

THE SHAH AND HIS ARMY ON THE EVE OF THE REVOLUTION

The one overriding fact of Iran's Imperial Armed Forces (IAF) was the supreme, absolute, and undisputed authority of Mohammad Reza Pahlavi.[17] The Shah considered himself first and foremost a soldier. He was a graduate of military schools and was promoted by his father to general on his twentieth birthday. Once in power, he viewed the armed forces as the fundamental support column of his regime and claimed, "If I can't be the Commander-in-Chief, I'll pack my bags and leave."[18] The destiny of the Iranian monarchy had become so intertwined with that of its military that the Shah described himself not as the state, like Louis XIV, but as the army.[19] He trusted few people outside of his immediate family, and he was most comfortable with high-ranking military officers, but even they fell victim to his paranoid tendencies. The Shah's closest friends were two senior generals, Hossain Fardoust and Mohammad Khatami, but his "divide and rule" modus operandi prevailed even over these two, whom he encouraged to be personal rivals.

The Shah routinely selected senior officers to run provinces, government ministries, and state enterprises. This was not unusual in the Middle East where political institutions and the military have "traditionally been intertwined and have performed overlapping functions."[20] The Shah's rule, in fact, "was based on the continuous expansion of the army," the bureaucracy, and the security services—in part to broaden his regime's thinning social base.[21] In Mohammad Reza Pahlavi's Iran, the military career was one of the few channels that allowed for upward social mobility, and military officers were generally assumed to be steadfast supporters of the monarchy and its modernization efforts. The Shah required all officers to swear an oath of loyalty to him, personally, and at every morning formation, military units recited a prayer for his welfare.

Under the Shah, the IAF had gone through frequent changes and personnel reshuffles in its senior ranks. Nevertheless, the IAF organizationally mimicked Western armies—particularly the US and the British militaries—from the service staffs down to the squad level.[22] The Shah, who was a skilled pilot, granted preferential treatment to the air force, while the navy was the smallest force and, until the mid-1960s, was more or less ignored as a branch capable of fighting. Aside from the heads of the navy and the air force, virtually the entire leadership of the Joint Chiefs of Staff as well as the directors of the various security services were army officers: in other words, it was hardly a genuinely *joint* staff.[23] In any event, the Shah may be said to have literally headed all three of the branches—showing up in the appropriate uniform when he visited their facilities—and nominal service heads were not permitted to communicate with each other unless he was present. As in many other dictatorships, Iran's regular armed forces were complemented with a smaller, elite force—the Imperial Guards—that was in charge of protecting the personal safety of the ruler and his family. The Imperial Guards consisted of twelve thousand men, most of whom were professional soldiers, although some of its divisions featured a mixture of enlisted and conscripted personnel.

THE RANKS

The morale of Iranian draftees—the rank and file of the entire Ground Forces consisted of conscripts—had been traditionally quite low for three principal reasons. First, conscription was not equitably implemented, meaning that young men from poor and predominantly rural families were the most likely to be called up. The IAF assigned many conscripts from the provinces, who did not complete their secondary education, to work as servants in the homes of officers as part of their military service. These troops were referred to as "Zero Soldiers" (*Sarbaz Sefr*) because of their low rank. They were largely sympathetic to the insurrection, and, during the revolution, they made up the bulk of the deserters.[24] Second, the remuneration of drafted soldiers was pitifully inadequate. While in the 1970s, lieutenants and generals were annually paid about U$14,000 and U$70,000, respectively, conscripts were only given U$365 (that is, U$1 per day).[25] Third, in view of their social background and usually deeply religious upbringing, most ordinary soldiers were very uncomfortable with the secular and often explicitly anticlerical atmosphere in the IAF. As early as 1977, commanders were worried enough about Islamist influences among their troops that they closed down prayer rooms on military bases.[26] Prior to the revolutionary upheaval, however, the army traditionally encouraged the servicemen's religious devotion as an antidote to leftist propaganda.[27]

The *homafars*—technical specialists or technicians—formed a separate caste within the IAF. They were relatively well trained and well remunerated, although their status was decidedly lower than that of officers. Following the completion of their training, they signed eleven-year contracts but were often forced to stay in the military after they fulfilled their obligations, owing to manpower shortages. Most *homafars* hailed from the lower-middle class, or even more modest socioeconomic backgrounds, and usually shared the religious outlook of the rank-and-file. Furthermore, *homafars* were not subjected to the extensive political indoctrination directed at the officer corps. For all these reasons, the conscripts and technicians were highly unlikely to protect—let alone fight for—a regime that was under siege by a broad-based opposition movement with deep religious overtones. Another, albeit indirect, reason for the deteriorating morale among IAF personnel of all ranks was the heavy American military presence in Iran.

As in most other armies, junior officers in Iran were less invested in preserving the ruling regime than their superiors. They had served for less time, received less indoctrination and perquisites, and were usually far more in tune with the attitudes of the general population than the military leadership. Junior IAF officers were strongly affected by the most negative aspects of the Shah's regime—deep-seated and widespread corruption, uneven modernization efforts that left rural areas behind, shocking income differentials, insensitive treatment of religious leaders, and the heavy presence of American personnel, ideas, and culture—which weakened their allegiance. Additionally, the training of junior and mid-grade officers was mediocre (especially in the ground forces), and their perquisites were limited. At the same time, junior officers—let alone the *homafars*—did not benefit from the vast opportunities for corruption (lavish trips abroad, gifts, bribes, etc.) that accompanied the military buildup and that had enriched so many of their superiors. All of these factors contributed to the loosening of their ties to the senior echelons of the IAF.[28]

The military leadership did not succeed in building the bonds with the junior officer corps, the *homafars*, and the rank-and-file that could have enabled the regime to survive—in all likelihood because they were oblivious to the critical importance of developing those ties. When the Ayatollah Khomeini and his allies began to test the linkages connecting the younger officers and NCOs to the regime, they found them to be easily severed and many soldiers receptive to their messages. Needless to say, the lack of attachment these soldiers felt toward the Shah and his corrupt top brass became a major factor in their response to the 1978–79 revolution. In short, while mid- and senior-ranking officers seemed overwhelmingly loyal to the Shah, there were deep divisions within the officer corps, on the one hand, and between officers and enlisted men, on the other. The conscripts, technicians, and junior officers—that is, the very soldiers who would face the demonstrators on the streets—could not be realistically expected to protect the regime from the opposition with whom they had much in common.

The Shah and His Generals

Like most dictators, the Shah was worried about the reliability of his generals, officers, and soldiers and did his utmost to secure his army's loyalty. He was directly involved in the day-to-day operations of the armed forces, supervised training programs, and personally vetted all entrants to the academy of his favorite service, the air force. He personally approved all promotions above the rank of major—which, in a military of over 400,000, translated to thousands of cases, annually. The most important criterion for advancement was not merit but loyalty to the regime. Mohammad Reza Pahlavi established multiple intelligence agencies to watch over military personnel and weed out potentially disloyal officers. State control over the army included a three-layer intelligence network with overlapping duties designed to foster competition between them: SAVAK, the Imperial Inspectorate, and the so-called J-2 Bureau which, as a formal part of the IAF, was tasked with gathering military intelligence.[29]

The Shah rotated top commanders to prevent them from developing their own support networks, established a classic "divide and rule" system, in which military leaders would never quite trust each other—just as he would not trust them—and cultivated resentment and competition among his generals to ensure that they would never be in the position to challenge his rule. Appointments and dismissals, even on the highest levels, were seldom adequately justified or even reported: there was no transparency regarding the rationale behind his personnel decisions. The most important rules for officers were to never create the impression that they were too comfortable or thought themselves irreplaceable in their position, never act independently or display initiative, and under no circumstances question the Shah's decisions, no matter how irrational they might have been.

In practice, the Shah's distrust of his generals compromised their ability to respond to the revolution. The service branch commanders reported directly to the Shah; they were only allowed to maintain contact with one another through the Shah's command staff or through the prime minister's office.[30] Regulations rendered lateral communication between high-ranking officers extremely difficult, and no general was permitted to visit Tehran or to confer with other generals without the Shah's explicit permission, which was granted on a case-by-case basis.[31] Consequently, even top commanders enjoyed very limited independent decision-making power. The Shah always made the final decision; if he was not available, progress on any given issue came to a standstill because his commanders were not permitted to act. Unsurprisingly, feedback mechanisms within the system were severely handicapped by the lack of confidence between principal actors. Commanders concealed mistakes, buried negative reports along crowded communication lines, and tried to avoid taking responsibility for their failures. At the same time, the Shah did not have the benefit of useful advisers because he had created an atmosphere in which those who questioned his wisdom did so at their peril.[32] This highly centralized system had several serious drawbacks, which were to become all too apparent in the crisis the IAF faced in the winter of 1978–79 and which virtually guaranteed the military's institutional paralysis after the Shah's departure from Iran.

The Defense Buildup

The Shah saw threats everywhere and believed that lavish spending on the armed forces would serve two ends: it would create a technologically sophisticated military powerhouse *and* increase the loyalty of his officers.[33] The plan was nothing if not grandiose: to become the supreme regional power in the Middle East with a military on par with the French armed forces by 1993.[34] The Shah conceived and then closely supervised the entire defense buildup and personally dealt with suppliers, not trusting his generals to do so. He believed that the IAF required the most sophisticated armaments, and he arranged the purchase of 150 F-14s to fly at a high altitude while equipped with the Phoenix missile as well as 300 F-16s to act as a protective force for these F-14 Tomcat fighters.[35] In fact, Iran was the only country other than the US to possess the state-of-the-art F-14 in 1978. Three circumstances aided the Shah in realizing his vision: Tehran's growing control over the production and pricing of oil; the completion of British withdrawal from the Persian Gulf in 1971, coupled with America's encouragement of its regional allies to assume responsibility for their own defense; and the 1973 Arab-Israeli War, in the aftermath of which the Shah successfully worked with Arab oil producers to cut production and drive up (nearly quadruple) oil prices.[36] His purchases of foreign armaments in the 1970s constituted "the most rapid buildup of military power under peacetime conditions of any nation in the history of the world."[37]

Although William Sullivan, the former US Ambassador to Iran, claimed that the weapons purchase program was not a major contributor to revolutionary turmoil in Iran, one suspects that the fast growth of the defense budget—from $293 million in 1963 to $7.3 billion in 1977—must have antagonized many progressive Iranians for several reasons.[38] First, even though the treasury was flush with money, millions of Iranians lived in dire poverty. Second, Iran had no obvious enemy and certainly no enemy possessing the type of arsenal that had required Tehran to purchase such expensive weapons. Third, the defense buildup quickly increased the number of foreigners, particularly Americans, on Iranian soil. Finally, the large-scale procurement of weapons served to exacerbate the already pervasive corruption within the IAF leadership, which could not but lower their societal esteem. When a former secret-police general asked the head of SAVAK how his agency was taken by surprise by the revolution, he responded, "General, we have been doing real estate."[39]

By the late 1970s, the IAF, with approximately 440,000 uniformed personnel, was the largest military in the region. On paper, it represented a formidable force, although in reality, it was less impressive for a variety of reasons. Ordinary army units lacked specialized instruction and experience in all but the most basic military tasks. The air force and the navy were better trained—partly a consequence of working more closely with American advisers—and their officer corps had more professional depth. Owing primarily to the stifling controls over personnel, officers did not have the opportunity to develop independent thinking, critical judgment, or professional initiative. Air force generals were so afraid of losing the Shah's beloved new planes that pilots were allowed to fly only in fair weather and during daytime hours.[40] Moreover, the personnel needed to properly maintain such complex weapon systems were never trained and the infrastructure (warehouses, workshops, hangars, etc.) necessary for their proper servicing was never built. In fact, the most technologically sophisticated components of the aircraft had to be shipped to the US for repairs and tune-ups. A US Senate report concluded that the Shah's forces would not be able to utilize their high-tech weapons, and both Ambassador Sullivan and President Carter's envoy, General Robert Huyser, agreed—something they did not do often—that most Iranian generals lacked the qualifications for their jobs.[41]

Both the Shah and his generals recognized the need to practice military maneuvers and involve both small and large formations in tactical exercises. Nevertheless, such activities usually weakened the Shah's control over commanders and underscored the institution-wide lack of confidence in personnel. Therefore, training exercises ordinarily lacked any challenging components that would have required officers to test and improve their problem-solving abilities.[42] In 1973, the Shah sent an expeditionary force of twelve hundred men to Oman to assist the pro-Western Sultan Qaboos's forces against Soviet-supported, left-wing guerrillas. The Iranian contingent soon grew to four thousand. They fought competently, but by no means spectacularly, and their commanders' lack of imagination made an impression on the British and Omani officers fighting with them.[43] Most conspicuously, IAF troops were unable to take advantage of their sophisticated equipment, which was far more advanced than their opponents' arsenal.

THE REVOLUTION: HOW DID IT HAPPEN?

Several turning points during the Iranian Revolution conveniently divide its course into distinct stages. The crisis that led to the revolution started in late 1977, when Reza Pahlavi chose to relax police controls and judicial procedures—a decision that served to revitalize and embolden opposition forces.

Some observers, like the former British Ambassador, Anthony Parsons, have opined that if the Shah had not liberalized, "he would still be on his throne, or rather his son would be."[44] This point lends credence once again to Alexis de Tocqueville's observation that "the most critical moment for bad governments is the one which witnesses their first step toward reform."[45]

Throughout much of the first half of 1978, the Shah professed his ignorance of any opposition to his rule and appeared supremely confident about his regime's stability.[46] Once he did seem to grasp the seriousness of the upheaval, he began to make contradictory gestures—ones that occasionally looked nonsensical and hinted at the overall confusion at the highest levels of decision-making. The increasingly unpredictable Shah's actions oscillated between repression and accommodation, which effectively precluded reconciliation with the moderate opposition and, at the end of the day, gradually reduced the regime's chances of survival. Put differently, the government's overall response throughout the crisis was counterproductive: its policies served to drive the liberal political opposition—composed in large part of initially moderate individuals with only perfunctory religious affiliation but democratic or at least reformist leanings—into the camp of the radical and uncompromising Islamist clerics.

The **first** stage of the revolution may be dated from the 7 January 1978 anonymous editorial, "Iran and the Red and Black Reactionaries," in the Tehran newspaper *Ettelaat*.[47] It described the exiled Ayatollah Khomeini in an obscene manner and suggested that he was a British agent, which enraged religious students and clerics. Two days later, security forces clashed with demonstrators who were denouncing the article in the holy Shia city of Qom, killing six; this incident precipitated protests in several major cities. Theology students staged a series of riots, in which seventy of them were killed by the authorities. These events commenced a cycle of demonstrations that lasted, with varying frequency and intensity, throughout the revolutionary period. In February and again in March, security forces ruthlessly suppressed rioting protesters in Tabriz—marchers chanted "Death to the Shah"—causing hundreds of casualties.

To appease the opposition, the Shah, who was incensed by the violence in Qom and elsewhere, fired General Nematollah Nassiri, the head of SAVAK, and replaced him with a more moderate general. He also sacked dozens of SAVAK officers—a measure that served to demoralize the security services. Further government actions in the summer included closing all gambling casinos and nightclubs, reinstating the Islamic calendar, and dropping the Minister of State for Women's Affairs from the government while elevating the director of Religious Endowment Organization to cabinet level.[48] These steps antagonized the moderate political opposition but failed to win over the radical Islamists.

On 19 August, the twenty-fifth anniversary of the 1953 coup, Islamic militants set fire to the Rex Cinema in Abadan killing at least four hundred.[49] Many enraged citizens (wrongly) blamed SAVAK agents for this tragedy and organized protests that gradually grew into massive rallies of hundreds of thousands, which eventually led to the resignation of the government. Importantly, demonstrators included not just students and middle-class groups but also factory workers who conveyed their growing alienation from the regime by staging strikes.

The **second** stage began on 27 August 1978, when the Shah replaced Prime Minister Jamshid Amuzegar with a former prime minister, Jafar Sharif-Emami, hoping that the latter would be more acceptable to the Islamist opposition. The new government was as subservient to the Shah as the one before it, although its professed intention to introduce some political reforms explained why it garnered support from a few members of the moderate opposition. The revolutionaries organized major demonstrations for September 4. Initially, the Shah ordered the military not to intervene, and instead, merely to place troops in highly visible locations; however, he later declared martial law and ordered the military to suppress demonstrations on September 7, trying to bring the crisis under control. This move backfired and, as it turned out, ushered in the most violent stage of the revolution.

One of the regime's several costly blunders in this period was pressuring the Iraqi government to expel Khomeini from the sacred city of Najaf, where he had been residing. Baghdad complied, and the ayatollah flew to Paris, where he received far more media attention than in Iraq—attention that helped him quickly become the de facto leader of the revolution. The newly announced amnesty for some of the regime's political opponents apparently applied to Khomeini as well, though he pledged that he would not set foot in his homeland as long as the Shah occupied the throne.[50]

On September 8, thousands of people—many ostensibly unaware of the imposition of martial law—gathered in Tehran's Jaleh Square for a religious rally. The troops ordered the crowd to disperse, and when protesters started to push toward the soldiers, the shooting began. Recent evidence shows that some of the gunfire came from professional agitators, trained in Libya and Palestine, who intended to escalate tensions.[51] This incident and the subsequent clashes between the protesters and the soldiers resulted in over one hundred dead, including demonstrators, police and military personnel—which was actually far below the figures (often in the thousands) cited by the opposition and Western journalists.[52] The Shah decided that the best way to deal with the situation would be to pander to the opposition and instructed Prime Minister Sharif-Emami to announce the dismissal and prosecution of seventy officers (including generals) and public officials for their roles in the disturbances of the previous months.[53]

Black Friday, as the Jaleh Square incident had become known, signified a major watershed, as it is often considered the point when any "hope for a compromise" between the regime and the opposition was extinguished.[54] An unending wave of protests commenced, from which the regime would never recover. In October, students took control of Tehran University. The military did not get involved, although it stationed armored personnel carriers just outside the campus while students had the freedom to organize and agitate inside. To further appease the opposition, the government cut the military's budget, announced an amnesty to all opposition members, and even allowed a number of radical students to return to Iran from exile—all of which only served to highlight the regime's inconsistent and confused approach to the on-going crisis.

In the first days of November, major clashes took place at the university between dissident students and the military, resulting in twelve dead and dozens of injured students. Significantly, some of the fighting was filmed and subsequently broadcast on national television. The government responded by severely reprimanding the commanders and troops involved. For the overworked and overstressed military, this might have been the last straw—from this point on, many officers ordered their soldiers to withdraw rather than to engage protesters, fearing further reprisals from their superiors.[55]

The revolution's appeal had expanded greatly by the start of this second phase to embrace new groups of individuals. Before August, the majority of the insurrectionists comprised middle class students and the followers of religious leaders. As a result of the fire at the movie theater, and especially Black Friday, a far larger segment of the population had become supportive of regime change; many of them were willing to join the protests. A large number were factory and oil industry workers, who organized frequent work stoppages. Aside from the obvious damage this did to the economy, their actions began to seriously hurt regime stability. Demonstrations grew, often reaching numbers in the hundreds of thousands, which would have been extremely difficult for a security force to control, even one that *was* resolute and experienced in crowd control (two attributes that were entirely lacking in the IAF).

On 6 November 1978, the installation of a military government, headed by General Gholam Reza Azhari, marked the beginning of the uprising's **third** stage. Only a few weeks before, many Iranians might have believed that a revolution and subsequent regime change was unlikely. But, although circumstances demanded a strong and willful prime minister with a clear set of priorities, someone who could quickly bring the protests to an end—many regime-supporters were hoping for the appointment of General Gholam Ali Oveissi, Tehran's military governor—the Shah chose Azhari, thereby, sealing his regime's fate. A mild-mannered man and mediocre military leader with unquestioned loyalty to the monarch, Azhari was certainly not the type of person demanded by the circumstances. In fact, some experts believe that the opposition's victory became all but inevitable with the appointment of Azhari's cabinet.[56]

Most Iranians anticipated that the Shah would give Azhari a carte blanche to restore order. This was not to be. The Shah remained very much in control and did not extend the cabinet the powers it needed to apply martial law effectively. Many people thought that the military government still had a chance to stem the tide of violence and protests and reestablish some semblance of stability. Certainly, the Shah could have still made compromises to isolate and undercut the Islamic militants, or he could have unleashed the full brunt of the armed forces on them, but he shied away from taking such direct steps.[57]

Azhari's government attempted to curb the uprising by expanded media censorship and closing down some universities, secondary schools, and, for a time, even the bazaar. The administration also placed armored tanks on the streets and made some threatening overtures toward the opposition, but these measures only achieved a few weeks of reprieve from the protests. From France, Khomeini called for a general strike on November 12, but Azhari's countermand that strikers return to their work was overwhelmingly heeded.[58] However, the relative calm lasted only a few weeks. Khomeini renewed his calls to keep pressure on the regime through work stoppages and protests, and to clarify his stance, he declared any government appointed by the Shah to be illegal. Demonstrations started up again in late November with impunity because the Azhari government was not prepared to enforce its own rules by taking decisive action against the opposition. Moreover, the regime moved to satisfy some of the opposition's demands, perhaps most importantly, by detaining former ministers and provincial governors and opening investigations into their alleged wrongdoings. It even recalled General Nassiri from Pakistan, where he was sent as ambassador, in order to prosecute him. These arrests had a toxic effect on the morale of the Shah's remaining supporters. By the end of this period, most people—who, unlike some of the political elites, saw the writing on the wall—stopped cooperating with the government entirely. At the same time, violence became more pervasive, particularly by December, when tanks drove through crowds of demonstrators, killing 135 in Qazvin.[59]

The ongoing crisis and the unceasing demonstrations wore down the Shah, and in late December, he embarked on a last-ditch effort to save his throne. In order to placate the opposition, he removed the military government, lifted martial law, and designated Shapour Bakhtiar as the new prime minister. In many respects, Bakhtiar, a man the Shah was known to dislike, was an even more curious choice than his predecessor.[60] A high-ranking member of Mossadegh's National Front and a long-term opponent of the Shah's rule, Bakhtiar had enjoyed no support either from the military or from the clerics, and he entirely lacked popular following— partly because, by heeding the Shah's call, he was immediately expelled from the National Front. Bakhtiar agreed to form a government on several conditions, most importantly that the Shah would leave Iran on a "vacation" as soon as the legislature approved Bakhtiar's government and that he would receive assurances of the military's support. In return, he promised to rule, rather than to reign.[61] This ill-conceived compromise began to unravel no sooner than it was reached. For one, the top military officials had little inclination to take orders from Bakhtiar, whom they thoroughly despised. And, unless anyone had doubts, Khomeini declared that obedience to Bakhtiar was equivalent to serving his master—Satan.[62]

The obvious marker for the **fourth** stage of the revolution is 16 January 1979, when the Shah and his family left Tehran for the last time.

The day after, as per the agreement, the legislature gave its vote of confidence to Bakhtiar's cabinet. The news of the monarch's departure in mid-January was greeted with an eruption of joyful celebration by hundreds of thousands. This period lasted until February 11, when the government collapsed and the armed forces surrendered to the revolution. Bakhtiar could never gain the confidence of the military leadership, and the population widely considered him "merely a fig leaf for the shah's departure, which, in turn, signaled significant erosion of the military's political power."[63] To be fair, it is hard to imagine that anyone could have saved the monarchy or held off the relentless wave of revolution by this time.

Nevertheless, Bakhtiar started out with some grand gestures, which included ordering the dissolution of SAVAK, freeing political prisoners, ending state censorship of the media, stopping the sale of oil to Israel, and cancelling $7 billion in arms contracts. He asked the opposition for a "honeymoon" of three months to prepare elections for a new legislative body that would decide the fate of the monarchy. But Bakhtiar held no political leverage; the opposition had no stake in his success, not to mention that its de facto leader, Khomeini, effectively forbade cooperation with any government appointed by the Shah. The ayatollah continued his militant—and by this time, extremely popular—calls for the monarchy's overthrow, simply considering Bakhtiar a traitor who did the Shah's bidding. In the meantime the large-scale demonstrations continued against Bakhtiar's government, demanding the regime be overthrown.

Days before Khomeini's return from exile, General Abbas Gharabaghi, the head of the highest military body, the Supreme Defense Council, met with the Khomeini's top advisers in Tehran in order to reach some sort of compromise that would end the growing violence in the capital and elsewhere. The opposition, however, had nothing to gain from negotiating with the regime. On February 1, when Khomeini landed in Tehran aboard an Air France Boeing 747, an estimated five million Iranians lined up along the streets to welcome him.[64] From that moment on the revolution's victory was beyond doubt. With the ayatollah's return, the military leadership was living on borrowed time.

At a press conference on February 4, Khomeini appointed Mehdi Bazargan, a prominent scholar and democracy activist, as the "real prime minister," creating a situation of overlapping governments and responsibilities. By this time, there were few people left who took Bakhtiar's government seriously, and indeed, Bazargan was negotiating for a peaceful transition not with the "other" prime minister but with representatives of SAVAK, the military leadership, and the United States.[65] Upon his return, the ayatollah invited the IAF to "be with us for their own good and the nation's good" and repeatedly warned the army elites that if they moved against the revolution he would declare a holy war against the military—a threat that was taken very seriously by the many devout soldiers.[66] Still, three days of serious skirmishes did take place between the revolutionaries, often supported by IAF deserters (mostly conscripts, *homafars*, and cadets), on the one hand, and troops loyal to the regime, particularly units of the Imperial Guard, on the other.[67]

On 11 February 1979, twenty-seven generals and senior officers of the Supreme Defense Council gathered to debate their course of action.[68] Even those most loyal to the Shah were in deep despair over the situation. Gharabaghi reminded his colleagues that the Shah's last order to them was to keep the army intact, safeguard Iran's independence, and support Bakhtiar's government. Nevertheless, the generals were not willing to intervene, well aware that their odds of successfully rallying the troops against a massively popular uprising were very low. Gharabaghi called Bakhtiar to tell him that the armed forces declared neutrality and would support neither him nor Bazargan's shadow cabinet. At 1:15 p.m., Tehran Radio announced the IAF leadership's unanimous decision to declare their neutrality in order to prevent further chaos and bloodshed.

THE FAILURE OF AMERICAN FOREIGN POLICY

In few modern revolutions was the relationship of the regime and its army with a foreign state as important as in the Iranian case. Among our case studies, none even comes close—not even Bahrain, which actually asked for and received help from abroad to put down the uprising there in 2011. Therefore, the Washington-Tehran nexus during the monarchy's final year is noteworthy, helping to explain why Washington's contradictory messages made the Iranian generals' predicament even more difficult, and why, ultimately, so many experts consider it one of the low points of American diplomacy.

The Shah was rightly nervous about Jimmy Carter's presidency, both because of its professed focus on human rights and owing to his own close association with the Nixon and Ford administrations and, especially, Henry Kissinger.[69] Throughout the crisis, Washington never showed that it had a clear plan for dealing with the revolution and repeatedly sent conflicting signals to Tehran. Little wonder that the Shah, according to some accounts, was "totally confused about the Carter administration's policies towards Iran" and strongly believed that the US government was "trying to embarrass him."[70] Until the last day of his life, Mohammad Reza Pahlavi was convinced that Washington was behind the Iranian revolution![71] The Shah's own feelings about America—and, more generally, the West—reflected two different misconceptions, often characteristic of Iranians: an exaggerated view of the power of the governments of the United States and the United Kingdom to "direct events" in Iran *and* a traditional openness to conspiracy theories.[72] Many Iranians on both sides of the political divide believed that Washington was currying favors with their enemies and, after the revolution, wondered with genuine perplexity, "why the US put Khomeini in power," convinced that nothing happened that America did not wish to happen.[73] Without a realistic understanding of how democracies worked, political and military elites in Tehran firmly believed that, for instance, the negative coverage of the Shah and his regime in *BBC* broadcasts reflected the wishes of Downing Street and not the facts of independent news analysis.[74]

The Carter administration's foreign policy record on the Iranian revolution is widely considered a humiliating fiasco. Seldom did a less able group of principal actors guide American diplomacy, especially during a major crisis so important to US national interests. The memoirs of the chief diplomats and politicians underscore their confused approach, ignorance of Iranian realities, wishful thinking, lack of close engagement until it was too late, and willingness to pass the blame onto each other.[75] Notwithstanding his oft-declared interest in human rights, Jimmy Carter toasted the Shah on New Year's Eve 1977 as "dearly beloved by his people" and called "Iran under the leadership of the Shah an island of stability in one of the most troubled areas of the world."[76] His administration supported the use of force and continued to assure the Shah of its backing—even after Black Friday and the installation of the military government. Some experts even argued that "one of the causes of the revolution was the indiscriminate American support of the Shah's regime."[77] Others certainly hold Carter ultimately responsible for the "confused and confusing policy that contributed to the disastrous American foreign policy loss in Iran."[78]

Zbigniew Brzezinski, Carter's National Security Adviser, was the most intent on exculpating himself from any failure over Tehran—even though he refused to tell Carter things he thought the president did not want to hear and, in the final stages of the crisis, wanted to give the Iranian generals a green light to stage a military coup.[79] Brzezinski subscribed to a rigid, Soviet-centric view of the world, and his condescension of

Secretary of State Cyrus Vance and the State Department "harmed any serious attempt to develop a realistic appraisal of events" in Iran—all the more because he relied on communications with Ardeshir Zahedi, Iran's ambassador to the US and a self-serving adviser to Mohammad Reza Pahlavi with vested business interests.[80] In short, Brzezinski and the National Security Council were not only "clearly in over their heads in the complex situation in Iran" but added insult to injury by undercutting Ambassador Sullivan and Secretary Vance, using the crisis to improve their own standings in the administration.[81]

Under these circumstances, it is hardly surprising that Sullivan received contradictory messages from Washington policy makers who simply did not want to believe—or just flat-out disregarded—his persistent dispatches that attempted to alert them to the imminent collapse of the Shah's regime. In view of Carter and Brzezinski's harsh criticisms of Sullivan, it is baffling that the president offered him another ambassadorship once his tour ended in Tehran.[82] In December 1979, Carter sent Huyser, a US Air Force general with close contacts in the IAF leadership, to try and stabilize the Iranian military, to prevent its generals' defection, and to nudge it toward cooperating with the Bakthtiar government: he achieved only limited success.[83] Huyser and Sullivan read the same White House dispatches, but they interpreted them quite differently.[84] They also disagreed over the capability of the IAF leadership to act independently, with Huyser holding far more charitable views of his colleagues than the ambassador.

These problems were exacerbated by failings in the American intelligence community, where there was an enduring dearth of understanding the magnitude of Iran's problems.[85] In August 1978, a CIA report concluded that Iran was "not in a revolutionary or even a pre-revolutionary situation;" in September 1978, the Defense Intelligence Agency projected that the Shah would stay in power for at least another decade![86] The CIA had insufficient resources dedicated to the country, and it did not engage outside experts who would have been able to inform its assessments. Some of the key assumptions the Agency held about Iranian politics could not be confirmed, which explained why intelligence officials believed that the Shah was strong and decisive. No one in the US government understood the role of religion or the importance of Khomeini as a revolutionary leader. Finally, analysts could not properly appreciate the Iranian opposition's nationalism and anti-Americanism, mainly because they associated these phenomena with terrorism. The shortcomings of American intelligence officials are all the more noteworthy when contrasted with the overwhelmingly better informed reading of the crisis by their Israeli colleagues.[87]

In sum, the conflicting signals emanating from the State Department and the White House, the selfish politicking of some of the principals, and the absent appreciation of the situation's gravity in the American intelligence community virtually ensured the incompetent handling of the crisis.

Dissecting the Army's Response

Until the fall of 1978, the Iranian military could have defeated the opposition with relative ease had it received an order to use all necessary means to do so. Whenever the opposition believed there was a high risk of the military using force indiscriminately against them—such as on June 5, September 8, and November 6—the protesters backed down.[88] As time went by, however, the revolutionaries had become apt at probing the limits of the regime's patience and understood ever more clearly that the Shah was not about to unleash his army against them. In fact, Mohammad Reza Pahlavi often told his commanders that he was unwilling to slaughter his subjects to save his throne and ordered them to "do the impossible to avoid bloodshed!"[89] Given the strong rebukes security forces received following serious bloodshed, it is hardly surprising that they gradually became more cautious when stifling protests.

Conscripts and the Revolutionaries

From the beginning of the uprising many commanders readily acknowledged that the loyalty of conscripts and NCOs was highly questionable for the simple reason that they overwhelmingly shared the values and concerns of the rebels. During the disturbances, the IAF decreed that the once-a-day loyalty oath had to be recited thrice daily, but it was ineffective. The soldiers had become ever more susceptible to Khomeini's "religious-nationalistic edicts to desert and join ranks with the revolutionary forces."[90] Like any revolting group worth its salt, the Iranian opposition focused on neutralizing and co-opting the armed forces. Toward that end, the revolutionaries' tactics included attacking army checkpoints and patrols and provoking security forces to shoot into crowds to incite anger and chaos but, perhaps more importantly, also using peaceful means, such as fraternization with the soldiers.[91] Marchers shouted to the troops, "Soldier, my brother, why do you shoot your brothers?" and "The army is part of the nation!" while Khomeini exhorted them, "Suffer slavery and humiliation no longer! Renew your bonds with the beloved people and refuse to go on slaughtering your children and brothers for the sake of the whims of this family of bandits!"[92] Fraternization was widespread and effective; demonstrators, often young female students, placed flowers into gun barrels and onto armored vehicles with promises of civilian clothing, hiding places, and bus tickets to the hometowns of would-be defectors. Leading clerics, including Khomeini, used their spiritual authority to remind soldiers that it was their *religious* duty to join the revolution and called on them to join the jihad against the "American-controlled" IAF.

Initially, the clergy pleaded with the officer corps trying to win military commanders over to their cause, but as time went by and the opposition's victory appeared more and more inevitable, the officer corps became increasingly isolated.[93] Moreover, clerical leaders also realized that they needed to address their messages to lower-level officers, who were younger and less invested in the Shah's regime than their superiors; besides, they were the ones who had direct contact with the troops. In these efforts, the opposition was quite successful: during the larger demonstrations, unit commanders tended to keep their soldiers separate from the protesters, withdraw them, and on occasion, even order them back to their barracks because they were so afraid that the conscripts would change sides.[94] Ayatollah Mohammad Hoseini Beheshti boasted to a US Embassy officer, "We control everyone below the rank of major."[95]

Already in November, there were well-publicized cases of large-scale insubordination among the soldiers, which usually translated into the refusal to fire upon protesters. In some instances, soldiers even killed officers. On December 11, for example, a group of draftees entered the officers' mess in the Lavizan barracks in north Tehran, killed at least fifteen senior officers, and injured many more.[96] By December, no fewer than a thousand soldiers defected daily—although given that the IAF's manpower stood at over 400,000, the army could have sustained this drain of personnel for several months. This final stage of the uprising was characterized by the rebels' increasingly intensive and successful campaigns to persuade soldiers to desert.

The main problem was that the officers understood that a large proportion of their conscripts—even those who chose to remain in the army—were practically useless as part of a potential fighting force against the revolutionaries.[97] Quite simply, for the underpaid and mistreated draftees, there was little reason beyond the threat of court martial to fire on crowds and every reason to desert, to fraternize with the revolutionaries, and ultimately, to join their side. As 1979 began, more and more units (particularly those of the *homafars*) defected to the revolution.[98] A week before the regime's collapse, a senior general complained that commanders could not rely on their troops to hold off the protesters, and so officers had to do much of the street fighting themselves.[99]

THE MILITARY LEADERSHIP AND THE FALL OF THE REGIME

The Shah was not clear about chains of command and did not delegate authority before he left Tehran, largely due to his growing lethargy and resignation about military issues. He apparently intended the army leadership to practice collegiate decision-making after his departure.[100] If true, this was certainly an entirely unreasonable expectation, given that he purposefully created an atmosphere where trust, collegiality, and mutual support were absent. Once the Shah left, top officials seemed to feel helpless and unable to take decisive action on their own. In a sense, it was like the members (the generals) of a deeply patriarchal family (the regime) suddenly losing the father (the Shah) who used to make all the decisions. The generals felt abandoned by the Shah and were completely bewildered about what actions to take in his absence.[101] In the wake of the Shah's departure, the rivalries between top military leaders—particularly between General Gharabaghi, the Chairman of the Joint Chiefs of Staff, and General Oveissi, the head of the ground forces—quickly intensified, while the commands of the navy and the Imperial Guard behaved as if they were leading entirely independent organizations.[102] Some, including Gharabaghi, planned to resign but were persuaded to stay and negotiate with Khomeini's top advisers.[103]

The IAF's chiefs were unable to come together and work out an effective response to the crisis. They could not decide whether to try to take control or seek a compromise with the revolutionaries. Perhaps the only thing virtually all of them agreed upon was that Bakhtiar's decision to allow Khomeini to return to Iran spelled disaster. Many thought that if any harm was to come to the ayatollah, a major and uncontainable carnage might result. The military, of course, could have easily shot Khomeini's plane out of the sky or bombed the school where he took up temporary residence, but it chose not to do so. Nonetheless, they had no notion of what to do once such an action had taken place because even the hard-liners in the top echelons of the IAF evidenced no real capacity or willingness to plan for a military takeover.[104] Very few supported

Bakhtiar and his government—in fact, several generals confessed after the revolution that they would have gladly staged a coup against Bakhtiar had the Shah, by then abroad, asked them to do so.[105] Even so, none of the Shah's military leaders were prepared to take power from him, in large part because they were not qualified to conduct large-scale independent actions on their own. One of the best candidates to lead a possible take-over, General Gharabaghi, actually complained that he had no experience with planning because the Shah had always handled plans.[106]

The majority of the generals remained faithful to the Shah after his departure, although some of them—including Fardoust, Gharabaghi, and SAVAK chief Nasser Moghadam—were received by Khomeini and/or Bazargan, which damaged their credibility among regime loyalists.[107] Gharabaghi is widely considered to have become a traitor; he was not held accountable by the Islamists, and his memoirs left a number of key questions insufficiently answered.[108] After the Shah's departure, both senior and junior officers realized that they might well pay the ultimate price for their loyalty in a new regime. With this fate before them, many formally resigned, but even more left the country.[109]

On February 9 at the Doshan Tappeh air force base, *homafars* enthusiastically saluted Khomeini's return, thereby provoking the Imperial Guards stationed in the same garrison. A few days of serious fighting ensued between the two groups, with both sides calling for help. While the air force commander approved the distribution of weapons to his men, the commander of the Imperial Guard unit defected to the revolutionaries and did his best to prevent reinforcements from reaching his erstwhile comrades.[110] At the Farahabad airbase, mutineers joined by civilian revolutionaries battled Imperial Guard units, eventually forcing them to retreat. *Homafars* and other noncommissioned personnel with access to the armories distributed weapons to the demonstrators. The fighting spread to other parts of Tehran, and the military ordered a city-wide 4 p.m. curfew, which was immediately denounced by Khomeini and observed by few. Elsewhere, commanders ordered their remaining troops not to return fire. In the provinces, some personnel simply abandoned their garrisons—in some cases, after shooting their superior officers.[111] On the morning of February 11, the rebels overtook all Tehran police stations and later seized control of the radio station. The fighting ended on February 12, according to local newspapers, leaving approximately 650 dead and 2,700 wounded over the three days of clashes. On both sides of the political divide, a total of as many as 10,000 Iranians may have died due to revolutionary activities from January 1978 to February 1979.[112]

We see here, as we will again in the other case studies, that an army such as the IAF, one designed to win conventional wars on the battlefield, is unprepared to control massive demonstrations. The absence of a proper riot police in Iran that specialized in managing and dispersing protests left the armed forces in a precarious position. The IAF lacked the proper training and equipment for dealing with such situations; the last time the army was used to suppress street demonstrations was in 1963, when it quelled an Islamist insurrection in opposition to the Shah's policies. One of the unintended consequences of the modernization of the IAF was that it lost whatever material and psychological capacity it held to execute its internal security functions effectively.[113] During the upheaval, street-level commanders tended to waver between the extremes of inaction and harsh suppression. The large crowds often prompted the inexperienced troops to overreact, leading to fatalities and further rounds of demonstrations and bloodshed, starting yet another cycle of violence.[114] Many local commanders took their cue from the military's lacking initiative and, for the sake of prudence, assumed a wait-and-see attitude, expecting instructions from their superiors that never came.

This is, then, how the region's largest armed forces came to their end. The IAF leadership's institutional torpor—owing to its inability and unwillingness to make independent decisions, the deterioration of relationships among the IAF's service branches, and the leadership vacuum left in the Shah's absence—allows us to better understand the 11 February 1979 declaration of neutrality by the Chairman of the Joint Chiefs, which, in essence, was tantamount to throwing in the towel.[115] Apparently, even Khomeini was surprised at how quickly the regime folded after his return.[116] Needless to say, the victors were not expected to, and did not, treat kindly any members of the military leadership who were unable to leave the country after February 11.[117]

CONCLUSION: A HARD CALL

Chorley correctly argued that an uprising could not triumph against a modern army that used its full strength, but fortunately for the Iranian revolutionaries, the army they faced did not use its manpower and resources to defeat them. In the early stages of the crisis, the Shah could have saved his throne with minimal bloodshed if he had ordered a resolute response from the military and the secret police. One SAVAK general contended that "he could have put an end to the demonstrations within a week if only the Shah had given him free rein."[118] Charles Kurzman, one of the most prominent experts on the Iranian revolution, believes that as late as October 1978 the fall of the Shah was "hard to foresee."[119] In fact, no major religious or secular leader, other than Khomeini, demanded to overthrow the Shah until November 5, when Khomeini assumed the overall leadership of the opposition.[120] During the course of the uprising, a number of generals approached the monarch, intending to convince him to use the "iron fist," but he repeatedly refused to do so.[121] In short, the military never received the unambiguous order to repress the demonstrations once and for all.

The Shah did not fully understand the nature of the challenges to his regime, nor the motivating forces driving the opposition. As one of his biographers recently put it, the defiance with which he initially viewed the massive demonstrations turned into disbelief, then disdain for his subjects, and, eventually, it collapsed into paralyzing despair.[122] The revolutionaries correctly viewed his compromises as signs of weakness, and his wavering, procrastination, and counterproductive measures steeled their determination as much as they baffled and frustrated his supporters, especially those in the military leadership. In his memoirs, the Shah explained his regime's defeat by saying that he had been unwilling to order the slaughtering of his own people. This may surprise those familiar with the brutal suppression of the opposition throughout much of his thirty-seven-year reign. Still, there can be little doubt that the Shah's concern, at least at this point in time, was genuine. On January 11, five days before his departure, he asked General Huyser, "Could you, as Commander-in-Chief, give the order to kill your own people?"[123]

The six main factors that I presented in chapter 1 generally explain how the army's responses to the revolution in Iran played one of the most important roles in determining the outcome of the revolt. The military's internal cohesion (I.1.) had considerable explanatory power in this case. Most particularly, the deep divide between officers and NCOs/soldiers (I.1.C.) essentially robbed the senior military officers of an effective force needed to fight the insurrection. The other components of the military cohesion variable were not decisive, although the troops' religiosity vs. the more secular orientation of the officer corps (I.1.A.), as well as generational divisions within the latter (I.1.B.), did make a difference in the generals' stance. The second most important factor, the distinction between volunteers vs. conscripts (I.2.) was a decisive issue in this case, given the unreliability of the drafted soldiers illustrated by their high desertion rate. The regime's treatment of the military, which is generally the third most important variable (II.1.) in my framework, had only one component that clearly made a major difference—the generals' lack of professional autonomy and authority to make decisions (II.1.D.). As demonstrated in this chapter, the generals' views of regime legitimacy (I.3.)—usually the fourth most significant factor—carried little weight since, for the overwhelming majority of military elites, this was not an issue: they had little uncertainty about the legitimacy of the Shah's regime.[124] The fifth factor—the size, make-up, and nature of the demonstrators (III.1.)—was another critical issue that influenced the military elites' responses to the uprising. The potential for foreign invasion (IV.1.) was not a serious consideration here, particularly because if the invasion of an American expeditionary force were to happen—and it was, indeed, an extremely remote possibility—then it would have favored the generals' side.

The regime's directions to the military (II.2.), another factor with decisive influence on the generals' decision-making process, is not among the top six variables, but it is captured in my framework. In this respect, the Iranian case is unusual since, most often, the head or heads of the ruling government do not display the kind of unpredictable behavior evinced by the Shah. Clearly, the monarch's own vacillation—between the suppression of and concession to the opposition—in his approach to the crisis denied the military leadership the clear, unambiguous directions they needed. Perhaps the most revealing anecdote regarding the fall of Pahlavi's monarchy is the one about Prime Minister Azhari meeting with Ambassador Sullivan on 21 December 1978, in order to explain the difficulty he had establishing law and order: "You must know this and you must tell it to your government. This country is lost because the king cannot make up his mind."[125]

Societal factors—aside from the aforementioned attributes of the demonstrations—also influenced the generals, particularly the popularity of the uprising (III.2.) and the opposition's successful fraternization strategy (III.3.), which resulted in the neutralization and, to some extent, even the co-optation of many conscripts, NCOs, and even some junior officers. Iranian society was resolutely hostile to the army, in part, because—unlike the armed forces in several countries discussed in this book—the Iranian army *was* an instrument of domestic terror, and many Iranians looked at it as, for all intents and purposes, "a kind of police that lived in the barracks."[126] Of the external factors the most influential was not, as I noted, the threat of a foreign invasion but the unusually close relationship the commanders had with their American colleagues and, more broadly, the regime maintained with the US government (IV.2.).

Table 1. Iran, 1979: Factors affecting the army's response to revolutions

	Iran
I. MILITARY FACTORS	
I.1. The Armed Forces' Internal Cohesion	5
I.1.A. ethnic, religious, tribal, and regional splits	2
I.1.B. generational divisions: senior vs. junior officers	3
I.1.C. divisions between officers and NCOs/privates	4
I.1.D. divisions between elite vs. regular units	1
I.1.E. splits between army, other branches, and security sector entities	1
I.1.F. sociopolitical divisions between military elites	0
I.2. Professional Soldiers vs. Conscripts	6
I.3. The Generals' Perceptions of Regime Legitimacy	1
I.4. The Army's Past Conduct toward Society	1
II. STATE FACTORS	
II.1. Regime's Treatment of the Military	3
II.1.A. taking care of the personnel's material welfare	2
II.1.B. taking care of the army	1
II.1.C. appropriateness of missions	2
II.1.D. the generals' professional autonomy and decision-making authority	5
II.1.E. fairness in top appointments	2
II.1.F. the military's prestige and public esteem	1
II.2. Regime Directions to the Military	6
III. SOCIETAL FACTORS	
III.1. The Size, Composition, and Nature of the Protests	6
III.2. The Popularity of the Uprising	4
III.3. Fraternization	3
IV. EXTERNAL FACTORS	
IV.1. The Potential for Foreign Intervention	1
IV.2. Foreign Affairs	4
IV.3. Revolutionary Diffusion	0
IV.4. Foreign Exposure of Military Officers	2

Top six factors are in bold.
Scale (0–6):
0 = irrelevant, not a factor
1 = of trivial importance
2 = of little importance
3 = somewhat important
4 = quite important
5 = very important
6 = critical, decisive

We must admit that the essential inaction of the Iranian generals and the institutional paralysis of the military at large would have been difficult to correctly predict, certainly in the early stages of the uprising when it could have been suppressed with relatively little effort. The main reason for this difficulty is the import of two "unknown unknowns" in the equation: the Shah's equivocation and the fact that he was gravely ill during the crisis and had grown increasingly lethargic and withdrawn as his disease progressed.[127] Who could have foreseen the indecisiveness of the Shah, whom even his close confidants considered a robust and resolute leader before the uprising? How could analysts know about his illness if even his own wife was apparently kept in the dark about it?[128]

This point is important for two reasons. First, it calls attention to the *timing* of one's analysis or prediction. Anticipating that the Shah would *not* ask his military to use all its might to stop the insurrection would have been extremely problematic before the fall of 1978. As time went by, and the monarch's irresoluteness continued and it became increasingly likely that his generals would not defy him—in part because they lacked the independence to do so, owing mainly to the Shah's control over them—it would have been easier to predict the army's inaction. Second, although some social scientists are loath to admit it, history often hinges on the actions, inactions, and attributes of individuals. One could hardly wish for a better illustration of this point than the Iranian revolution. For those who knew the Shah there is no doubt that had he been healthy, he would have been far more decisive *and* defiant, and would have gone to great lengths to save his throne.

3

Burma, 1988 and 2007

Until its tentative political reforms began in late 2010, Burma[1] may well have been one of the most isolated and impenetrable countries in the modern world, perhaps second only to North Korea.[2] On rare occasions when news about the country appeared in the world's newspapers, it was nearly always for the wrong reasons: the ruling generals' inadequate responses to natural disasters or their brutal suppression of peaceful demonstrations. This general opacity, Burma experts have long warned, applies even more to military affairs: there is much that we simply cannot know about Burmese armed forces, especially given the all-pervasive propaganda campaign of the post-1962 era.[3]

The Burmese uprising that is most fresh in experts' minds is the 2007 "Saffron Revolution," when thousands of usually docile monks marched and demonstrated against the ruling military regime. Nevertheless, "Saffron Revolution" was a bit of a misnomer. First, the robes of the monks were not "saffron" but more of a maroon or reddish brown color—though the desire to add this event to the growing list of "color revolutions" might have been understandable.[4] Second, the 2007 events in Burma, as some observers noted, did not satisfy rigorous definitions of "revolution," given that the monks did not use or threaten to use violence, nor did they seek to bring about a systemic political change. Nonetheless, the "Saffron Revolution" was a "bottom-up mass popular challenge to the established political regime and/or its ruler(s)" and thus easily conforms to my definition as outlined in the introduction. *The* most significant challenge Burmese generals have faced to their rule since independence took place nearly two decades earlier, in 1988, when hundreds of thousands of protesters led by university students threatened to unseat their regime.

The primary example we will explore in this chapter is usually called the "Four Eight Uprising" because it started on 8 August 1988 (8-8-88) and occasionally referred to as the "People Power Uprising," is but I decided to also include in the analysis the "Saffron Revolution." Having two such events occur approximately two decades apart in the same country, and in a rather similar sociopolitical environment, presents an appealing opportunity for comparison, allowing us not only to gauge the differences according to my primary interest (the generals' responses to these upheavals) but also to appraise the changes in the armed forces, the disparities in the organizational characteristics of the opposition, and the reaction of the outside world.

The underlying causes of both uprisings lay in the people's frustration—pent-up for decades—with the military dictatorship, the economic mismanagement and failure of the "Burmese Way to Socialism,"[5] the widespread systemic corruption, and the often brutal police repression and human right violations. Given the relative obscurity of Burma, I devote the first part of this chapter to a sketch of the setting for the 1988 uprising, mainly by looking at the country's recent history and the nature of General Ne Win's regime. In the second part, I analyze the main characteristics of the 1988 People Power Uprising and then explain the armed forces' responses to it. In a brief section that follows, I identify the key relevant political and military developments of the nearly two decades that separate the two upheavals and then move on to examine the 2007 "Saffron Revolution." In the concluding section, I summarize my findings and entertain the question of whether or not experts could have reasonably anticipated the army's stance and tabulate the relative weight of each of the factors that influenced the generals' disposition toward the two uprisings.

BURMA BEFORE THE PEOPLE POWER UPRISING

Burma is a Southeast Asian country bordering on India, Bangladesh, China, Laos, and Thailand, with a current population of well over 50 million people.[6] The British colonized Burma in three stages, corresponding with the three Anglo-Burmese Wars (1824–26, 1852, and 1885). It was administered as an adjunct to the Raj (British India) until 1937 and remained under an unusually destructive colonial rule that enfeebled traditional elites. World War II brought further miseries: the retreating British destroyed much of Burma's infrastructure, and the country was occupied by Japanese forces that were joined by the local anti-British army, which adopted three names as the war progressed: Burma Independence/Defence/National Army. Additionally, tensions over allegiances between ethnic Burman and major ethnic minorities, like the Chins, Kachins, and the Karens were exacerbated; the latter issue has never been satisfactorily resolved and has remained a persistent problem in Burmese politics ever since. Nearly four years of Japanese occupation (1942–45) brought some major changes to the country by partially dismantling the British system of colonial rule, encouraging social mobilization, and offering military training to many of those who would become so influential once Burma became independent.[7] In May 1945, the British colonialists returned, but Burma received its sovereignty three years later.

In many respects the political history of independent Burma is the history of its armed forces, the *Tatmadaw*. According to the military's own propaganda, "Only if the Armed Force is strong, will the Nation be strong," and "the *tatmadaw* is the mother and father" of the people.[8] Since independence, civilian governments were in charge only for short periods of time in Burma: 1948–58 and 1960–62. As in other states with heavy military political influence, like Egypt and Pakistan, even during de facto civilian rule, the generals were not far removed from the locus of power. The military sided with the allies in March 1945. Its top general, the deeply revered Aung San (the father of the democracy activist Aung San Suu Kyi), negotiated Burmese independence with the British, though he was assassinated six months before it came about. The *Tatmadaw* had fought the communist uprisings and the decades-long insurgency of ethnic minorities, and had managed to keep the country together in spite of very real external threats in the 1940s and 1950s. For all these reasons the *Tatmadaw* has not only been the most important formal institution in Burma but also has been highly regarded for much of its existence by large segments of Burmese society.

At the time of independence, Burma's army was small, poorly organized, and modestly equipped. By the 1962 coup, the *Tatmadaw*, commanded since 1949 by Ne Win, had grown to a force of 100,000 officers and men. From then on, owing to numerous restructurings and the addition of new commands, the army's size steadily increased to 184,000 at the end of Ne Win's rule (1988), although the defense budget grew only modestly during the first two decades of military rule as a result of the regime's acceptance of foreign military aid.[9] It should be noted that the generals were careful with receiving defense assistance from abroad and, in fact, turned down numerous offers in order to safeguard their neutrality during the Cold War. Indeed, despite its economic troubles, Burma insisted on paying for some new military hardware.[10] As in so many other late-developing countries, the military leaders were convinced of their rightful political role, especially in view of what they considered the inept and corrupt civilian elites.

In 1962, General Ne Win mounted a coup d'état, arrested the civilian political leadership, and established a despotic, nationalistic, and xeno-phobic military regime that was in place until the 1988 uprising. Those behind the coup justified their actions by citing the gross incompetence of Prime Minister U Nu's government and its declaration of Buddhism as the state religion through the State Religion Promotion Act of 1962, which, the generals contended, would have irrevocably alienated the already unsettled non-Buddhist minorities and would have made the preservation of the union all the more difficult. The *Tatmadaw* set out to build a new political system in which the military was to dominate both politics and economic policy.

Ne Win and his colleagues established one of the most enduring military regimes of modern times, aided not only by their monopoly of the coercive apparatus but also by some genuine support, especially early in their tenure.[11] At the head of the regime was the Revolutionary Council, composed of eight members—all but one active-duty military officers and all but one holding multiple portfolios. Naturally, all of these individuals enjoyed the confidence of Ne Win, the person whose two-and-a-half-decade rule had shaped contemporary Burma more than anyone else. A few months after seizing power, he established the Burma Socialist Programme Party (BSPP), which, following the 1964 abolition of all other parties, became the key political organization of the regime. Virtually all high-ranking military officers received seats on the BSPP's Central Committee. All government employees had to undergo a BSPP-devised, three-month political indoctrination and military training course in what was quickly becoming a model totalitarian state.

Until 1971, however, the BSPP remained mainly a party of the military and governmental elites. Only then did it turn into a mass party similar to its Soviet Bloc counterparts. Afterward, party membership was essentially a prerequisite for professional advancement and access to some goods and services. In 1974, the BSPP's leading role in society was written into the new civilianized constitution, and Ne Win relinquished his military position to become Burma's president. As in socialist one-party states, the regime established BSPP committees within the *Tatmadaw* and tasked them with ensuring proper ideological indoctrination and the faithful execution of party policies by military personnel. The fact that Ne Win resigned as head of state in 1981 but kept his position as the BSPP's chair until 1988 hints at the party's importance in the state.

During the 1974–88 period, Burma had become an "indirect military regime," a "national security state" in which the military junta's own conception of the country's and the armed forces' interests became conflated with national interest.[12] In short, Burma turned out to be a fairly loyal representation of the kind of garrison state Harold Lasswell described many years ago.[13] Ne Win wanted to create a self-sufficient, unified, and strong Burma, free of any dependence on or intervention from foreign powers; in practice, this meant increasing roles for the armed forces, an uncompromising stance toward political opposition of any sort, and a socialist blueprint for developmental economic policies. The latter turned a resource-rich country into an economic disaster. In 1987, the United Nations listed Burma as one of the world's poorest and least developed countries.[14]

Courageous civilians—particularly students and monks—time after time, publicly protested the regime's harsh policies. Demonstrations and labor strikes, many of them mobilizing thousands, disrupted years of quiet. Most of the protests were motivated by economic policy changes, price rises, or new privations, although some had a clearly political character. For instance, the imposition of military rule in 1962 was followed by demonstrations that continued into 1964, notwithstanding mass arrests and imprisonment.[15] The funeral of U Thant, the Burmese General Secretary of the United Nations (1961–71), in 1974 occasioned protests against the Ne Win regime—envious of U Thant's international stature and genuine domestic popularity—which wanted him buried without any ceremony. The military responded to the disturbances by declaring martial law and recalling troops deployed in border areas to the capital.[16] Most of these incidents, usually focused in urban centers, culminated in the armed forces' heavy-handed suppression of any dissent. The *Tatmadaw* had developed considerable capacity to subdue these sporadic upheavals, owing to its near-continuous fight against ethnic insurgents.

It is impossible to understand Burma without appreciating the role Theravāda Buddhism, the oldest surviving branch of Buddhism, plays in its society.[17] Buddhism is perhaps the most defining characteristic of ethnic Burmans, who make up 60–70 percent of the country's population (depending who is doing the counting).[18] Prior to colonialism, all formal education was conducted in Buddhist monasteries. In a deeply spiritual and superstitious society like the Burmese, monks continue to enjoy extraordinary public esteem; indeed, they are so revered that many laypeople are reluctant even to step in the shadows they cast for fear of giving offense.[19]

Burma's generals have frequently avowed their devoutness by participating in Buddhist ceremonies and offering large donations to the monks and their monasteries.[20] The government's promotion of Buddhism is particularly discernable during political crises and has been used to shore up its eroding legitimacy.[21] Ne Win's regime initiated a pagoda-building project, culminating in the tyrant personally raising the spire—a symbolic act, since it was a royal prerogative in the past—and publicly showering gifts on loyal monasteries.

At the same time, the generals also made a concerted effort to control the monks. The Buddhist religion lacks the strict church hierarchy of some of its Christian counterparts—most especially the Roman Catholic Church—and as such, it is far more difficult to bring under state domination. In order to remedy this "problem," Ne Win's regime set out to formally institutionalize Buddhist organizations by creating the Supreme Sangha Council (*Sangha Maha Nayaka*) through which it intended to take a role in the administration of pagodas and monasteries and to register all monks. One of the specific objectives of this campaign was to make *sayadaws* (senior monks or abbots) accountable for the political activities of monks in their monasteries. Prior to the 1988 revolution, many of the then approximately 150,000 monks and some of the leading abbots harbored deep grievances against the regime and strongly disapproved of the BSPP's campaign to wrest away control over the Buddhist religious hierarchy.[22]

THE PEOPLE POWER UPRISING OF 1988

By the late 1980s, Burma was clearly falling behind its neighbors owing to the effects of a quarter century of political isolation and socialist-inspired economic policies.[23] The economy was in shambles, and even some brave individuals within the ruling elites began to tentatively question the direction the country was taking. In September 1987, Ne Win's regime took two significant economic steps. First, it abolished compulsory procurements and liberalized trade in nine major agricultural products, including unprocessed rice—a move that "brought to question the very foundation of the economic system."[24] Second, in an astoundingly senseless move, the government declared all large-denomination *kyat* (the Burmese currency) notes to be worthless, without any grace period, and replaced them with a new series of bills. The upshot was catastrophic for those with any cash savings—and those who had savings tended to keep them in cash—because they instantaneously lost their value. These policies ushered in a period of growing popular discontent and tension that had only intensified throughout the winter.

WHAT HAPPENED?

Revolutions are often started by something relatively trivial. The proverbial spark that lit the fuse of Burma's uprising was a brawl in March 1988 between some young men in a Rangoon teahouse. The police responding to the incident overreacted, killed one student, and then refused to apologize or take responsibility for its actions, which resulted in an eruption of conflict. College students from the Rangoon University of Technology, soon joined by their colleagues from Rangoon University, protested the miscarriage of justice. The government's poorly calibrated crackdown against the demonstrators on March 16 resulted in dozens of casualties: security troops chased students into Inya Lake in central Rangoon where many of them drowned, forty-one students suffocated to death in an overcrowded prison van, and a number of female students were gang-raped by soldiers in what became known as the "Red Bridge incident."[25] The next day the authorities arrested thousands of students and closed down universities in an attempt to regain control of the situation. It did not work: the uprising spread both in the capital and into cities and towns across the country, where such protests were unprecedented. On May 30, the regime reopened the universities, but they once again became hotbeds of opposition activity. Three weeks later thousands of students marched in the capital and were attacked by riot police. Nearly one hundred people, including twenty on the government's side, died in the resulting skirmishes.[26] Especially in Rangoon and Mandalay, the students succeeded in disrupting daily life and continued to draw more people to their cause with their increasingly explicit prodemocracy and antigovernment slogans.[27]

In response to the deepening crisis, the BSPP convened an extraordinary congress on July 23, at which the 78-year-old Ne Win announced, much to everyone's surprise, his resignation as party chairman *and* proposed a referendum on the arguments for and against a multiparty system. At the same time, Ne Win also issued a warning to protestors, "When the army shoots, it shoots to hit," lest there be any confusion about the military's determination.[28] The party congress voted down the referendum idea and elected Vice Chairman Sein Lwin—one of the commanders who ordered soldiers to shoot at student activists in July 1962—as Ne Win's successor. Sein Lwin's response to the expanding protests was to declare martial law in Rangoon on August 3, but it did not have the desired effect; demonstrations not only continued but spread further to provincial cities and began to attract not just students but monks and citizens from all walks of life. A growing number of workers and state employees left their workplaces to join marchers, heeding the students' calls for nationwide strikes planned for 8 August 1988 (a date some astrologers considered favorable), a day that saw as many as a million people in the streets.

On August 8, the government deployed troops to contain the demonstrators, who had become increasingly belligerent and violent. First, the soldiers shot into the air, but when that seemed ineffective, they turned their guns directly at the crowds. In many cases, the protesters fought back and, according to the authorities, killed thirty troops. On August 12, universities were once again closed down, and Sein Lwin—only in office for a couple of weeks—resigned as party chief to be succeeded by, Dr. Maung Maung, a civilian who was one of the more moderate members in Ne Win's retinue. Neither these personnel changes nor Maung Maung's decisions to lift martial law and order the troops to stand down appeased the protesters. The growing demonstrations brought life in the capital to a standstill: offices stayed closed because their staff could not get to work, radical students occupied the Ministry of Trade building, railways and airports ceased to function, and, by extension, state administration was almost paralyzed. On September 10, the *Tatmadaw* disassociated itself from the BSPP, which—given that the Burmese government had heretofore been ruled through the military, effectively ended the party's viability.

In the meantime, the movement had continued to expand and—as is usually the case with uprisings—the protesters' demands had become more radical and now included the establishment of a parliamentary democracy. Another new development was the emergence of nonstudent leaders—among them U Nu, Tin Oo (the *Tatmadaw*'s former Chief of the General Staff), and, most importantly, Aung San's daughter, Aung San Suu Kyi. Nonetheless, these individuals had no way to control the movement that had never become institutionalized, and so remained remarkably disorganized. Some student and worker groups had come to be increasingly aggressive, mobs began to loot shops, prison inmates started to riot, and no one in the ranks of the opposition possessed the ability to scale back the protests or restrain unruly protesters.

It was in this context that some regime leaders—it has never been firmly established exactly who—eager to reestablish public order, directed the armed forces leadership to carry out an internal coup, which the generals executed on 18 September 1988.[29] The takeover, led by generals Saw Maung and Than Shwe, forced out Maung Maung after only a month in office and established a direct military dictatorship under the ruling authority of the newly established State Law and Order Restoration Council (SLORC), a twenty-one-member military junta headed by Saw Maung. Although the foreign media referred to it as a "coup," it would be more appropriate to call what occurred a "self-coup," "pseudocoup," or even "leadership change"—after all, it is a strange coup indeed that features no tanks staking out strategic points, no suspension of the constitution, and no political leaders arrested.[30] Indeed, in the first few hours following the radio broadcast announcing the SLORC, the only movement in the streets was thousands of enraged citizens marching in protest—though not for long. The authorities immediately declared martial law, which included an 8 p.m.–4 a.m. curfew. A few minutes after 10 p.m. (on September 18), soldiers began firing warning shots to disperse demonstrators still on the streets and then turned their guns directly at them. The intensive violence lasted for a couple of days; by September 21 the carnage, which took the lives of at least three thousand protesters, was over. Rangoon was quiet, and a new era had begun.

Explaining the Generals' Responses

In this case, the discussion of state and external factors can be brief. Immediately, we must consider that—in contrast with the Iranian state and the other polities we will examine in the rest of this book—Burma in 1988 was fundamentally a military regime. Therefore, several of the variables explaining the generals' responses to this revolution, in particular those that relate to the state, possess limited explanatory power. For instance, in a praetorian (i.e., military-dominated) state, one would expect the government to treat the armed forces, that is, itself, in a manner that is satisfactory to the generals. Similarly, the factor I called "regime directions to the military" (II.2.) is also not tremendously helpful in explaining the armed forces' responses; after, all the ruling generals themselves decided how to engage the demonstrators. Even though the BSPP leadership included some civilians, they served at the pleasure of the generals and certainly had enjoyed exceedingly modest genuine decision-making autonomy. In fact, we can rate the impact of all state variables a "0" on the generals' decision-making, with a tentative "2" for the "military's prestige and public esteem" (II.1.F.) because the top brass surely did not want to alienate Burmese society and lose its support as a result of their overly harsh response to the uprising.

Only one external factor played any appreciable role, and that factor, the threat of a foreign invasion, was actually quite important. Burmese generals, ever mindful of threats from abroad, did fear a potential invasion, and the appearance of a US fleet of five ships off the coast of Burma on September 12—ostensibly to evacuate American citizens—played into those fears.[31] Even though neither Washington nor any other foreign government did anything to substantiate the military elites' fears, it is important to underscore that we are concerned with the Burmese generals' own *perceptions*, not whether or not they were realistic. The other external factors were essentially irrelevant. The student movement did not succeed in enticing a single major international actor to offer, much less to deliver, any tangible support.

MILITARY FACTORS

Let us take a look at the Burmese military in 1988 to gauge the weight of military variables. Most importantly, the *Tatmadaw* was fundamentally a solidly united organization that had never had a mutiny within its ranks. Some experts considered its esprit de corps the strongest of all the Asian armed forces (I.1.).[32] This is not to say that occasional strife did not emerge in the *Tatmadaw*. Already in the 1960s, rival groups formed in the higher echelons of the officer corps—not based on an ideological or policy position, but around leading generals or service branches (such as infantry or intelligence), or regional commands (I.1.E.). In some cases, the officer groupings were primarily organized around their membership in military academy or officer training school classes, as has been the case in the Indonesian, South Korean, and Thai armed forces. In fact, one expert described the *Tatmadaw* as "a collection of finely balanced institutional and personal loyalties."[33] As such, these factions never posed a threat to the internal stability of the armed forces; if there was even the slightest danger that they might, the dissenting faction member were marginalized, purged, or jailed.[34] For example, a 1976 officers' plot to assassinate Ne Win, which posed no serious threat to its intended target, was followed by a massive purge.[35] In 1983, former military intelligence chief Brigadier General Tin Oo, who many regime insiders expected to succeed Ne Win, was purged along with his service branch, which was thought to have gained too much power and institutional autonomy.[36] At the same time, one expects that there had to be some discontent among the *Tatmadaw*'s senior echelons, since many of these generals were denied promotions as a result of stagnation at the very top, where no mandatory retirement age applied.

In spite of these issues, there was no reason to believe that the Burmese military would split in its response to an uprising. Still, I believe that the overall "Internal Cohesion" factor (I.1.) had a decisive impact on the generals for several reasons. First, throughout much of their existence, the abiding concern of the Burmese armed forces has been the *possibility* of a rift in the *Tatmadaw*.[37] There were strong institutional memories of the disastrous mutinies of the 1940s and 1950s, which nearly saw the country collapse. Given that the military regime depended on its coercive power (exercised primarily through the army), the loyalty and cohesion of the armed forces was essential for continued military rule, which also included unity, independence, and sovereignty. Even if a split was unlikely in 1988 (and in 2007), it was a tremendous concern for the military regime, leading us to believe that one of the most important reasons for the army's violent response to the demonstrations was that the protests might cause a schism in the *Tatmadaw*.

This lends credence to some observers' belief that what finally forced the *Tatmadaw*'s hand on September 18 was the appearance of some soldiers among the marchers. At first they were mostly junior airmen from a nearby air force base, but later, a growing number of young sailors and soldiers joined them.[38] There are those who question this view and, while conceding that a few units in the navy and air force *were* reported to have joined the demonstrators, insist that their numbers were "so small as to be insignificant."[39] In their view, the growing disorder and the increasingly violent nature of protests was more likely a "final straw" that spurred the reprisals on September 18. Given the generals' near paranoia regarding the inviolability of the *Tatmadaw*'s unity, and the notion that, again, we are interested in explaining the perceptions—regardless of whether or not those perceptions were based on fact—that guided the generals' decision-making process, I prefer the first explanation.

Unlike in many other revolutions, the vast majority of personnel in all branches of the Burmese armed forces, most of whom *were* enlisted soldiers, did not evidence any hesitation about confronting demonstrators or opening fire on unarmed protesters on the streets (I.2.).[40] Why is this an important point? The soldiers, after all, were volunteers, not draftees: although there has always been a legal framework allowing for conscription in postindependence Burma, it has never been used. Until 1988, the army was made up purely of volunteers, although some specialists, such as doctors, were forced to serve in the army to pay back the government for their education.[41] This fact is noteworthy because, unlike most enlisted soldiers in professional armies, Burmese army volunteers were treated poorly by the army as an institution, which offered low pay and few benefits, and by their commanders, who routinely mistreated and humiliated them. These young men in uniform essentially suffered from the same miserable living standards and the same stifling political suppression visited on Burmese society. Even junior officers (I.1.B.) and NCOs (I.1.C.) had plenty of reasons to be dissatisfied, given that they were also inadequately remunerated and frequently abused by their superiors, and yet they remained loyal to the regime. So how to account for this anomaly?

What explains the fundamental unity of the Burmese military and its soldiers' willingness to shoot their fellow citizens is the remarkably potent combination of the Burmese army's strong emphasis on internal discipline and their strict approach to authority coupled with the soldiers' blind loyalty to and fear of their superiors, their modest education, and their deeply held superstitions, which were easily exploited by their commanders. As any successful socialist army, the *Tatmadaw* had developed an extremely capable propaganda machinery. By all accounts, the military had been able to persuade its officers and enlisted men—as well as large segments of the rest of society who were indoctrinated beginning in primary schools—that it had a central role in achieving and then maintaining Burma's independence and territorial integrity as well as protecting its Buddhist heritage, and no other institution or political movement (had they been permitted to exist) could be an acceptable alternative. It ought to be recognized that these beliefs were not just the product of clever regime propaganda, but, at least in 1988, they were *sincerely held* by many in the officer corps, in the ranks, and in large portions of the civilian population, as well.[42]

More specifically, in late summer 1988, the *Tatmadaw* gave all outward signs that it had succeeded in convincing its personnel—officers, NCOs, and privates alike—that those taking part in the demonstrations were not just traitors but also communists who wanted to destroy the state and/or were in the employ of foreign countries. This nonstop barrage of propaganda effectively checked whatever influence the student movement might have had on the soldiers, convinced them of the indispensability of continued military rule, and incited them to denounce the disorder and violence represented by the opposition. In sum, Burma's military regime, unlike so many ruling regimes that fell victim to revolutions, succeeded in turning its ill-treated soldiers into shooters.

Another "military variable" that should not be dismissed out of hand is the armed forces' view of the regime—in this case a military regime (I.3.). Although certainly, as a general rule, the top brass and members of the officer corps are the beneficiaries of a military regime, in some cases they might very well want to give up power and return to the barracks, due to their suffering from what Samuel Finer called "governance fatigue."[43] There are quite a few examples that readily come to mind, such as Ghana in 1969, and South Korea and Chile in the late 1980s.

Nevertheless, Burmese generals had no intention of turning over control at this point, as they so clearly confirmed following the 1990 "mostly free" elections in which regime-supported candidates fared extremely poorly. Therefore, in this context, abdicating power was not a factor for the *Tatmadaw* elites to consider.

SOCIETAL FACTORS

The size of demonstrations continued to grow, and by August–September 1988, the number of participants reached hundreds of thousands in Rangoon and millions across the country. The sheer size of the crowds confounded the political leadership (III.1.). Notwithstanding some earlier protests, the regime had not faced anything like the student-led popular uprising in their quarter century of governing. The generals were so worried that they brought in units that had previously been fighting against border-area insurgencies to suppress the revolution. They calculated that these troops—many uneducated and from faraway regions—would prove immune to the protesters' potential fraternization efforts (III.3.). The unprecedented size of the demonstrations was the most important factor in the generals' decisions—along with their fear of a rift in the military.

Although the opposition movement had several important achievements to its credit—most importantly, its ability to mobilize large numbers to join demonstrations and antiregime activities—on balance, it was far from a formidable foe for the military. The protesters included different segments of the Burmese society, but the student-led opposition was unable to draw into the uprising two potentially significant participants: critical masses from Burma's large agricultural population and the country's ethnic minorities, some with well-organized and battle-hardened guerrilla forces. Additionally, the opposition was only partially successful in attracting the active participation of Buddhist monks, whose more extensive involvement might have been symbolically invaluable. Some monks served the demonstrators by organizing protection for neighborhoods once the police and the army no longer discharged their law-enforcement functions. Nevertheless, many monasteries remained outside of the uprising, at least in part due to the regime's successful control over them. The spreading chaos and the violence perpetrated by some demonstrators seemed to turn off large portions of the population. As in other revolutionary contexts—for example Poland in 1980–81 or contemporary Syria—it seems that many Burmese were increasingly exhausted by the chaos, having reached what one might call "uprising fatigue," and were keen to resume their lives even under continued military rule.

In some settings, as we saw in the Iranian case, fraternization is an effective tactic, but Burmese protesters, despite some minor feats, were unable to enlist a large number of soldiers, let alone higher ranking military personnel, to their side. It is also worth noting that professional military personnel, even if they would have contemplated changing sides, might well have reckoned that they would have been unlikely to fare well if the military regime had been defeated. It did not help that the movement had also turned increasingly violent: protesters killed Military Intelligence Service agents they suspected of being provocateurs, tried and executed individuals accused of being traitors before "people's courts," burned down a police station (murdering officers who fled the flames), and even invented stories of rape by soldiers to mobilize opinion against the regime.[44]

Clearly, the students were inexperienced and in over their heads in dealing with the authorities.[45] They unwisely dismissed out of hand concessions offered by Maung Maung and would not consider any outcome other than the immediate replacement of the ruling elites with an interim government which, realistically, was extremely unlikely to happen. Moreover, they continued to challenge and harass soldiers who were withdrawn on August 24. Just as importantly, student leaders did not recognize the regime's missteps and, therefore, could not exploit them to their own ends.

Despite numerous attempts, the students were unable to unite the movement's principal organizers into a single leadership council that could have managed the disparate strike committees and provided overall guidance to the uprising. On the contrary, the actions of some of key opposition figures ended up deepening the divisions within their own ranks. For instance, when U Nu announced his shadow government and declared himself the country's legitimate prime minister on August 26, other opposition leaders, like Aung San Suu Kyi, failed to rally behind him. In fact, in a speech delivered at Rangoon's famous Shwedagon Pagoda on the same day, she asked participants to continue to support the military adding,

> I feel strong attachment to the armed forces. Not only were they built up by my father, as a child I was cared for by soldiers. I would therefore not wish to see any splits and struggle between the army which my father built up and the people who love my father so much.[46]

In short, the student movement was quite adept at generating mass support but less capable and skilled in channeling that support to achieve its desired political outcomes.

At the end of the day, the most important reason for the failure of the 1988 revolution, as Christina Fink so aptly put it, was the regime's ability

> to regain control because the generals could command the obedience of enough of their officers and soldiers. Although some soldiers did join the movement, or refused to shoot, there were plenty who did not desert but stayed to pull the trigger as they were told.[47]

THE TWO DECADES BETWEEN THE UPHEAVALS

In order to understand the political environment in which the 2007 "Saffron Revolution" took place, we need appreciate how and why political life, military rule, and the opposition movement had changed in the nineteen years between the two uprisings. This section aims to do just that.

For the new SLORC leadership, the 1988 uprising signaled the emergence of a new "threat" to their rule—the citizenry whom they now regarded as "objects of distrust and potential enemies."[48] The SLORC reacted to this threat by establishing a harsher totalitarian regime that was even less open to compromise. The generals suspended the 1974 Constitution and abolished all national political institutions from the BSPP era. They tightened political controls, prohibiting, for instance, unsanctioned gatherings of more than three people. The regime also shut down the dynamic free media outlets that sprang to life in 1987–88. Instead, it put in place an effective system of censorship; maintained a stream of undiluted propaganda on radio, television, and billboards; and relentlessly persecuted opposition activists who remained in Burma. In 1992, Saw Maung resigned, citing health concerns, and was succeeded by another hard-liner, Senior General Than Shwe, who headed the junta—renamed in 1997 the State Peace and Developmental Council (SPDC)—until 2011.

The beginning of the SLORC regime also marked a generational shift in the *Tatmadaw*'s senior officer corps as younger officers replaced Ne Win's contemporaries. Although the military government always had an undisputed single leader (Ne Win, Saw Maung, Than Shwe), rivalries among the most senior generals had seldom completely ceased.[49] Power struggles within the leadership occasionally surfaced, most manifestly in 2004 when Prime Minister (and former Chief of Intelligence) Khin Nyunt was alleged to threaten Than Shwe's position. Khin Nyunt was a pragmatist who was open to dialogue with the opposition and said to consider some limited political reforms, thereby evoking the ire of the SPDC hardliners. For Khin Nyunt, an ethnic Chinese fluent in English, the kiss of death was when Chinese leaders dubbed him the "Deng Xiaoping of Burma."[50] He was purged and held under house arrest until 2012. Tensions between service branches, particularly infantry and intelligence, continued to occasionally resurface until 2004, when almost the entire military intelligence apparatus—most of them supporters of or allied with Khin Nyunt—was purged.[51] Another enduring cleavage persisted between generals serving in the *Tatmadaw*'s central administration in the capital, on the one hand, and regional commanders, some of them directing combat in the border areas, on the other. By 2007, the top brass had removed practically all high-ranking officers supportive of liberalization.

In May 1990, the regime held a surprisingly free multiparty election, where it was represented by the BSPP's newly organized successor, the National Unity Party (NUP). Aung San Suu Kyi led the opposition's National League for Democracy (NLD), which originated in the 1988 uprising. One cannot help but wonder why an all-powerful military dictatorship held relatively free elections? What could they possibly gain? The simple answer is that the military regime was convinced that it would triumph at the polls and expected this victory to strengthen its legitimacy and popular support.[52] The privileged, rich, and corrupt ruling elites could think this way only because they were entirely out of touch with the downtrodden, demoralized, and poor general population that, for the first time, had a chance to freely express its political preferences.

In the end, the NUP suffered a crushing, humiliating defeat, winning just 21.9 percent of the popular vote and only 10 seats in the 492-seat constituent assembly, while the NLD garnered nearly 52.5 percent of the ballots and 392 seats (several dozen other parties, most representing national minorities, shared the rest). The SLORC was stunned, refusing to honor the results and arresting NLD activists. If the regime was isolated from its citizenry in 1990, they became even more alienated in 2005, when the government decided to move the capital to Naypyidaw—a planned city of surreal proportion, 240 miles north of Rangoon. The new capital, built at enormous cost, was a politicoadministrative enclave, ostensibly conceived to make it more difficult for potential foreign invaders to overthrow the regime.

Political elites also finally realized the general population's deep-seated discontent with their living standards and responded by discarding the socialist economic model and replacing it with a more market-oriented approach. The direct effect of the new policy was large-scale corruption and the brazen exploitation and export of Burma's considerable natural resources (timber, precious gems, gold, etc.) for the personal gain of the top military leadership and their family members. This partly explains why the economy had continued, at best, to stagnate with a per capita gross domestic product (GDP) in 2006 that was half that of Bangladesh or Laos.[53] After 1988, millions of Burmese went abroad to work and escape the harsh political and socioeconomic realities in their homeland. Poverty went hand-in-hand with government ineffectiveness, as measured by the World Bank. In 2005, Burma's score of 2.4 percent was by far the lowest among eleven Southeast Asian countries, significantly lower than those of Cambodia (14.8 percent) and Laos (12 percent), let alone Singapore (99.5 percent) or Malaysia (80.4 percent).[54]

Several noteworthy developments took place in the military between 1988 and 2007. First, the number of armed forces personnel had doubled to approximately 400,000, and its equipment and training facilities had undergone a comprehensive modernization program. The army leadership realized that it needed a larger force to face not just potential challenges from abroad but also to suppress domestic upheavals. Significant increases in defense expenditures—although the precise figures are difficult to estimate[55]—allowed for higher pay and more extensive privileges for officers. As in many other armies serving under dictatorships, personal loyalty trumped merit where professional advancement was concerned. The unintended but logical consequence of the *Tatmadaw*'s expansion were lower recruitment standards, accompanied by the escalation of disciplinary problems, and sinking morale among the soldiers. The regime required village and town leaders to fill recruitment quotas, and the selected local youngsters were rarely the best and brightest.[56] The army leadership employed various coercive measures to expand the military—claims that children as young as fifteen had been tricked into enlisting or even kidnapped by army recruiters surfaced in numerous instances—and placed restrictions on people wanting to leave the *Tatmadaw*.[57] Significantly, however, even at this point, the army did not formally implement a national conscription scheme. (The provision permitting conscription was retained in the new [2008] constitution, presumably to give the government the option during national emergencies.[58])

Aside from expanding the armed forces, the generals also augmented the capabilities of the police and intelligence agencies to shore up the regime's defense against future domestic confrontations.[59] In addition, the

SLORC brought under its control a number of organizations—some of them were newly established, such as the Union Solidarity and Development Association (USDA) in 1993—to serve the military's needs and support its policies.[60] Given the large membership of some of these groups, they also proved useful as vehicles for the junta to control ever larger segments of the population. Burmese generals were similar to their colleagues in many authoritarian states, insofar as they discouraged passing bad news up the chain of command. This trait, in turn, dropped them even further out of touch with the general population.

Second, the need to transfer soldiers from insurgencies on Burma's frontiers to suppress the 1988 uprising in the cities made the regime recognize the critical importance of resolving or at least stabilizing the conflict with ethnic minorities. The generals succeeded in negotiating, one by one, cease-fire agreements that included granting different degrees of autonomy with at least seventeen armed ethnic organizations. A side benefit of these pacts was that they allowed the junta to gain control over prized trade routes and made their wholesale export of the country's riches all the easier, which is the third important military-related development of this era.[61] Namely, the liberalization of the economic system went hand-in-hand with the military's growing rent-seeking activities. The *Tatmadaw* increased its participation in the national economy by, for instance, creating military-managed or military-backed companies, renting out regimental facilities, and selling electricity. The generals also formed a number of large holding companies that fully owned and ran small- and medium-sized tax-exempt enterprises. One of the biggest, the Union of Myanmar Economic Holding, Ltd., controlled fifty-one firms in 2007.[62] The culture of impunity and the growing temptations fostered by expanding opportunities greatly increased large-scale corruption, something that was unusual during Ne Win's rule.

Between the two upheavals, significant changes took place in Burma's foreign relations, as well. After 1988, Western interest in Burma had increased, even if it was manifested by the withdrawal of economic aid and the introduction of a range of sanctions against the military government. Aung San Suu Kyi, who received the Nobel Peace Prize in 1991, had become the focus of Western diplomatic, political, and media attention; in fact, one expert claimed, "No living foreigner has shaped contemporary US attitudes toward a single country more than Aung San Suu Kyi."[63] The junta, therefore, reluctantly turned toward China, India, and Thailand for support and much needed economic and commercial opportunities. These countries and members of the Association of Southeast Asian

Nations (ASEAN), which Burma joined in 1997, also sensed the potential business ventures that lay in closer relation to the generals' regime and not only seemed little perturbed by their policies but, in fact, extended sustained regional support to them.[64] ASEAN states in the 1990s and 2000s were rather wary of Burma becoming a "satellite of China," but they underestimated the junta, which was quite apt at playing one regional power off another and exploiting regional rivalries to their advantage.[65]

In sum, the military regime had only become stronger in the nearly two decades after the 1988 revolution. At the same time, the opposition's woes had continued, as it not only had failed to come together but, in fact, had been fragmented even further following the uprising. This notion was demonstrated by the dozens of parties—some ninety-three in all—that ran candidates in the 1990 elections. Afterward, the junta successfully isolated the opposition movement's leaders by confining them in jails, prison camps, or in their own homes. The most emblematic opposition leader, Aung San Suu Kyi, spent much of the 1988–2011 period under house arrest. The NLD, the organization she founded, did not succeed in embracing all those in opposition to the military regime, in large part because its leaders were not willing to compromise. Aung San Suu Kyi, herself, received a fair amount of criticism for not focusing on unifying the organization, for continuing to surround herself with the unimaginative octogenarian men of the NLD's Central Executive Committee (often referred to as "the Uncles") who were ill-equipped to reach compromises with the regime, as well as for failing to mobilize opposition forces and obtaining the support of young people.

The junta continued its prolonged efforts to control Buddhist monks, while at the same time convince the population of its piety. To boost their legitimacy and demonstrate their direct connection to the past, the generals even adopted some of the ceremonial functions of ancient kings. Their campaign included some bizarre episodes—one example, Senior General Saw Maung's public declaration that he was the reincarnation of King Kyanzittha (1030–1113), one of the greatest Burmese monarchs.[66] Meanwhile, the SLORC and then the SPDC continued to pressure abbots to join local state-controlled *Sangha* committees, which more or less effectively oversaw their monasteries' activities. The regime routinely arrested recalcitrant monks and harassed their monasteries in order to compel them to rein in their wayward brethren. The harassment of the abbeys took on renewed emphasis after 1996, when the Ministry of Religious Affairs charged the NLD with infiltrating the *Sangha* in order to champion the party's cause and commit subversive acts against the government.[67] To be fair, the generals preferred to use the carrot rather than the stick in their dealings with the monks. They proudly claimed to be guardians of Buddhism and to preserve and promote Buddhist sites, which included building pagodas and granting gifts. It is somewhat ironic, then, that the "Saffron Revolution" was led by the monks who rose against the generals.

THE 2007 "SAFFRON REVOLUTION"

The growing poverty and economic dislocations had already motivated some isolated demonstrations during the summer of 2007. The regime's announcement, without any warning, of a five hundred percent increase in the price of fuel (gasoline, diesel, and compressed natural gas) on August 15—likely to have been an extremely unwise ad hoc step to alleviate a cash-flow problem[68]—however, became the direct cause of an uprising that, in the end, brought tens of thousands of people into the streets. This was by far the largest opposition protest in Burma since 1988 and, while it, too, failed, it might well have planted the seed of the eventual liberalization process that began three years later. The chronological parameters of the "Saffron Revolution" extend from the August 15 government announcement and ended with the junta's suppression of the demonstrations on September 26–28 and can be conveniently divided into three stages.

Phase 1: August 15–September 4

The unannounced five-fold increase in the price of fuel was a heavy blow for poor Burmese—and the vast majority of Burmese *were* very poor[69]—because it multiplied their transportation, cooking, and lighting costs (outside of Rangoon, electricity—which was generated by gas generators—was sporadic). Consequently, people's ability to donate food to Buddhist monasteries greatly diminished, which became an existential problem for Burma's hundreds of thousands of monks. Moreover, many destitute citizens who were unable to provide for their children traditionally took them to monasteries to be fed, a mission the monks could no longer perform. This desperation sent people to the streets as early as August 19, when small, peaceful, and silent demonstrations took place in Rangoon to protest the price increases. Experienced opposition activists led and organized most of these protests. Local authorities, in turn, did their best to identify and arrest them, usually at night, hoping to stop the demonstrations.[70]

Phase 2: September 5–21

On September 5, just as the fuel protests began to die down, several hundred monks in the central Burmese town of Pakokku organized a march that soon attracted the support of the townspeople to demand the withdrawal of price increases. In response, *Swan Arr Shinn* thugs—*Swan Arr Shinn* ("The Strong Ones") being a state-supported, state-trained paramilitary organization affiliated with the USDA—severely beat many monks, and security forces fired rubber bullets into the crowd of marchers, possibly killing one (a claim that has never been confirmed). It is important to emphasize that in a deeply devout society such as the Burmese, to physically harm unarmed, peaceful Buddhist monks is considered an extraordinarily cruel and repulsive act. Five days later, the "All Burma Monks' Alliance" (ABMA) announced its formation and began to circulate a petition on the Internet that quickly spread to monasteries across the country. The document made four demands to the SPDC—apologize for the Pakokku incident; withdraw the price increases; release all political prisoners, including those incarcerated in the current protests; and immediate dialogue with the "democratic forces"—and set the deadline for meeting them on September 17.[71]

On that day, the monks, who had waited for the regime's apology in vain—the SPDC made some donations but also increased security around monasteries—turned over their alms bowls, indicating that they would not accept donations from members of the armed forces and their families, a serious offense to lay Buddhists who would now be unable to acquire "merit." On September 18—an auspicious date as it was the nineteenth anniversary of the military takeover—monks in numerous cities and towns followed the example of their Pakokku brethren and marched, denouncing the regime. They often did so in heavy rain, wearing only their robes and flip-flops, a sight that did not fail to move many pious Burmese.[72] More and more citizens stood with the monks to protect them from the authorities. The ABMA called on all monasteries to join the boycott, although some of them refrained—likely because their very survival depended on public donations.[73] The SPDC rewarded these monasteries with generous gifts for refusing to join the boycott. Otherwise, the regime's coercive apparatus appeared to be mostly unruffled: apart from videotaping the growing protests, they allowed them to unfold.

Phase 3: September 22–28

The difference between phases 2 and 3 is primarily the size of the protests —in phase 3, hundreds of thousands of people participated in the demonstrations at one point or another across Burma—and the growing resolve of the regime to stamp them out. On September 22, tens of thousands of monks and mostly young opposition sympathizers marched in Rangoon, demanding not just economic and political reforms but, increasingly, the overthrow of the military regime.[74] About five hundred monks broke off from the crowd and were inexplicably allowed to pass through a military checkpoint in order to visit Aung San Suu Kyi. She came to the front gate of her compound to address them—this was the first time she was publicly seen in four years—and her presence and support galvanized the protests.[75] When demonstrations had grown to fifty thousand people in Rangoon, some carrying NLD banners and chanting antiregime and prodemocracy slogans, the regime began to lose its theretofore remarkable composure. Brigadier General Thura Myint Maung, the Minister for Religious Affairs, called on the Supreme Sangha Council to order all monks back to their monasteries and prohibit their political activism, but these instructions had only limited effect. The general blamed the NLD, the Communist Party of Burma (which had virtually no influence on the events), foreign agents, and media organizations (the British Broadcasting Company and the Voice of America, in particular) for inciting the protests. On September 25, the state-run newspaper, *New Light of Myanmar*, published several mostly ineffectual directives, ordering the monks to end their political activities and prohibiting further demonstrations. On that day, too, the regime imposed a curfew, began the large-scale arrest of protesters, and surrounded monasteries.[76]

The junta waited for nearly a week before it resorted to large-scale violence. The final crackdown began on September 26, when soldiers, riot police, and *Swan Arr Shin* goons assaulted unarmed monks and took hundreds of demonstrators into custody. Loudspeakers on army trucks ordered people off the streets, to obey the newly announced curfew and the prohibition of public gatherings. Soldiers first fired warning shots in the air, but when protesters refused to disperse, they trained their guns against the people. It took the generals three days to restore order in Rangoon as well as the rest of the country. Meanwhile, army units raided more than fifty monasteries, arrested monks they considered to be ringleaders, and sent thousands of others back to their home villages.[77] The ABMA's leader, U Gambira, a 28-year-old abbot, was arrested and charged with treason—he was later sentenced to sixty-eight years in prison, though he received amnesty in January 2012.[78]

All in all, the SPDC regime acted with noticeably more restraint than in 1988, although it is important to stress that the challenge to the regime was considerably more modest in 2007. There are no entirely reliable casualty figures that have been independently confirmed; however, according to numerous sources, the crackdown resulted in thirty-one dead, including a Japanese press photographer, and seventy-four "disappearances," although activists and some foreign media organizations initially published far higher numbers.[79]

EXPLAINING THE MILITARY'S RESPONSE

Were the generals' reactions to the upheaval surprising? The most important point regarding the army's reaction to the "Saffron Revolution" is that, as Burma expert Andrew Selth noted, "despite claims of confusion and dissension within the regime, its response to these disturbances was never in doubt."[80] The most important factors behind the SPDC's reaction to the upheaval, just as in 1988, were the *Tatmadaw*'s cohesion (I.1.) and, even more so, the size of the demonstrations (III.1.)—or, perhaps more correctly, the very fact that there were demonstrations.

If anything, the military regime was more powerful in 2007 than two decades before and was not in serious danger of falling for a number of largely predictable reasons. Most important, while the entire *Tatmadaw* leadership might not have endorsed using violence against the unarmed monks, the generals certainly remained united in their desire to stay in power. The top officials *were* the regime, the armed forces were professional, and the rebels, once again, were unable to persuade soldiers to support their cause—perhaps because would-be defectors realized that they might well have to pay the ultimate price if the uprising failed and, realistically, the chances of that failure were exceedingly high.[81]

The *Tatmadaw*'s officer corps was more cohesive and its personnel better paid, better equipped, and generally better off than two decades before. The military leadership was probably apprehensive about the demoralizing effects the threat of religious boycott might have on the soldiers (I.2.) most of whom, along with their commanders, were practicing Buddhists.[82] Nonetheless, as in 1988, the years of indoctrination, training, esprit de corps, and the magnitude of anticipated sanctions punishing disobedience once again overrode whatever misgivings the soldiers might have had about turning their guns against the demonstrators. Additionally, many of the soldiers that were used against the demonstrators were selected from battle-tested infantry combat units whose loyalty was not doubted. Still, the violent repression of the deeply revered monks was a formative moment in Burmese state-society relations, as it marked the strongest threat to the remaining legitimacy of the junta.[83]

Fundamentally, while the regime became stronger than it was two decades earlier, the opposition appeared to be weaker (III.1.). Although given the resolve and unity of the generals' coercive machinery, this was more or less an unwinnable uprising, the numerous failures of the opposition are difficult to ignore. As I noted above, not all monks joined the protests. Bearing in mind that estimates put the number of monks at approximately 400,000 to half-a-million,[84] only a fraction of them appear to have actively participated. Although marchers who joined the monks included students, NLD members and sympathizers, and other prodemocracy activists, once again, the opposition was unable to tap into the two huge reservoirs of potential supporters: blue-collar workers and peasants. Moreover, the democracy movement, if indeed one can call it that, had no widely acknowledged leadership and no apparent coordination: the protests seemed to be unplanned and to have come about in an almost haphazard manner. The NLD itself had become even less of a unifying force, because young people could not abide by its internal dynamics, which resembled the rigidly hierarchical "democratic centralism" of Leninist parties. After nearly twenty years, the NLD was still lacking a coherent strategy, was unable to modify or diversify its tactics, and had essentially no leverage to force the generals into negotiations—leaving it no realistic chance of undermining state authority.[85]

With respect to technology, the "Saffron Revolution" was different from the previous uprising because ordinary Burmese were not misled by the false reports of state-owned media or rumors that the generals could deny. For the first time, their main source of information was amateur videos, where they could see images of the regime's repression of their fellow citizens captured on personal electronic devices and posted on the Internet. The regime realized the power of this new technology only when the content had already become widely available. To prevent further reports and the dissemination of film clips, the junta shut down the Internet on September 28 and did not restore service for a week.[86]

Ironically, even though the 2007 upheaval was far smaller than the People Power Uprising, it attracted a great deal more international attention.[87] It is also ironic that the "Saffron Revolution" drew international attention mostly *after* the generals had already suppressed the protests. Powerful international actors, like the United States, France, Great Britain, and the European Union, imposed some travel restrictions and limited sanctions against Burma, but regional powerhouses, such as China and India—that is, those with more proximity to, more investment in, and, therefore, more leverage over the junta—elected to do little more than announce that they were "monitoring the situation."[88] In the end, it is hard to disagree with seasoned Burma experts who noted, "It is highly unlikely that the generals proceed according to advice or threats from foreign experts or officials" and "Burma's military government seems impervious to external influences."[89]

CONCLUSION

After having learned about Iran's successful revolution in the previous chapter, we considered failed uprisings in this one. On the surface, the Burmese military might seem quite similar to its Iranian counterpart, but on closer inspection, it turns out to be rather different, and even a superficial comparison of the Iranian opposition in 1978–79 shows it to be very different from the Burmese student movement of 1988 and the monk-led marchers of 2007.

What immediately sets the Burmese generals apart from their Iranian colleagues is that they were the de facto rulers of their country. Although the generals in Rangoon, and later, Naypyidaw, were no strangers to factionalism, it is important to understand that these cleavages centered not on different worldviews but on personalities, and they did not compromise the military's commitment to preserving the regime and, when necessary, suppressing the opposition. This is the main reason that the generals' decisions to defend their positions of power were hardly surprising. The *Tatmadaw* also had a great deal of combat experience, given its long-standing battle against ethnic minority insurgents. Another significant factor in favor of the military government was that, certainly in 1988, it had enjoyed deep-seated support in several major quarters of Burmese society. The regime was skillful in manipulating particularly the large majority of uneducated and poor ethnic Burmese, who genuinely believed its propaganda of safeguarding independence and upholding national unity, battling communists and hostile minorities, and preserving and promoting Buddhism. Accosting and humiliating monks in 2007

Table 2. Burma, 1988 and 2007: Factors affecting the army's response to revolutions

	Burma 1988	Burma 2007
I. MILITARY FACTORS		
I.1. The Armed Forces' Internal Cohesion	6	4
I.1.A. ethnic, religious, tribal, and regional splits	0	0
I.1.B. generational divisions: senior vs. junior officers	1	1
I.1.C. divisions between officers and NCOs/privates	2	2
I.1.D. divisions between elite vs. regular units	0	0
I.1.E. splits between the army, other branches, and security sector entities	2	2
I.1.F. sociopolitical divisions between military elites	2	2
I.2. Professional Soldiers vs. Conscripts	4	2
I.3. The Generals' Perception of Regime Legitimacy	0	0
I.4. The Army's Past Conduct toward Society	1	1
II. STATE FACTORS		
II.1. Regime's Treatment of the Military	0	0
II.1.A. taking care of the personnel's material welfare	0	0
II.1.B. taking care of the army	0	0
II.1.C. appropriateness of missions	0	0
II.1.D. the generals' professional autonomy and decision-making authority	0	0
II.1.E. fairness in top appointments	0	0
II.1.F. the military's prestige and public esteem	2	2
II.2. Regime Directions to the Military	0	0
III. SOCIETAL FACTORS		
III.1. The Size, Composition, and Nature of the Protests	6	6
III.2. The Popularity of the Uprising	4	4
III.3. Fraternization	3	2
IV. EXTERNAL FACTORS		
IV.1. The Potential for Foreign Intervention	3	0
IV.2. Foreign Affairs	0	0
IV.3. Revolutionary Diffusion	0	0
IV.4. Foreign Exposure of Military Officers	0	0

Top six factors are in bold.
Scale (0–6):
0 = irrelevant, not a factor
1 = of trivial importance
2 = of little importance
3 = somewhat important
4 = quite important
5 = very important
6 = critical, decisive

called into question this last claim and prompted the subsequent erosion of the regime's legitimacy. One aspect that stood out during both crises was the soldiers' willingness to suppress unarmed civilians. The military's indoctrination campaign, the soldiers' low levels of education, and the threat of punishment for disloyalty go far in explaining this point.

Certainly, the Burmese generals had a far easier job suppressing the opposition than their colleagues in Tehran. One of the surprising things we learned in this chapter is the inability of the Burmese opposition to develop a strategy, unite, coordinate activities, learn to compromise, and find ways to exploit the regime's weaknesses. Quite simply, for a cohesive military force like the *Tatmadaw*, the Burmese democracy movement hardly presented a daunting challenge either in 1988 or in 2007. In fact, the latter upheaval mobilized a far smaller number of people and was accompanied by far less violence which, in turn, allowed the military to exercise some restraint in its suppression tactics. Unlike the demonstrators in Tehran, the students and monks in Burma were remarkably ineffective in persuading a critical mass of soldiers, who in most cases were their contemporaries, to defect from the armed forces. An important similarity between Iran and Burma is the religious leaders' decision to distance themselves from and, in the former, forthrightly oppose the regime, confirming Goodwin and Skocpol's long-ago contention that such a development makes it exceedingly difficult for authoritarian rulers to maintain their political legitimacy.[90] In Iran, the Shah's regime never recovered, while in Burma, the generals were compelled to accommodate the religious establishment as much as possible, though at the same time resolutely opposing the monks' challenges to their regime.

All in all, seasoned Burma experts were not—or, in any event, should not have been—surprised at the outcome of these upheavals. As Chorley contended, a revolution would have no chance against an army willing to use all of its resources to suppress it. The generals commanding the *Tatmadaw* were certainly ready to do that, and their job was made easier by the failings of their opponents. In sum, predicting that the Burmese army would suppress the uprisings and prevail both in 1988 and in 2007 could not have been any easier.

4

⌒ᕼᕮ⌒

China and Eastern Europe, 1989

In the following two chapters, we will examine upheavals—or, in some cases, regime change—in a group of states where the virus of revolution spread from one besieged capital to another. The Soviet Union politically, economically, and militarily dominated the six East European states—Bulgaria, Czechoslovakia, East Germany, Hungary, Poland, and partially, Romania—from the end of World War II. Although Soviet control was extensive in the first decade, afterward, domestic political approaches varied as Moscow's reins became looser. Poland and Hungary had become relatively liberal—although Poland, less consistently so—as their leaders were carefully probing the limits of Soviet tolerance. Both experienced major social upheavals (Poland in 1956, 1970–71, 1976, 1980–81; Hungary in 1956) with important and prolonged domestic political consequences.

The four other communist states continued to tow the conservative line, with each marked by unique characteristics. Czechoslovakia's leaders decided upon a deeply authoritarian path following the 1968 Prague Spring, a reform movement that pursued "socialism with a human face" and ended with the Warsaw Pact's[1] invasion. East Germany had stuck to a steady conservative course throughout the Cold War, its elites all too aware of the temptations of freedom and democracy just a stone's throw away. No noteworthy opposition activity took place in either Bulgaria or Romania, and both had steered a conservative line. The key difference between them was that the former was Moscow's most loyal European ally, while the latter the most troublesome.

The Soviet Union had established multifaceted military control over all of these countries, with the exception of Romania, after the 1960s. The East European armies were the servants not of national but of supranational—that is, Soviet and Marxist-Leninist—interests. The USSR stationed tens of thousands of troops in Czechoslovakia (1968–91), East Germany (1945–93), Hungary (1945–91), Poland (1945–93), and Romania (1945–58);[2] many of their barracks were located next to the native armies' bases, just to ensure their loyalty. The East European states, with the partial exception of Romania, were not independent in any real sense. Communism was imposed, literally, at the point of Red Army bayonets, and the prolongation of state-socialist rule was guaranteed by Soviet hegemony.

In the 1980s, numerous research projects attempted to gauge the reliability of Warsaw Pact armies.[3] The findings differed from country to country, and analysts did not always agree about their conclusions. In general, they were deeply skeptical of the East European conscript armies' willingness to protect the unpopular posttotalitarian regimes from domestic revolts. The uprisings against socialism were suppressed by Soviet/Warsaw Pact military power or the implicit or explicit threat of intervention, which is why the rise of Mikhail Gorbachev to the top of the Soviet political hierarchy was of decisive historical importance for East Europeans.

In 1986, the year after his ascension in the Soviet communist party, Gorbachev and his foreign minister, Eduard Shevardnadze, came to recognize that the status quo in Eastern Europe could not be maintained.[4] Once Gorbachev embraced reforms, East European communist party chiefs could no longer justify their refusal to liberalize or use the threat of Soviet military suppression to maintain control. Once Gorbachev made it clear—officially so in July 1989—that the USSR would no longer interfere in the domestic affairs of its satellites, the rug was pulled from under the feet of the dictators in East Berlin, Prague, and Sofia. And once the region's opposition groups realized they would not be crushed by Soviet tanks, they boldly forged ahead, confident that their own conscript armies were not going to shoot them. The result was the collapse of all of these communist regimes within six months after Gorbachev's declaration.

In contrast, the People's Republic of China (PRC) has always been a fully sovereign socialist state. By the late 1980s, Deng Xiaoping's policies of economic reform and societal liberalization were nearly a decade old and had brought positive, tangible changes to the lives of many millions of Chinese. Deng also initiated, albeit more cautiously, the modernization of the Chinese armed forces. Nevertheless, there was minimal *political* liberalization in the PRC; furthermore, the political liberalization process ongoing in Poland, Hungary, and the Soviet Union alarmed the Chinese Communist Party (CCP) elites, while it emboldened intellectuals and students eager to increase the pace and reach of reforms.

Much of this chapter is devoted to two bona fide revolutions, one failed and one triumphant: China and Romania. Even though the two countries were quite different, the fundamental causes of the uprisings were rather similar. The communist dictatorships allowed no political liberties in either China or Romania, but the protesters demanded more freedom and, eventually, democracy. One major difference in the causes that spurred the upheavals is that while in both countries' economic woes were among the main reasons for the revolt, in China, the overall economic situation was actually improving; however, protesters were upset about the corruption and inflation that were side effects of Deng's reform program. In contrast, economic conditions in Romania were steadily deteriorating, adding to the population's deepening dissatisfaction with the regime.

Dividing our attention between two main case studies necessitates a somewhat condensed exposition, but its inclusion will reward us with an interesting comparative opportunity. In order to appreciate the process of revolutionary diffusion and the role of the other five communist armies in what were, more or less, peaceful regime transitions, it seems useful to consider them in the analysis, even if in a truncated form. We will follow the East European and Chinese upheavals chronologically starting with the smooth transition of power in Poland and ending with the Romanian revolution.

POLAND AND HUNGARY

Poland and Hungary experienced no revolution but peaceful and carefully negotiated transfers of power from communist to postcommunist political elites. There was no military (or even police) involvement in these groundbreaking events. The first salvo of this change occurred in August 1988, five years after the martial law that forced the Solidarity movement underground was lifted and Minister of Internal Affairs Czesław Kiszczak announced talks with the opposition groups. There were three major reasons for the the Polish United Workers' Party (PUWP) elites' willingness to begin the so-called roundtable negotiations that were conceived to devise a framework for partially free elections. First, the economic reform policies of General Wojciech Jaruzelski, Poland's president and communist party leader, failed, owing to the passive resistance of large segments of Polish society, the regime's lack of legitimacy, and difficult economic conditions. Second, the opposition largely had recovered by 1988 and organized waves of crippling strikes in May and August 1988 that signaled the Polish workers' readiness to challenge the status quo. Third, by this point, Gorbachev recognized the imperative for East European states—which had become a growing economic burden on and a political liability for Moscow—to initiate political and economic reforms. Gorbachev visited Warsaw in July 1988 and persuaded Jaruzelski that reconciliation with the opposition was not only possible but, in fact, desirable.[5] The results of the June 1989 elections astonished the communist leadership— just as they did the Burmese generals following the 1990 elections there— and even surprised Solidarity supporters: the opposition won all but one of the contestable seats.[6] Two months later, Solidarity advisor Tadeusz Mazowiecki became prime minister, commencing Poland's transition to democracy.

There was no real danger that the armed forces would be used against the opposition in 1989. Following the first round of elections, some feared that the Supreme Court might invalidate the results, but Jaruzelski allowed the election process to take its course and committed to respect its outcome. In any event, the Polish army as an institution was not opposed to political reforms.[7] Experts agree that the army would have refused to turn their guns against the people, even if they had been asked.[8] In 1988–89, it was a cohesive organization, without any deep internal divisions. Up to the moment in October 1981 when he became the First Secretary of the PUWP—that is, Poland's de facto ruler—Jaruzelski had enjoyed an enormous amount of authority within the armed forces. In the words of Edward Gierek, the PUWP's chief in 1970–80, Jaruzelski "arranged the armed forces as he pleased" and conducted the military's affairs with minimal party interference.[9] From that point on, however, he started to lose the support of many line officers.[10]

After the repression of Solidarity, the army lost much of its societal prestige, though most Poles still trusted it far more than the police, let alone the security forces. Ordinary people still looked to the army to guarantee the peacefulness of the regime transition process.[11] It was a conscript army, and the vast majority of its soldiers were just as disillusioned with the communist regime as the rest of society. In 1989, the Soviet Union stationed about thirty thousand troops in Poland; at no point was their intervention mentioned by anyone.[12] In fact, Moscow continued to encourage a peaceful political settlement without influencing developments—a position that, as we shall see, the Soviet leadership consistently maintained everywhere in Eastern Europe throughout 1989.

The end of Hungarian socialism was even less dramatic: there were no strikes, no societal upheaval, not even large protests directed against the regime.[13] The main public event was the June 16 ceremonial reburial of the 1956 Revolution's martyrs, overseen by the mostly reformist leadership of the Hungarian Socialist Workers' Party (HSWP) but also featuring key opposition leaders and attended by 250,000 at Budapest's

Heroes' Square. The last communist defense minister, Ferenc Kárpáti, assured the government that the military remained loyal to the regime, but the top leadership clearly recognized that socialism in Hungary was finished. In fact, it was the defense ministry's commandos that raided the arsenals of the 60,000-strong paramilitary Workers' Guard—supposedly the regime's last line of defense—to make sure that its members did not do anything imprudent on the day it was disbanded.[14] On that day, 23 October 1989—which happened to be the thirty-third anniversary of the 1956 Revolution—the Republic of Hungary was proclaimed (to replace the communist "People's Republic" designation).

No one of any consequence in the Hungarian communist party or government apparatus gave serious consideration to deploying the armed forces or the Workers' Guard to save the regime. In any case, it would have been unthinkable for Hungarian conscripts to use their guns against the people—even more so than in 1956. It was Hungary's Warsaw Pact ally, Czechoslovakia, whose communist party leader, Miloš Jakeš, volunteered the Czechoslovak People's Army to "help" put a stop to Hungary's reform movement.[15] Jan Fojtík, the man in charge of ideological matters in the Czechoslovak Communist Party, urged his colleagues in Budapest to move in a "more forceful manner." Fojtík's opposite in the HSWP, János Berecz, reportedly replied,

> The basic lesson to be drawn from the history of socialism is that the military solution is no solution. The Polish army was the best in the bloc, and we were glad when Jaruzelski introduced martial law [in 1981] but even he was unable to consolidate.[16]

In sum, then, the transitions in Poland and Hungary could not have been less violent. The regimes' commitment to peaceful change, coupled with Moscow's insistence that the Soviet Union would be no more than an interested observer, also guaranteed the acquiescence of the top brass in Warsaw and Budapest. Few people would have expected these armies to shoot at their fellow citizens to save an illegitimate and bankrupt political regime in 1989.

CHINA

Like so many revolutions, the upheaval in China started as a spontaneous demonstration. A few hundred students from the University of Political Science and Law went to Tiananmen Square in central Beijing to lay a wreath in memory of the reformist CCP Secretary-General Hu Yaobang, who was purged after vocally supporting the protesting students in 1987 and who died on 15 April 1989. The tribute to Hu turned into a "democracy movement"—a seven-week-long cycle of demonstrations, protests, and hunger strikes that was eventually suppressed by the People's Liberation Army (PLA) on June 3–4.

Most of the early protesters were from Beijing and Beijing Normal Universities, but they were soon joined by others from different colleges. In fact, students from twenty-one institutions of higher education formed a "United Students' Association" a few days after the initial protest to coordinate their activities.[17] Workers, businesspeople, even party functionaries, and military personnel participated in the events alongside the students at various times. On May 4, for instance, crowds cheered a group of protesters from the CCP Central Committee Propaganda Department who carried banners proclaiming that, henceforth, they would only publish the truth![18] On May 17, a group of army administrators, dressed in camouflage, joined a grand procession marching down on Chang'an Avenue—bordering on Tiananmen Square—in support of the students chanting, "Down with corruption!" and "We demand democracy!"[19] Although activities centered in Beijing, the protests spread to many other cities, as well.

Predictably, as the weeks went by the students' demands became more radical. The movement that started with honoring Hu Yaobang quickly shifted to criticize the widespread corruption and high inflation, both of which were thought to be the consequence of Deng Xiaoping's economic reforms. During the course of the uprising, the protesters' demands became even bolder, eventually including sweeping political reforms such as freedom of the press and of assembly. Fundamentally, the students' objective was to push the regime to move toward genuine democratization. Throughout the revolution, they claimed the moral high ground, and their "carefully worded moralistic appeals and scrupulously nonviolent deeds paradoxically raised the stakes in the eyes of China's leaders."[20]

The first major regime response to the protests came on April 26, a few days after students began boycotting their university classes. There was nothing conciliatory about the tone of the CCP's reaction, which was conveyed through an editorial in the *People's Daily*, penned by Premier Li Peng, the second-ranking CCP leader. The article contended that the protests were creating turmoil and relayed a stern warning to the demonstrators, claiming—falsely—that "an extremely small number of people with ulterior motives" was "taking advantage of the young students' feelings of grief for Comrade Hu Yaobang to spread all kinds of rumors to poison and confuse people's minds."[21] As so often happens, an action designed to intimidate backfired and steeled the students' resolve to continue the unrest.

The CCP leadership's opinion of the demonstrations was not undivided. Although most of the party elite viewed the protests with growing apprehension, one party leader—just as Hu in 1987—openly sided with the students and sharply decried the proclamation of martial law that marked the beginning of the party's clampdown. Zhao Ziyang, who led the CCP's reformist wing, appeared on national television on May 4 to express his sympathy with the students' demands and instantly became their hero. He considered the tone of the April 26 editorial unduly harsh and pleaded with the party hard-liners to extend conciliatory gestures toward the protesters. He was rebuffed. On May 19, Zhao visited the young protesters on Tiananmen Square—together with Li Peng, who refused to meet the students after Hu's funeral—and tearfully begged them to give up their hunger strike and save their lives. Zhao clearly saw what others did not: in effect, the hunger strikes and the continued occupation of Tiananmen Square "turned the [students'] movement into a moral crusade and a zero-sum game," and "from then on, a head-on collision was almost inevitable."[22] On the same day, Zhao's prostudent sentiments and categorical refusal to support a violent crackdown resulted in banishment from the party leadership and house arrest for the rest of his life.[23]

Others who questioned using force against the demonstrators included eight retired senior generals who published a letter in a Shanghai newspaper on May 20, the day martial law was proclaimed. In the following days, Deng Xiaoping dispatched top military officers to personally persuade them to change their minds, clearly explaining the Party's view of the unfolding situation to them. The mission succeeded, the old generals relaxed their opposition—it may well be that they just wanted to feel relevant and be consulted.[24] In any case, after Zhao, who had no power base in the military, lost the face-off with Deng and the hard-line leadership, no alternative was left but the eventual repression of the democracy movement.

Soviet President Gorbachev ended up an unwitting "participant" in the Chinese events, owing to his trip to Beijing on May 15–17. The visit—long in planning and conceived to underscore the reconciliation between the two communist parties—could not have come at a more awkward time for the Chinese, for whom it became a diplomatic humiliation. They could not risk spoiling the meeting by suppressing the demonstrations but could also not receive their guest on Tiananmen Square as was customary for high-ranking dignitaries. To make matters worse, Gorbachev's visit further galvanized the demonstrations; on May 17 and 18, the protests attracted well over a million people and inspired some students to start a hunger strike.[25] In turn, the continuing protests and Li Peng's inability to persuade the students to back down hardened the regime's resolve to deal with the crisis, decisively.

By the end of May, the demonstrations had become a popular movement—one that was still dominated by students and intellectuals—that Mao would have been proud of, except that it was directed against his own communist party.[26] Protests sprung up in over one hundred major urban centers, many even with the participation of some industrial workers; however, relatively few workers joined the demonstrations because they were displeased with the increasingly chaotic situation. When they did join, they did so as individuals and not as parts of a bloc because of the hold state enterprises had over them.[27] In the end, Deng and his close associates—six men and one woman with some of the longest and most distinguished CCP careers, often referred to as the "Eight Elders"—agreed that the mounting chaos could only be stopped by declaring martial law and, subsequently, deploying the PLA against the demonstrators. Deng—who, like Mao, relinquished most of his titles—formally headed the CCP's Central Military Commission (CMC), the organization in charge of the regime's entire coercive apparatus. The CMC was actually run by its vice chair, Yang Shangkun, a long-time Deng confidant and one of the longest-serving party leaders.

On May 19 and 20, several units from the Beijing Garrison Command of the Beijing Military District were ordered to the city. By May 23, large contingents of PLA and other security troops entered Beijing. Deng and his colleagues were so confident in these soldiers that they did not instruct them about how to react if they were met with resistance, and they issued no maps for them to plan alternate routes.[28] As it turned out, the troops faced large crowds of ordinary citizens who successfully stymied their mission: many people began to fraternize with the inexperienced and bewildered soldiers. As Li later admitted, the conscripts had no tear gas, rubber bullets, or any sort of riot control gear, let alone appropriate training to deal with the situation.[29] The CCP chiefs recognized that the operation was a fiasco and withdrew the troops from the city on May 26.

On June 2, the CCP leadership branded the upheaval a "counterrevolutionary riot"—falsely implying that the protesters were armed and had shed blood—and ordered the troops to move into the city center.[30] In the "second coming" of the PLA, its soldiers were given unambiguous objectives: clear Tiananmen Square utilizing all necessary means, including using live ammunition against the people. Somewhere between 150,000 and 350,000 soldiers were stationed in Beijing's outskirts, waiting for the command to begin the operation. This time, they were drawn from all over the country—in part, to discourage fraternization—representing more than half of China's army groups. Soldiers, most wearing uniform but many in civilian clothes to aid their infiltration into the city, began to move into Beijing days before the violence began, some as early as May 27. Most of those in civilian clothes were unarmed, their weapons were brought in by trucks. Many local residents who recognized conscripts in civilian clothes taunted and humiliated them—some draftees were actually beaten up during the nights prior to the crackdown.[31] People chanted slogans and sprayed graffiti on walls— "Don't Betray the People!" and "Is the People's Army Afraid of the People?" and "Never Trust the Mother-fucking Government!"—to persuade advancing troops to back off.[32] Protesters also tried to appeal to the troops' sense of historical responsibility, crying, "If you dare to raise your hands against the people . . . history will forsake you. . . . You will remain condemned through the ages." As it turned out, none of this mattered.[33]

Late June 3, loudspeakers placed all over the city center repeatedly called on people to clear out and go home. Once the shooting began, weeks of remarkable civilian self-control and military discipline gave way to pent-up feelings of anger and frustration.[34] Many of the soldiers involved in the operation were eighteen- and nineteen-year-old conscripts who had never received any training on riot control or how to deal with unruly crowds. The consequence was a force that was out of control, often targeting innocent bystanders, bicyclists, medical personnel, and people looking on from nearby buildings. Another result of the soldiers' lack of discipline and preparedness was the high incidence of injuries and deaths caused by friendly fire.[35] The official death toll was 331, although outside observers estimated the number to be between 900 and 3,000, but no fully reliable figures are available.[36]

Could the Army's Response Be Predicted?

Let us return to our framework to answer the questions that should help us decide whether the PLA's response could have been anticipated.

MILITARY FACTORS

In the PLA, as in all armies, internal cohesion (I.1.) is one of the quintessential objectives. In all *communist* armies, this unity is cultivated and enforced by a complex web of military and party institutions. The CCP's dominance of the military—most of the party's early leaders were military commanders who helped win the war against the Nationalists in 1949—is the most important attribute of Chinese civil-military relations. Most top commanders in 1989 joined the PLA during or before the civil war, fought to establish the communist regime, and, for four decades, were its privileged beneficiaries; as such, they were highly unlikely to turn against it over student protests. From the very beginning, the party had a symbiotic relationship with the armed forces, and the CCP penetrated the PLA from top to bottom through three critical organizations that ensured military compliance with party authority: the political commissars (i.e., political officer system), the party committee system, and the discipline inspection system.[37] The PLA's response to the crisis was only moderately impacted by issues of institutional cohesion (hence the "3" in this rubric). Components such as ethnoreligious splits, divisions between various types of units and services, or sociopolitical cleavages between military elites were simply irrelevant. Divisions between senior and junior officers, aside from a very few cases, were also inconsequential; slightly more important were the differences between the officer corps and a minority of conscripted soldiers. Nevertheless, the army's political officers were successful in isolating the soldiers— in particular those units that participated in the army's second deployment—from information emanating from outside sources and convinced them that the protesters wanted to overthrow the party and would bring further chaos.[38]

The fact that the CCP was a conscript army (I.2.)—as were all communist armies—did make a difference, given some comparatively minor disciplinary issues that a volunteer army might not have experienced; however, with a large number of inadequately trained young draftees, one would expect some disciplinary problems. According to reports, about four hundred conscripts (that is, approximately 0.11–0.26 percent of the troops involved), who were reported missing at the end of the operation, might have deserted. Some soldiers marched with the students and even chanted antiregime slogans as late as May 23.[39] The most noteworthy case of dereliction of duty, however, was not of a draftee but that of General Xu Qinxian, the son of a legendary PLA general. Xu blamed his inability to command his troops—the Thirty-eighth Army, which was based in Baoding (some seventy-five miles south of Beijing) and regarded as a showcase unit by the Party—on the slow healing of his broken leg. Xu was repeatedly warned—and personally so by Yang Shangkun— that disobeying a military order would get him court-martialed, but Xu remained unyielding. He was later stripped of his command, CCP membership, and Beijing residence permit and sentenced to a five-year prison term.[40] Following the uprising, the PLA investigated the participating units and concluded that ninety-two percent of them had shown "good or relatively good party style and discipline" and most of those whose performance invited criticism were reprimanded rather than charged, suggesting that their offenses were minor.[41] So, in spite of a few instances of insubordination, not a single unit defected from the CCP during the suppression of the demonstrators; the vast majority of officers and soldiers discharged their duties and supported the regime, even if their professional performance in the final phase—due mostly to inadequate training—raises questions.

The most important reason—hence, the "6" on my 0–6 scale—motivating the army to suppress rather than join the opposition movement was its conviction that the CCP regime was legitimate (I.3.), such that it enjoyed the support of the vast majority of the population and nearly all the armed forces personnel. There were large demonstrations occasionally attended by hundreds of thousands of people, but virtually all of the nonstudent participants called for policy changes, not the toppling of the regime. In any event, the demonstrators represented a small proportion of the Chinese population of nearly 1.2 billion. The relative and absolute importance of the party's control of and trust in the armed forces was best illustrated by the following snippet of conversation: at a May 17 meeting of the CCP leadership, Zhao argued for more patience with the protesters, but his colleagues voted him down. Deng, apparently, insisted that the PLA now had to be used:

"I have the Army behind me," he [Deng] is reported to have boasted.

"But I have the people behind me," Zhao replied.

"Then you have nothing," retorted Deng.[42]

Deng's hard-edged directness followed the old axiom about communist politics: the primacy of force over the expendable subjects of the party-state, or, as Mao famously said it, "Political power grows out of the barrel of a gun." Once the demonstrations metamorphosed from annoyance to something that threatened regime stability, Deng and the top party leadership did not hesitate to turn to the army. And they did not hesitate because they well knew that they had the generals' support.

STATE FACTORS

In order to appreciate the relevance of the state factors, we must understand that communist states are one-party states, where the communist

party is, in fact, a far more important political actor than the state apparatus (which is predominantly staffed by communist party members and
is controlled by the party). So how could one describe the CCP's treatment of the PLA (II.1.) in the summer of 1989? In the 1980s, the PLA had
undergone a modernization campaign with the objective of producing a
younger, leaner, better-equipped and structurally streamlined organization. These reforms were partly in response to developments that the CCP
leadership viewed with some concern but that were the results of Deng's
concurrent economic transformation drive. Military service and soldier-
ing as a profession had lost some of their luster as the civilian economy
generated more lucrative and stimulating opportunities, and corruption
in the armed forces had increased.[43] Owing to the army's reorganization,
approximately one million military personnel had to leave the service;
some of them were unhappy with their lot.

The rapid inflation that accompanied Deng's economic reforms also
made the lives of soldiers and others who lived on fixed incomes (II.1.A.)
more difficult. The decreasing defense outlays—the PLA's share of the
state budget declined from 17.2 percent in 1980 to 7.5 percent in 1988—
and the growing importance of personal ties must have caused some discontent among the top brass.[44] In short, the military faced some difficulties, but there is not sufficient evidence to support the blanket statement
that there was "apparent disunity in the ranks;"[45] moreover, the PLA was
still widely considered one of the most highly respected Chinese institutions (II.1.F.).

Clearly, some officers and soldiers were not happy that the party
leadership ordered them to suppress the demonstrators, albeit only after
weeks of chaos. Nevertheless, this sort of mission (II.1.C.) was certainly
not "inappropriate" in a communist state, where the army's involvement
in "political" affairs and domestic security was considered perfectly normal and legitimate.[46] In fact, maintaining domestic security and, if necessary, protecting the survival of the regime has always been one of the key
missions of the PLA, as it has been for all communist armies.

One issue that seriously affected the Chinese generals' responses to the
crisis was that, as I noted above, they did not receive clear instructions
prior to the first troop deployment in Beijing (II.2.). June Teufel Dreyer
wrote that the troops who moved into the city on and around May 23
"seemed reluctant to take action against the students."[47] Their "reluctance" stemmed from the fact that they did not have plain orders, most
of them did not even have live ammunition, and they were dumbfounded
by the protesters, many of whom enthusiastically fraternized with them.[48]

No wonder that these conscripts, "mostly rural youth who were less educated and less sophisticated than the university students" and "who [had] never walked through a city let alone rehearsed combat in one" were not only hesitant to shoot at the protesters but, in fact, were entirely unprepared for what they encountered on Tiananmen Square.[49]

At the beginning of the upheaval, a minority of commanders were unclear about what the protests meant, did not have accurate information, and even formed "reading groups" to develop the "correct" assessment of the events while continuing to support the Party. To avoid confusion among the commanders, the regime soon began to brief military officers—from captains to army group generals—underscoring that the demonstrations signified growing turmoil and, therefore, martial law and, ultimately, military action were necessary to restore order. Yang, at least, must have been satisfied with the results because on May 13 he confidently reported, "The thinking in the army is fully in line with the Central Committee and the Central Military Commission. These protests are not going to spread to officers or soldiers in the military."[50]

SOCIETAL AND EXTERNAL FACTORS

As the demonstrations went on week after week, as the disorder continued to mount, as the students became increasingly radical, all but a few of even the previously hesitant commanders were persuaded that the deepening chaos had to be stopped. The protests mobilized hundreds of thousands across the country in what amounted to an unprecedented criticism of the CCP regime and clearly shocked the military leadership, which wanted a speedy return to normalcy (III.1.). "The army's past conduct toward society" (I.4.) was not an important factor—recall that the PLA enjoyed high public esteem—for the generals, but the level of support the students received in urban areas, plus their adeptness in fraternizing with the conscripts (III.3.), clearly motivated them to resolve the crisis.[51]

As I noted above, Gorbachev's visit to China was a sidebar to the democracy movement. Chinese political and military leaders viewed his reforms in the Soviet Union with concern and his laissez faire attitude toward the political developments in Eastern Europe with disapproval. They were alarmed by the collapse of communist rule in Poland and Hungary—ironically, June 4, the day of repression in Beijing, was also the day of the first partly free elections in Poland— and its effects on the students (IV.3.), fearing that these developments would undermine the legitimacy of communist rule in China.[52] In fact, some analysts have claimed that one of the reasons that Deng, Li, and Yang were willing to use violent means to suppress the uprising stemmed from their fear of the East European changes.[53] In turn, according to Mary Sarotte, the bloody crackdown on Tiananmen Square aided Gorbachev's decision to embark on a peaceful course of political transition in the USSR.[54]

Several experts argued that the military's intervention was not a foregone conclusion. In a book published in 1990, the revisionist historian Lee Feigon contended, "In late May the final outcome of the protests was still quite ambiguous."[55] The school of thought he represented interpreted the reluctance and hesitation on the part of a small minority of soldiers and commanders as an indication that the PRC's response to the upheaval was not a clear-cut case. Analysts of this ilk noted that during the CCP's past internal divisions, the PLA was also divided—during the Cultural Revolution (especially in 1967) and the succession to Mao in 1976—but in both cases, the majority of the army eventually lent its support to the dominant party faction.[56] Thus, this argument goes, given that the CCP was far from united at the early stages of the 1989 unrest, expecting the PLA to suppress the upheaval without internal debates would have been a folly. The resolute peacefulness of the student demonstrators, the fact that the PLA was an army of conscripts, the negative effects of the economic reforms on the PLA and its professional personnel, and the growing popularity of the protests especially in urban areas all cautioned against hasty predictions of a swift and decisive intervention. All of these are, to be sure, factors to be seriously pondered.

Nevertheless, the PLA was (and is), more than anything, the army of the Chinese Communist Party. It is critically important to recognize that, in stark contrast to its East European counterparts, the CCP enjoyed a great deal of support from the vast majority of ordinary people. PLA commanders owed their privileged societal position to the CCP, and virtually all of them were its card-carrying members; when clear directions came from the party leaders, only a tiny minority appeared hesitant to carry out their orders (I.3., II.2.). Ultimately, most well-informed and level-headed analysts would have predicted that, when necessary, the PLA's generals would use force to protect the regime—after all, in a very real sense, they *were* the regime. Given the historical context and the political situation, the "failure of the June Fourth movement was inevitable," as was, I argue, the PLA's role in its suppression.[57] As the veteran China expert and on-the-scene observer Orville Schell conceded a quarter century later, to think that the regime would "never get this genie back in the bottle . . . of course . . . was a very naïve presumption."[58]

EAST GERMANY

In the early fall of 1989, the leaders of the German Democratic Republic (GDR), intent on celebrating the fortieth anniversary of their state, might well have feared that this would be the last. They had many serious concerns, even apart from the developments in Poland, Hungary, and the Soviet Union. Perhaps the most alarming of these was the exodus of East German citizens to West Germany.[59] Just as in Beijing five months earlier, Gorbachev's visit—he was in East Berlin to attend the festivities—once again marked an important juncture in the crisis. He annoyed the leaders of the Socialist Unity Party (*Sozialistische Einheitspartei Deutschlands* or SED) by urging them to introduce political and economic reforms, and his very presence stimulated the opposition and strengthened its determination.[60]

The upheaval that led to the end of communism in the GDR largely manifested itself through a series of peaceful, well-organized, and steadily growing demonstrations—at times mobilizing tens of thousands—in major cities such as Leipzig, Dresden, and East Berlin. In East Berlin on October 7–8, with Gorbachev's plane barely off the tarmac, some sixteen thousand police (not military) personnel were deployed against the tens of thousands of protesters—of whom they arrested 1,047—on the order of Minister for State Security Erich Mielke, who "screamed at the police, 'Club those pigs into submission!'"[61] The authorities deployed units of the National People's Army (*Nationale Volksarmee* or NVA) alongside the police and the workers' militia (paramilitary detachments organized by workplace) in Dresden on October 9. Their orders were to break up the march without using deadly force, but "the size of the demonstration took the authorities by surprise and exposed a lack of resolve among police and army units."[62] Recognizing the situation, the police chief instructed his forces, without authorization from his superiors, to sheath their truncheons. The next day, twenty opposition representatives met with Dresden Mayor Wolfgang Berghofer in what was the first instance of official "dialogue" between East German officialdom and the people.

The demonstrations in Leipzig took place every Monday, the most momentous one on October 9.[63] The authorities promised a robust response, readying a large contingent of security forces—police, State Security (Stasi), paramilitary units, and some fifteen hundred NVA troops[64]—to challenge the marchers, even going as far as distributing live ammunition. The situation was defused by the "Leipzig Six"—three midcareer SED officials and three prominent figures from the city's art and intellectual community, among them Kurt Masur, the conductor of its famed Gewandhaus Orchestra. The party bureaucrats requested, but did not receive, instructions from SED headquarters in East Berlin, eager to prevent violence and avoid having to take responsibility for it. When no direction was forthcoming, they decided to work with the intellectuals. Together, they composed a plea for peace and dialogue, which was distributed to clergymen and repeatedly broadcast on local radio stations. Once the security forces understood that party officials wanted to avoid violence, they quickly followed suit and issued the necessary orders to their subordinates.[65] Egon Krenz, SED General Secretary Erich Honecker's heir apparent, tried to take credit for the peaceful outcome, but he fooled no one: he had approved the appeal of the Leipzig Six *after* it was made public.

On the critically important night of October 8, the authorities effectively handed over power to the Leipzig demonstrators instead of opting for a Tiananmen Square-style solution.[66] On October 17, four days after he prohibited the use of force against peaceful demonstrators, his colleagues removed Honecker from leadership and replaced him, as it turned out for a mere forty-six days, with Krenz. On November 9, the East German authorities opened the gates to the Berlin Wall. In less than eleven months, the GDR was unceremoniously dissolved and Germany reunified.

Ultimately, for a hard-line political approach to succeed, reliable and resolute military forces are necessary.[67] The East German army was not such an organization in October 1989. Many experts considered it the most reliable military in the Warsaw Pact, given the regime's all-out, decades-long effort to indoctrinate it with the requisite Marxist-Leninist values and its unusually close relations with the Soviet troops occupying the country. Quite possibly, the NVA would have been more reliable than the other East Bloc armies in an external defensive scenario,[68] but that is a rather low bar to clear, given the grave reservations about those armies' likely performances. More to the point, the NVA soldiers' willingness to suppress peaceful demonstrations—*particularly* in as confusing and heavily charged a political context as the one in October 1989—was doubtful. Why?

The East German regime's decision not to use lethal military force against the protesters was not a foregone conclusion.[69] One important reason for the NVA's reluctance to inflict bloodshed was that the SED Politburo was divided on the issue of applying deadly force, and with time, the number of skeptics had only grown. Although Honecker and Krenz— along with Romania's Nicolae Ceauşescu—were among the few East European politicians to openly applaud the crackdown on Tiananmen

Square, many in the GDR party elite were fearful that a "Chinese solution" to the protests would have unforeseeable consequences that would further undermine their rule.[70] In other words, broad agreement on an approach to the crisis, which was an indispensable prerequisite for the consistent use of force, was simply lacking in the GDR political leadership. Consequently, the SED chiefs did not give clear instructions to their generals because, owing to their own perplexity, they *could not*.

The authorities were stunned by the size of the protests and the resolve of the demonstrators. Mielke, notwithstanding his aforementioned combative exhortations to his security forces on October 6, admitted to Honecker later during the crisis, "We can't beat up hundreds of thousands of people!"[71] Moreover, senior police and army commanders were acutely aware of the growing doubts and lack of discipline among their troops.[72] NVA officers openly admitted their frustration with and resentment of the situation they found themselves in: compelled to rough up peaceful protesters, leading soldiers who in many cases would rather risk being court-martialed and imprisoned than obey their superiors, and, in general, being forced "to do the party's dirty work."[73] Many soldiers publicly expressed sympathy with the demonstrators and, not surprisingly, those who spotted their parents, siblings, and acquaintances in the crowds were especially troubled. Furthermore, virtually all the male protesters ages 25–60 served as NVA conscripts themselves and understood the soldiers' predicament. Few of them thought that the troops would use live ammunition against them.[74] In the end, thousands of draftees deserted and joined the exodus from East Germany. There was to be no shooting of protesters.

None of this could have happened without the cooperation of the 380,000 Soviet forces stationed in East Germany. General Boris Snetkov, the head of the Soviet occupation forces, acted on the strict orders of Moscow and Soviet Ambassador to the GDR Vyacheslav Kochemasov and made sure that his troops stayed in their barracks. The Kremlin, determined to avoid even the appearance of any sort of interference in the unfolding events, ordered its forces not to react in any way, even in the case of extreme provocation.[75]

BULGARIA

Todor Zhivkov began his term as the General Secretary of the Bulgarian Communist Party (BCP) in 1954, and for thirty-five years, he had managed to surround himself with people of questionable competence but seemingly unwavering loyalty. By mid-1989, however, his support in the Politburo began to falter for a number of reasons. First, the economy was deteriorating quickly. Second, firmly opposed to reforms of any consequence, Zhivkov was bewildered by the political developments in Eastern Europe. Finally, his close associates, several of whom aspired to succeed the 78-year-old, were alarmed by the quick promotions of his son, Vladimir, through the BCP hierarchy. (As we will see in the last chapter, dynasties are seldom popular in putative republics.) On 10 November 1989, just a few hours after the Berlin Wall fell, Zhivkov was replaced in a civilian-military palace coup led by Foreign Minister Petar Mladenov.

What role did the military play in Zhivkov's ouster? For decades, General Dobri Dzhurov, the long-serving defense minister, was one of Zhivkov's closest colleagues in the top party leadership. Dzhurov also thoroughly controlled the Bulgarian People's Army; therefore, acquiring his support was of paramount importance for the would-be putschists.[76] Dzhurov agreed not only to ensure that Zhivkov could not fight back but also to tell his old comrade that if he refused to resign voluntarily there would be a Politburo resolution to remove him from office.[77] Mladenov's instinctive reaction to the first mass demonstration that took place in the capital on December 14 illustrated just how little had changed after Zhivkov's resignation. Mladenov, facing the specter of a revolution, was captured on camera as he called for tanks to be used against the protesters.[78] Fortunately, no one took him seriously; the tanks stayed in their barracks, and Bulgaria organized free and fair multiparty elections in June 1990.

As Moscow's closest allies in the region, BCP leaders were eager to get Gorbachev's blessing of their coup. At the July 1989 Warsaw Pact summit in Bucharest, Mladenov told the Soviet president of the BCP's plans to replace Zhivkov, but the response he got, "This is entirely your business. You have to sort it out yourselves," was less than what he had hoped for. In late October, when Zhivkov began to understand that his position was under threat, he asked the Kremlin for an urgent meeting, but Gorbachev refused to meet him, reminding him that the Soviet Union was "neutral" about the BCP's personnel changes and was not going to interfere.[79]

CZECHOSLOVAKIA

In January 1989, Václav Havel received a nine-month prison sentence for his dissident activities. On 29 December 1989, he became president by a unanimous vote of Czechoslovakia's Federal Assembly. By the late 1980s, his country had become stuck in a deep-seated political, economic, and societal malaise; the Czechoslovak Communist Party (CSCP) had virtually no legitimacy left and no genuine societal support. As in East Germany, the death-knell of the communist regime was sounded by peaceful demonstrations, attracting large crowds to Prague's historic Wenceslas Square. Although all of the demonstrations were organized by the Civic Forum, a coalition of opposition groups, the most important of these took place on November 17. It was also the most memorable because on this day the police and specially trained antiterrorist units of the Ministry of Interior (MoI) viciously beat up and arrested several hundred of the fifty thousand protesters, most of them students. The brutality of the security forces spurred further mobilization, strengthening the protesters resolve—just as we have seen in other cases and will see again in the next chapter—and driving the preparations for further demonstrations that included a general strike ten days later.[80]

The tipping point, however, was the November 20 protest on Wenceslas Square, where the over 200,000 participants included not just students but also workers and ordinary people who were not usually taken to risk their livelihood by appearing at antiregime rallies. On that day, significant protests also took place in other large cities, such as Brno and Ostrava. By November 25, when the number at Wenceslas Square increased to a reported 500,000, the workers' presence was part of the routine and only regime stalwarts were surprised at their extensive participation in the general strike two days later.[81]

At no point was the military deployed against the people—in all likelihood because few in the leadership believed that conscripted soldiers or even line officers would have obeyed the party's orders. Another reason was that the CSCP leadership—just as their East German comrades—was divided on the issue, with hard-liners like Jakeš, Fojtík, and Prague CSCP Secretary and People's Militia boss Miroslav Štěpán backing continued robust police action, while a number of their colleagues sharply dissented.[82]

Defense Minister Milán Václavík raised the possibility of a "military solution" and, on November 17, even issued orders for the possible use of military force and urged the party leadership to put the militia and the Czechoslovak People's Army (*Československá lidová armáda* [ČSLA]) on alert.[83] As it turned out, this was more bluster than common sense on Václavík's part, and not a single ČSLA soldier was ordered out of his barracks during what has become known as the "Velvet Revolution."[84]

The communist regime essentially fell on November 22, when Václavík declared on national television that the army would not get involved in the protests. For anyone familiar with the Czechoslovak military, this was hardly much of a surprise: most experts agree that the vast majority of ČSLA soldiers would not have fired at unarmed citizens, and certainly not by November 22, when the communist regime's goose seemed thoroughly cooked.[85] On the same day, CSCP General Secretary Miloš Jakeš decided to call on the People's Militia—a paramilitary group of twenty thousand well-remunerated loyalists, mostly factory workers—to attack the demonstrators, but the militia categorically refused.[86]

The Czechoslovak army might well have been the least reliable Warsaw Pact army.[87] Traditionally known for its lackluster fighting spirit, the morale in and the social esteem of the ČSLA had plummeted following the 1968 Prague Spring and had come to reflect the deep-seated apathy of the general population.[88] Because of the small number of qualified young men who were willing to choose the military profession, training time at military colleges had to be repeatedly reduced. Like all communist armies, the ČSLA served the communist party, not the country, and after 1968, that party had become synonymous with repression, stagnation, and servile fealty to the Soviet Union.

Gorbachev had no personal involvement in the collapse of Czechoslovak communism, and the party leaders in Prague were clearly aware that there was no use asking for his support to save their rule. In fact, a senior Kremlin official informed Jakeš directly that he could not expect any political or military help from Moscow.[89] As in the GDR, the seventy-five thousand Soviet troops stationed in Czechoslovakia ceased all activities during the upheaval to avoid even the appearance of partiality.

ROMANIA

Romania's revolution in December 1989 was the exception to the rule of more-or-less peaceful regime change elsewhere in Eastern Europe. This case also hints at the chaos and anarchy that often surround revolutionary upheavals. As a result, there are still numerous issues regarding the revolution, including specific events and the participation of the armed forces, that have not been satisfyingly explained, and it is likely that we will never know exactly what really happened. A small library could be stacked with books on the Romanian revolution—many of them written soon after the last shots were fired, and some of them by individuals who had personal stakes in propagating their versions of the events. The most reliable account in English is Peter Siani-Davies's *The Romanian Revolution of December 1989*, a painstaking, hour-by-hour reconstruction of events with an insightful analysis of the revolution's dynamics.[90] Siani-Davies, too, readily admits all the things that we do not—and quite possibly will not ever—know for certain and offers sensible assessments of the relative merits of contending viewpoints, studies, and participant recollections.

What Happened?

At the end of the 1980s, Romania was in many ways a bizarre communist dictatorship, likened to "the Ethiopia of Europe" by an insightful Romanian commentator.[91] Beginning in the early 1980s, food and electricity rationing encompassed most of the country, and human rights violations and secret police monitoring of ordinary citizens were perhaps the most extensive in Eastern Europe. The vast majority of Romanians lived lives of quiet desperation, but the regime's propaganda apparatus constantly told them that they were fortunate to be alive in a "golden epoch" of unparalleled achievement under the wise guidance of Nicolae Ceauşescu. A delusional dictator whose cult of personality rivaled that of Stalin and Mao, Ceauşescu stood at the apex of this sultanistic regime, where oppression was so stiflingly effective that not a single opposition group was organized nor an underground publication printed throughout the communist period.[92] In Romania, "There was no bond between the ruler and the ruled, merely despair and a deep-seated hatred ready to flare at the earliest opportunity."[93]

That opportunity presented itself on 15 December 1989. On that day, thousands of ethnic Hungarians entered the streets of central Timişoara to protest the forced eviction of their dissident Calvinist pastor, László Tőkés. They were soon joined by ethnic Romanians, and the demonstration's focus quickly assumed an antiregime character. Initially, Ceauşescu instructed his local minions to let the protest go ahead; probably he expected it to peter out, but it did not. In fact, for the next couple of days the demonstration quickly grew. Agents of the feared secret police, *Securitate*, instigated an attack on and looting of some public buildings to create a pretext for the repression that followed.[94] Army units and other security forces deployed tear gas and water cannons against the protesters. On December 17, Ceauşescu angrily ordered the army and the police to suppress the protest with live ammunition, and that is what they did—killing dozens of mostly peaceful and unarmed people. Still, the demonstrations continued, as did the sporadic gunfire of the security forces.

Ceaușescu made three strategic mistakes that directly contributed to his and his regime's end. They are lesson-worthy for those who want to successfully resist uprisings. First, confident that the security forces were in control of the situation in Timișoara, Ceaușescu left for a state visit to Tehran on December 18. By the time he returned two days later, the unrest had spread to several cities across the country, and containing the revolutionary fervor had become extremely difficult. Also by this time, some army units had switched sides and joined the revolution, while a number of commanders withdrew their troops to the barracks, fearing fraternization and the passing of weapons from conscripts to demonstrators. (Lesson No. 1: Do not underestimate the potential threat protests pose. Focus all your energies on the crisis until it is fully resolved.)

Second, oblivious to how quickly a seemingly supportive large crowd can become an angry mob—after all, this was not a danger he had ever had to face in the past—Ceaușescu called for a mass rally to display support for his regime the day after his return from Iran (December 21). At the rally in central Bucharest, he blamed "imperialist espionage services" for inciting turmoil in Romania and announced some conciliatory measures (e.g., a ten percent increase in the minimum wage) that already had been approved a month earlier.[95] By this time, Ceaușescu was so divorced from reality and from ordinary Romanians, and the regime's propaganda of the "Soviet threat" had so diminished in popular perception, that he did not realize that his old bases of legitimacy had crumbled entirely. The event, broadcast on national television, quickly turned into an unruly anti-Ceaușescu and antiregime protest, one from which the Romanian Communist Party leadership would never recover. Violent clashes erupted between police and mostly young demonstrators (thirteen of whom were killed) and spontaneous protests broke out all over the capital. Security forces trying to clear the streets used live ammunition against civilians. Overnight and into the morning of December 22, *Securitate* and riot police units killed about thirty-five people; however, upon hearing reports of dissension within the military, the crowds started fraternizing with the troops and chanting, "The army is with us!" which, to be sure, was partly a strategic effort by demonstrators to make it so. At this point, the tanks were withdrawn from the city's center. Such fraternization, which we saw also in Iran and China as well as in Timișoara a couple of days earlier, often leads generals to pull back their forces and assess the emerging situation. In Romania, the tanks were never again deployed against the people. (Lesson No. 2: Do not do the opposition's work for them by creating chances for mass mobilization.)

Third, believing that someone had to pay the price for the continuing chaos in Bucharest and elsewhere, Ceauşescu made the fateful mistake of assigning blame to Defense Minister General Vasile Milea. According to the dictator's stenographer, when confronted, Milea replied to the raging Ceauşescu that he searched the military code and the constitution and "did not find a single paragraph in which it says that the army of the people must fire on the people."[96] Within minutes he was dead, either shot by a *Securitate* detail on Ceauşescu's orders or taking his own life. Once the regime publicly announced his suicide on the morning of December 22, Milea instantly became the revolution's martyr. At that moment, virtually all army commanders who might still have been undecided about how to respond to the uprising abandoned Ceauşescu and joined the revolution.[97] (Lesson No. 3: Avoid creating martyrs who might unite people—especially your armed forces—no matter how unlikely martyrs they might be.)

In a last-ditch effort, Ceauşescu attempted to address the demonstrators from the balcony of the Central Committee building on December 22, but he was shouted down. He and his wife, Elena, fled Bucharest and eventually ended up at the base of an antiaircraft artillery regiment in Târgovişte, where they were taken into protective custody. In the meantime, the fighting intensified between security forces of various stripes and civilians on the streets of Bucharest even as a new transition government, the National Salvation Front (NSF), began to take form. After a heated debate, the emerging NSF leadership came to the conclusion that only the quick liquidation of the Ceauşescu could make counterrevolutionary forces lay down their weapons and, thus, stop the bloodshed. And so, that is precisely what they arranged: after a hasty trial Nicolae and Elena Ceauşescu were unceremoniously executed by a firing squad on Christmas Day, ten days after Pastor Tőkés's parishioners began their vigil.

Once the NSF announced the demise of the Ceauşescus, the shooting began to taper off. Nonetheless, the fighting did not entirely stop until 6 January 1990. What occurred in the meantime was rather strange: various units of the security forces (i.e., army, *Securitate*, militia) along with armed citizens were fighting "terrorists" supposedly intent on hijacking the revolution, but it was never entirely clear who was fighting whom and, more specifically, who exactly the so-called terrorists were. As a result, people were mistaken for "terrorists" and fired upon for having a shade darker skin (e.g., "Arab terrorists" or Gypsies), speaking a foreign language (e.g., Hungarians), wearing "suspicious" clothing or the "wrong" uniform, being in the proximity of a building that ostensibly housed "terrorists," or, most often, just for being in the wrong place at the wrong time. According to NSF leader Ion Iliescu, these "terrorists" were few in number and were practically indistinguishable from the general population. In contrast, Silviu Brucan—a prominent NSF member—claimed that they were four thousand elite *Securitate* sharpshooters trained in urban guerrilla warfare. Then again, those who knew Brucan also knew that most of what he said needed to be independently confirmed and, of course, this could not be,[98] though a 2012 volume written by a former military prosecutor unequivocally identified the "terrorists" as *Securitate* personnel.[99] In any event, the extensive violence that occurred December 22–January 6

> can only be understood if it is firmly placed within the context of the prevailing heady atmosphere of elation, tinged with fear, suspicion, and rumor, and a total breakdown of political and social control, which saw the effective erosion of all constraints of behavior. In this atmosphere of anarchy, the first task of the new leadership was the reestablishment of public order.[100]

What Was the Army's Role, and Could It Have Been Predicted?

The seeds of Romania's actual autonomy from Moscow were sown by the USSR's withdrawal of its occupation army in 1958, and one of its clearest manifestations was Ceauşescu's decision not to provide troops for the Warsaw Pact invasion of Czechoslovakia a decade later. Correspondingly, the Romanian army, unlike the other East European armed forces, was independent of Soviet military command, had its own military doctrine and defense strategy, and "a relatively untarnished reputation as national defender rather than an instrument of communist repression."[101] At the time of the revolution, the principal coercive apparatus at Ceauşescu's disposal consisted of the 140,000-strong army (95,000 of whom were draftees); the paramilitary patriotic guard, which had a large putative membership but an actual core body of 12,000; and forces under the command of the MoI (the feared *Securitate* or security police of 38,682, the militia or regular police of 32,595, and the 15,000-strong border guards).[102]

A number of senior army generals were unhappy with Ceauşescu's foreign and military policies. He alienated some of these by depriving them of the opportunity to socialize and collaborate with their erstwhile colleagues, owing to Romania's minimal participation in the Warsaw Pact.[103] Many in the top brass as well as in the officer corps were demoralized by the army's modest fighting capacity and its doctrine: "the entire people's war," which deemphasized military capability in favor of massive popular participation.[104] This doctrine permitted defense budgets to stay low; indeed they were frozen throughout most of the 1980s. A significant proportion of the conscripts' time in the army was taken up not with training but with construction and agricultural work, as draftees were being used as free labor for the state. The need to be engaged in such nonmilitary "missions" characterized the armies of many socialist states, but the extent of this phenomenon was far greater in Romania. Furthermore, Ceauşescu demanded that military units become self-sufficient and supply their own food. In practice, this meant that many garrisons doubled as chicken or pig farms, surrounded by the omnipresent cloud of stench. It is not hard to imagine what this side job did to the professional esteem of the Romanian officer corps.[105] Professional military personnel were also unhappy with their inferior salaries and perquisites as well as basic resources, especially compared to those of *Securitate* employees.[106]

Although some senior army commanders favored overthrowing the Ceauşescu regime, many line officers were reluctant to commit themselves to a revolution initially headed by what they saw as "a few crazy poets and intellectuals."[107] According to General Nicolae Militaru, who was appointed as the NSF's defense minister on December 26, top military officials had contemplated deposing Ceauşescu as far back as the mid-1970s: they planned an aborted coup attempt in 1984 and hatched a plot to overthrow Ceauşescu in February 1990, but the revolution overtook the conspirators.[108]

As in China, most of the conscripts were undisciplined and poorly trained for the task at hand. Consequently, friendly fire was the cause of a large proportion of the deaths and casualties of the revolution—1,104 killed (493 in Bucharest) and 3,352 (2,200 in Bucharest) wounded. In one of the best known cases, RPA troops guarding the international airport in Otopeni, near Bucharest, opened fire on a truck bringing reinforcements to join their side—killing forty soldiers and eight civilians—mistaking them for "terrorists," owing to a lack of basic order and proper communications.[109] According to Valentin Gabrielescu, the chairman of the Senate inquiry that studied the violence and bloodshed during the revolution, most of the deaths were civilians,

> Innocents caught in the crossfire between panic-stricken soldiers and civilians firing at terrorists. . . . As well as the army and the police, thousands of civilians were armed and under the stress of false rumors and false dangers . . . everyone fired at everyone else. It was chaos.[110]

Most Romanians held their conscript army in high esteem, particularly when contrasted with the militia and the *Securitate*. The army was seldom involved in domestic repression; it was a national institution and an organic part of society, rather than separate from it. Military officers had to line up for goods and services in the ubiquitous queues just like everyone else—in sharp contrast to most of their colleagues in other East European armies, who could shop in special stores. In other words, there was little disconnect between society and the armed forces in Romania. Most male demonstrators served as conscripts in their youth and understood the pressures the draftees were under. No wonder that, in many instances, demonstrators moved eagerly forward to embrace and fraternize with RPA troops. Few of them would have expected the soldiers to use their guns against them to save Ceauşescu's regime, and in the rare occasions when they did, the protesters were incredulous.[111]

There is no doubt that at least *some* regular army units opened fire on the demonstrators in the first few days of the revolution in Timişoara, Cluj, and elsewhere.[112] Exactly when and how many are questions difficult to answer due to the many rumors spread by *Securitate*, militia, RPA, and paramilitary units, each blaming the others for shooting civilians. Still, numerous sources claim either that the army did not shoot at people and/or that many cases of the soldiers firing at the protesters were actually *Securitate* agents wearing RPA uniforms.[113] Substantiating these allegations is virtually impossible. One can confidently say, however, that the vast majority of the senior army officers and their units had gone on record by December 22 as supporting the revolution, many of them emphatically declaring, "The army is with the people."[114]

Unlike in the other East European cases, Moscow had no control over the Romanian Communist Party and military elites, and its influence on the Romanian revolution was modest. The relationship between Bucharest and Moscow was frosty, at best. A Soviet leader who was willing to consider meaningful political reforms and socioeconomic liberalization was obviously bad news for a died-in-the-wool Stalinist like Ceauşescu. When Gorbachev visited Romania in 1987 and dropped some hints regarding Bucharest's discriminatory ethnic minority policy and the dangers of nepotism, Ceauşescu duly ignored them.[115] The Romanian leader was so upset about the events of 1989 in Eastern Europe that he even proposed a Warsaw Pact intervention in Poland when he learned about the formation of the new Solidarity government in August 1989.[116] Ironically, Moscow was even more against interfering in Romania than Washington, although suggestions that the United States actually encouraged a Warsaw Pact invasion of Romania are incorrect.[117] US Ambassador to the Soviet Union Jack F. Matlock Jr. *was* told by the State Department that Secretary of State

> Baker was concerned that Gorbachev might think that any intervention in Romania, however justified—say, to extract Soviet citizens—would violate the understanding [US President George H. W.] Bush and Gorbachev had reached during their [2–3 December 1989] meeting in Malta. (That the Soviet Union would not intervene in East Europe and that the US would not "take advantage" of the changes there.) We were quite aware that there would be no intervention to preserve the Ceausescu regime. Therefore . . . I was instructed to make clear that, if violence in Romania should spread and threaten Soviet citizens, Bush would not consider attempts to extract them contrary to the understandings at Malta.[118]

So, when it was reported that Soviet Foreign Minister Shevardnadze was "categorically opposed" to Washington's "stupid" idea that the USSR invade Romania, which, he feared "might make a martyr out of Ceaușescu," he was not given accurate information about American intentions by his subordinate, most likely Deputy Foreign Minister Ivan P. Aboimov.[119]

Was the army's stance toward the Romanian revolution predictable? This outcome was, in my view, "somewhat challenging" to anticipate and only after the mass rally in Bucharest could analysts forecast with confidence the RPA's decision to join the revolution. First, there was less known about Romania in the West than about the other East European states, in part owing to the aforementioned dearth of opposition activism and *samizdat* (i.e., self-published and illegal) publications coupled with the Ceaușescu regime's across-the-board propaganda and media manipulation. Second, the fact that some army units—not just *Securitate* and militia troops—*did* turn their guns at unarmed people in the early days of the revolution must give us some pause. How can we explain it? The answer lies in the consideration of several factors: the severity of the Romanian regime, the lack of opposition activity in Romanian society that soldiers could have been familiar with, the heavy-handed indoctrination of conscripts, and the authorities' confusion in the early days of the revolution. We must also consider that those commanders who might have ordered their soldiers to open fire on demonstrators were themselves manipulated and fed erroneous information by their superiors in Bucharest.

It is clear that those who relayed Ceaușescu's orders to the officers in the armed forces did so very reluctantly, and it was only a matter of time—a few days, as it turned out—until the vast majority of commanders turned against the regime. Several generals in the RPA leadership went to great lengths to avoid the responsibility of firing on demonstrators. Deputy Defense Minister General Victor Stănculescu, for instance, had his right leg put in a plaster cast to avoid having to appear at headquarters to face Ceauşescu.[120] (One wonders if Stănculescu learned this trick from PLA General Xu Qinxian.) General Milea most probably committed suicide.[121] We know that by December 22 the RPA's support of the uprising was indisputable.

Many weighty factors in my framework suggest that the RPA would *not* save the regime. There was an important split between the military and the *Securitate* (I.1.E.); the RPA was a conscript army that was treated poorly by a regime (I.2.) that, in turn, was widely despised (I.3.). Moreover, the demonstrations were large, peaceful, and representative of the entire society (III.1.). Indubitably, the revolution was extremely popular (III.2.), and relations between the people and the RPA were agreeable (I.4.). Foreign intervention on the side of the Ceauşescu regime was also not in the cards (IV.1.); however, given the context and the bewilderment about the "terrorists," it is not surprising that it took a couple of days for the military to figure out that foreign invaders were not behind the events. The generals' decision-making was little affected by Romania's foreign affairs—aside from some "undesirable" allies in the Middle East, by 1989 most prudent governments shunned Ceauşescu's tyrannical dictatorship—but the fate of the other East European communist regimes had certainly made an impression on them (IV.3.).[122] All in all, while the army's support of the revolution was neither inevitable nor immediate, it was not surprising.

CONCLUSION: WHAT CAUSED SUCH DIFFERENT MILITARY RESPONSES?

Strictly speaking, Poland, Hungary, East Germany, Czechoslovakia, and Bulgaria did not experience revolutions in 1989. The first two countries went through negotiated power transfers that transpired without as much as a broken window. East German leaders actually did deploy the army on a very limited scale alongside the more extensively utilized various security and police units, but at no point did NVA soldiers turn their guns against the protesters. In Czechoslovakia, the soldiers never even left their barracks, while there is no evidence that in Bulgaria anyone even thought of calling them out, other than Petar Mladenov's off-the-cuff threat in the midst of a demonstration that was captured by an alert cameraman. All of these armies were relatively cohesive institutions, treated generally well by the communist state. Nonetheless, the East European communist regimes thoroughly lacked popular legitimacy. Additionally, the demonstrations were large, peaceful, and representative of society, and the upheavals were very popular. Also important, in the two countries where the political leadership appears to have contemplated the deployment of the military against the people—East Germany and, less seriously, Czechoslovakia—they were deeply divided on the matter and thus unable to issue unambiguous and binding orders. Furthermore, all of these were conscript armies, and most of the draftees shared the pervasive disenchantment and hopelessness of late-socialist societies. In brief, anticipating—say, in early 1989—that armies would not use their guns against their fellow citizens would have been a "no-brainer" for Poland and Hungary, relatively easy—especially considering its past history—for Czechoslovakia, but somewhat challenging for East Germany and Bulgaria.

The Chinese and Romanian armies reached their decisions in a very different manner, ultimately turning their guns against unarmed people. At first, the PLA was somewhat hesitant to violently suppress the students on Tiananmen Square, but when ordered to, the soldiers did just that. In Romania though, in a reversal of the Chinese case, the army joined the revolution after a few instances of conscripts actually shooting at protesters. How to explain these differences?

First of all, in Beijing officers and soldiers obeyed the instructions of the party leadership with only very few notable exceptions. It is important to recognize that soldiers followed orders during their first deployment on May 19–20, but Deng Xiaoping and his colleagues underestimated the crisis and expected demonstrators to desist once they encountered the essentially weaponless troops. In other words, the operation was a debacle not because of the PLA but owing to the miscalculation of its civilian masters. In contrast, their Romanian counterparts, in the end, actually fought for the revolution. But there is also an interesting similarity between these two forces: both the PLA and the RPA were *professionally* unprepared for their task of controlling and dispersing crowds because they were not previously called upon to conduct such operations.

One might argue that, actually, Deng Xiaoping and his colleagues were relatively patient: their decision-making was calculated, they made sure that commanders "correctly understood" what the protests meant, they took care to build consensus even as they were willing to marginalize contrarians, and they only declared martial law and deployed the troops

Table 3. China and Romania, 1989: Factors affecting the army's response to revolutions

	China	Romania
I. MILITARY FACTORS		
I.1. The Armed Forces' Internal Cohesion	3	4
I.1.A. ethnic, religious, tribal, and regional splits	0	1
I.1.B. generational divisions: senior vs. junior officers	2	1
I.1.C. divisions between officers and NCOs/privates	1	1
I.1.D. divisions between elite vs. regular units	0	0
I.1.E. splits between the army, other branches, and security sector entities	0	5
I.1.F. sociopolitical divisions between military elites	2	0
I.2. Professional Soldiers vs. Conscripts	3	3
I.3. The Generals' Perception of Regime Legitimacy	6	5
I.4. The Army's Past Conduct toward Society	0	0
II. STATE FACTORS		
II.1. Regime's Treatment of the Military	2	5
II.1.A. taking care of the personnel's material welfare	2	4
II.1.B. taking care of the army	3	4
II.1.C. appropriateness of missions	2	4
II.1.D. the generals' professional autonomy and decision-making authority	0	3
II.1.E. fairness in top appointments	0	2
II.1.F. the military's prestige and public esteem	0	3
II.2. Regime Directions to the Military	3	1
III. SOCIETAL FACTORS		
III.1. The Size, Composition, and Nature of the Protests	5	5
III.2. The Popularity of the Uprising	3	3
III.3. Fraternization	3	3
IV. EXTERNAL FACTORS		
IV.1. The Potential for Foreign Intervention	0	1
IV.2. Foreign Affairs	1	1
IV.3. Revolutionary Diffusion	3	4
IV.4. Foreign Exposure of Military Officers	0	1

Top six factors are in bold.
Scale (0–6):
0 = irrelevant, not a factor
1 = of trivial importance
2 = of little importance
3 = somewhat important
4 = quite important
5 = very important
6 = critical, decisive

when they thought that their regime's stability was in danger. The deliberate crisis-management in Beijing was sharply contrasted by the confusion, overreaction, and strategic errors of Ceauşescu and the Romanian Communist Party leadership.

Even more important were the disparities in terms of regime legitimacy and the leaders' personal stature among the population, in general, and the armed forces, in particular. The overwhelming majority of Chinese considered the Communist Party to be China's legitimate ruling entity.[123] More to the point, the PLA's readiness to obey orders on June 3–4 can be attributed to the respect and loyalty of military leaders to Deng, personally. Unlike political leaders in the East European communist states in 1989, Deng was revered as a member of the founding generation of the PRC with extensive experience in military affairs. Conversely, most Romanians—including RPA personnel—viewed the communist regime as entirely bankrupt and had no respect for Ceauşescu. This overwhelming sense of a lack of regime legitimacy, which increases as revolutions ripen, reveals a startling parallel between the East European socialist states and the Shah's Iran.[124] Unlike Honecker, Jakeš, Zhivkov, not to mention the Polish and Hungarian communist leaders, Ceauşescu refused to back down. He was so far removed from the reality of what life had become for ordinary Romanians during his quarter-century-long rule, so caught up in his own cult of personality that he was unable to recognize—as the transcripts of his "trial" clearly demonstrate—the wave of history that was about to roll over him.[125] He and Libya's Muammar Qadhafi alone in the pantheon of dictators featured in this book share the dubious distinction of being murdered by their own people. But, perhaps, this is not so surprising after all. As the *Washington Post*'s Meg Greenfield wrote at the time,

> Ceauşescu killed himself. He choked on his own arrogance, greed, and unimpeded ascent to what seemed and, for a while was, absolute power. . . .
> By the time he faced the execution squad, he had lost any capacity he might have had to see and hear what was really going on around him.[126]

There were differences in the societal factors that made an impact on the generals' stance vis-à-vis the uprisings in China and Romania. Although the students' movement ended up mobilizing one million people, it did not enjoy the support of the majority of China's population.[127] In contrast, there was no doubt about the massive popular support of the revolution in Romania. Moreover, while most demonstrators on

Tiananmen Square and elsewhere demanded policy changes and the fine-tuning of Deng's reforms, in Romania, nothing but the regime's overthrow would have satisfied the protesters.

External factors figured significantly in the upheavals we examined in this chapter. Other than China and, to a lesser extent, Romania, these states were not independent in any meaningful sense; however, that changed in 1989 with Mikhail Gorbachev's explicit pledge of noninterference. The import of this assurance from Moscow would be hard to overstate, given that it reversed the threat of Soviet military action that, in fact, had been the guarantee of survival for East European communism for over four decades. Gorbachev's visits to Beijing and East Germany inspired the protesters and steeled their resolve, and his consistent refusal to support old dictators cleared the road for the democratic opposition. Revolutionary diffusion, too, played a role, as it moderated the behavior of some regime stalwarts in East Germany and Czechoslovakia but, clearly, worked its magic in the opposite direction in China and Romania. Seeing the writing on the wall, Deng and Ceaușescu wanted to make certain that they did not meet the fates of communist leaders elsewhere and redoubled their efforts to save their regimes. The disparate outcomes, ultimately, reflect the different judgments of their soldiers and their citizens of their regimes' legitimacy.

5

The Middle East and North Africa, 2011

The uprisings that spread through large swaths of North Africa and the Middle East were touched off by the self-immolation of a fruit vendor, Mohamed Bouazizi, humiliated by a low-level municipal official in the dusty central Tunisian town of Sidi Bouzid in December 2010. The initial protests became massive demonstrations; the upheaval spread first throughout Tunisia, then to several countries bordering on Tunisia, then farther afield in the Arab world. The avalanche of popular dissatisfaction eventually redrew the political map of the region. Four long-entrenched republican dictatorships—Tunisia, Egypt, Libya, and Yemen—were toppled by late 2011. In a fifth republic, Syria, the conflict between the regime and the protesters soon metamorphosed into a civil war, which was still raging at the time of this writing (June 2015). The upheaval was accompanied by considerable bloodshed in only one of the eight Arab monarchies, Bahrain, where the authorities easily repelled the challenge to the regime.

The armies of the Arab republics received considerable scholarly attention in the 1960s and 1970s. This was not surprising, after all, their leaders were former military men who came to power after mounting coups d'état. In the last forty years, however, there has been very little research on the armed forces of most Arab states. Several of these regimes were politically stagnant, their armies had become integral parts of the state's coercive apparatus and staunch supporters of the regimes. Thus, it perhaps appeared to many Middle East scholars and analysts that there was no pressing reason to study their political role. This notion is one of the main reasons that Western intelligence communities, as I noted in the introduction, were apparently just as baffled as the public at large by the relatively quick collapse of the rules of Hosni Mubarak, Muammar Qadhafi, Zine el-Abidine Ben Ali, and Ali Abdullah Saleh. Clearly, their regimes were not nearly as firmly entrenched as they appeared to be.

One of the principal reasons why recent Middle Eastern and North African (MENA) events took so many observers by surprise was the sheer opacity of these countries, especially their military establishments. Gathering reliable information about MENA armies has been extraordinarily difficult. In just a three-page span in her recent book, Sarah Phillips, one of the few Western academics who can claim to be an authority on Yemen, qualifies her assertions about Yemeni military affairs with phrases such as "a point of great contention," "shrouded in secrecy," "notoriously inaccurate self-reported statistics," "extremely vague," "an unknown quantity," "casting further doubt on the reliability of any figures presented," and "accurate figures are still impossible to obtain."[1] It is hard not to be sympathetic to the researcher's plight. Until recently, MENA armed forces appeared to be unquestionably dedicated to the autocracies they served, and, in part because they were so little studied, few would have thought that these armies might disobey their political overlords.

In this chapter, the primary focus is on the military's role in the six Arab-majority states where considerable bloodshed took place: Bahrain, Egypt, Libya, Syria, Tunisia, and Yemen. Aside from the first, a tiny island kingdom in the Persian Gulf, each of these countries was or is ruled by a sultanistic regime under the sway of a despot bound by no apparent term limits: Mubarak, Qadhafi, Bashar al-Assad, Ben Ali, and Saleh, respectively. In order to gauge the differences between these six states and those where demonstrations took place but bloodshed was minimal, I expand the analysis briefly to include the Arab monarchies, especially Oman and Morocco. Because we will be discussing more individual cases in this chapter, they must necessarily receive somewhat less extensive coverage than others we have previously examined, but I hope that the gains in comprehensiveness and the chance for comparison will outweigh the loss in detail.

The immediate, direct causes of these uprisings were, of course, quite different; however, the "demonstration effect" was certainly unmistakable, as the revolutionary "virus" that originated in Tunisia jumped from one country to another—circulating among countries that shared many historical and modern experiences based, in part, on a common language and religion.[2] Moreoever, the principal underlying causes were broadly similar throughout the region. The vast majority of citizens were deeply discontented, owing to a volatile combination of numerous political, economic, and sociocultural reasons. The seemingly well-entrenched autocratic regimes that were accountable to no one did not bestow even the basic political freedoms—freedoms of expression, association, and movement, or opportunity for meaningful political participation—onto their subjects. In some cases, they maintained state of emergency laws for decades, and, of course, did not allow free and fair elections. The incompetence and profound corruption of the regimes was manifested in a deep-seated economic malaise that was characterized by extremely high unemployment rates—especially among youths, even those with college degrees—rising food prices, and the enrichment of narrow political and economic elites juxtaposed with the growing poverty of tens of millions across the region. Discrimination based on gender, religion, ethnic-tribal membership, sexual orientation, socioeconomic class, and other attributes were part of the daily lives of most Arab citizens.[3] In short, there were many reasons for people to join the uprisings once the sparks turned into fires.

Some commentators seeking to find patterns among the Arab uprisings suggested that they failed in countries where rulers told the military to open fire but triumphed in places where rulers could not stomach killing citizens.[4] That suggestion is incorrect. Among our six cases, where substantial violence occurred, every ruler ordered his military and/or security agencies to suppress protests by force (including lethal force). In some cases, the generals said yes; in others, they said no, because they calculated that their own and their country's interests would be best served by regime change. The eight states in this chapter can be grouped into four categories, defined by how the regular military—as distinct from special elite units and security detachments—responded to the revolt. In Tunisia and Egypt, the soldiers backed the revolution; in Libya and Yemen, they split; in Syria and Bahrain, they turned their guns against the demonstrators; and in Morocco and Oman, they did not get involved at all. What explains the disparities?

Siding with the Rebels: Tunisia and Egypt

There are major differences between these two countries in terms of the processes that led their military leaders to the decision to support the rebels, the complexity of the factors affecting their response to the uprisings, and ultimately, the predictability of the outcomes. Nonetheless, they both came to the same conclusion, to let their respective heads of state fall rather than turn their guns against unarmed protesters.

Tunisia

Tunisia was the country where the wave of unrest began in mid-December 2010. When it became apparent that the police and security forces would not be able to stop the quickly spreading street demonstrations, President Ben Ali unleashed gangs of thugs and his elite Presidential Guard against the protesters. The decision to use lethal force against peaceful demonstrators virtually ensured the radicalization of the uprising. Once it became clear that the security forces were unable to control the demonstrators, Ben Ali ordered Army Chief of Staff General Rachid Ammar to deploy his troops to suppress the uprising. Although until this point the army was more or less a passive observer and did not interfere as the police attacked the protesters, General Ammar rejected the order and placed his men between the security units and the protesters, thereby effectively saving the revolution and forcing Ben Ali into exile.[5] Why did Ammar act this way? Why did the army take the side of the protesters? A closer look at Tunisian civil-military relations reveals that this outcome should not have been unexpected.

MILITARY FACTORS

Ben Ali's predecessor, Habib Bourguiba, had deliberately kept soldiers out of politics during his three decades as president (1957–87), even banning them from joining the ruling party and withholding from them the right to vote. Although in 1978 and 1984, the army answered the government's call to restore order following civil disturbances, the generals resented being told to assume police functions and were happy to have their men return to barracks as soon as the crises had passed.[6] A military academy graduate, Ben Ali became a police-state apparatchik who overthrew Bourguiba bloodlessly in 1987 and continued the policy of keeping the armed forces on the political sidelines.[7] Unlike most other North African armies, Tunisia's had never even attempted a coup, had never taken part in making political decisions, had never been a "nation-building" instrument, and had never joined in economic-development schemes. Ben Ali kept it a small (approximately 30,000 personnel, in contrast to the considerably larger interior ministry forces [about 49,000 men, plus up to 30,000 informers]), marginalized, and modestly funded force that was focused on border defense.[8]

Tunisia's army has been remarkably free of internal divisions of any sort. For the most part, the officer corps is traditionally drawn from the coastal Sahel; this relative homogeneity is offset, however, by the rank and file, who are conscripted from all over the country.[9] The armed forces are widely considered by Tunisians as a *national* institution in contradistinction to the Presidential Guard, the police, and the security organizations. The military's institutional rivals have been the various security organizations under the control of the Ministry of Interior (MoI).

STATE FACTORS

Ben Ali's Tunisia was a police state. As in many other sultanistic regimes, it was a place where the regular military found itself overshadowed by far larger, more amply funded, and more politically influential security agencies run by the MoI. Not surprisingly, the military resented its institutional rivals, particularly the MoI's 12,000-strong and highly privileged paramilitary National Guard, the backbone of the security forces that received fifty percent more funds in 2010 than the entire armed forces (whose procurement budget, at $70 million, was the lowest in the Arab world).[10]

Undistracted by politics and despite its meager budget and equipment, the Tunisian military came to rank among the Arab world's most professional forces. With its comparatively disadvantaged status and its officers' disdain for the notorious corruption of the presidential clique, the military had no special stake in the regime's survival and no strong reason to shoot fellow Tunisians on the regime's behalf. Ben Ali allowed his militias to attack demonstrators and to loot with impunity, which could not but enrage the army whose personnel maintained its professionalism throughout the crisis.[11] As soon as Ben Ali found himself forced to turn to the soldiers as his last resort, he was doomed. According to some accounts, it was General Ammar who persuaded Ben Ali to leave and told the demonstrators, "The army is the guarantor of the revolution."[12]

SOCIETAL FACTORS

The initial protests condemning Bouazizi's humiliation spread quickly throughout Tunisia and turned into mass demonstrations with the participation of a veritable cross section of society. Ben Ali's conciliatory speeches were useless, particularly as dozens of protesters fell victim to the violence unleashed upon them by the police and militias. The demonstrations were overwhelmingly peaceful, although, as the days went, by not all protesters took the brutal response of the security detachments lying down.

In no Arab country has the military been more clearly distinct from the regime in power: indeed, in Tunisia, the term *la grande muette* ("the big silent one") is often used to describe the army's noninterference in public affairs.[13] The population maintained an overwhelmingly positive view of the armed forces, in which a one-year service for young men was compulsory; in fact, the military *was not* identified by Tunisians as part of Ben Ali's coercive apparatus.[14]

There could be also no doubt about the popularity of the revolution. During the nearly quarter-century-long reign of Ben Ali, society became increasingly polarized with an ever-smaller section benefitting from business opportunities, corruption, and the ruling gang's largesse, while the resentment of the rest of Tunisians had gradually built up. As in other Arab republics, political succession was an issue in Tunisia, as well, where Bourguiba was the first self-proclaimed Arab president for life (1975) and where Ben Ali's much-hated wife, Leïla, was rumored to have her eyes on the presidency. On 14 January 2011, a nation-wide general strike turned into a celebration of Ben Ali's departure to Saudi Arabia.

EXTERNAL FACTORS

In order to counterbalance the close professional ties that had developed between Tunisian security agencies and their French counterparts, Ben Ali sent a high proportion of his military officers for training in the United States, where some were exposed to programs on the principles of civil-military relations under democracy. The majority of Tunisian army officers had significant exposure to Western, particularly American, military personnel and had ample opportunities to build and professionally benefit from these relationships.[15]

Egypt

Although Egypt's generals also opted to back the uprising, their road to that decision was by no means as clear and straightforward as the path that Tunisia's senior soldiers trod. For the first two-and-a-half weeks of the uprising in Egypt, the country's military elites hedged their bets. They worked quietly to advance their position in the government, while some army units were actually detaining and abusing protesters or enabling the police to assault them. Troops themselves never actually fired on the people; however, nor did the army prevent demonstrators from filling Cairo's Tahrir Square.[16] On January 28, the resistance of the police and the Ministry of Interior's Central Security Forces (CSF) collapsed. The regime responded by sending in the army: officers and conscripted soldiers in tanks and armed personnel carriers were deployed in and around downtown Cairo. This course of events suggested that Mubarak was losing his grip on power.[17]

When security agents and President Mubarak's loyalists unleashed extensive violence on February 2, whatever credit his regime still had with the people was shattered. The generals concluded that Mubarak's mix of concessions (agreeing not to seek reelection or have his son succeed him) and repression (the February 2 attacks) had failed, and rising violence and disorder would only hurt the military's legitimacy and influence. Even the Republican Guard—a division-level force in charge of protecting the presidency—opted not to defend the regime. Thus, on February 10, the nineteen-member Supreme Council of the Armed Forces (SCAF) concluded that it was no longer worth defending an 82-year-old, out-of-touch dictator with no acceptable successor; it assumed control of the country and, the next day, forced a reluctant Mubarak to step down and head for internal exile.[18]

MILITARY FACTORS

The Egyptian army is a cohesive organization with no appreciable ethnoreligious splits. Although Egypt is home to the sizable Coptic Christian minority, few Copts choose the military as a career—quite possibly, due to the antipathy toward their brethren and their perception of a "glass ceiling" that limits their advancement in the armed forces—and thus, Muslim-Christian relations within the armed forces are not a source of tension.[19] As in many other armed forces, junior officers resent the extensive privileges of the top echelons of the officer corps.[20] Still, the complex web of the army's interests, allegiances, and the entire officer corps' dependence on military networks helps explain why it retained its cohesion during upheaval.[21] As in Tunisia, the major split is not within the military but between the military and the security establishment. The growing political clout of the MoI had eclipsed that of the traditionally more influential defense establishment approximately two decades prior to the Arab Spring.[22]

Egypt's military is based on mandatory conscription. For those with no education or only basic schooling, conscription is for three years. A large proportion of these soldiers receive minimal training—illiterates who enter the army are most likely to leave the same way—and are often posted in front of some state building or facility for the duration of their time in the military. Those who have at least completed their secondary education tend to be drafted for one year. Most draftees of both categories consider the time spent in the military "as an unfortunate yet temporal ordeal."[23] The conscripts represent every region of the country and help make the army a truly national institution.

The Egyptian armed forces are a massive and powerful organization whose top leaders enjoy broad decision-making authority. The Minister of Defense and Military Production from May 1991 until August 2012,

Field Marshal Mohamed Hussein Tantawi, was Mubarak's close associate for decades and ran the military without interference. The chiefs of the service branches, as well as that of the elite Republican Guard, were all vetted and approved by Mubarak. Nevertheless, analysts have long raised problems regarding the professionalism of the military. According to two experts,

> the Egyptian army is not the tight professional force that many consider it to be. It is bloated and its officer corps is indulged, having been fattened on Mubarak's patronage. Its training is desultory, maintenance of its equipment is profoundly inadequate, and it is dependent on the United States for funding and logistical support.[24]

Others note that the military has been in an intellectual and social decline and, partly because its salaries fell below those of the private sector, it is no longer one of the top career choices for middle-class youths. Furthermore, working-class or low-income applicants to officer schools are disadvantaged both by the high cost of attending and the definite prejudice against them at such institutions.[25]

STATE FACTORS

The stance of the Egyptian military vis-à-vis the demonstrators was a less predictable outcome than the one in Tunisia for several reasons. To begin with, Egypt's armed forces have long been privileged in a way that Tunisia's never were, even with the superior political influence of the MoI. The Egyptian military remained a key part of the support base for Mubarak (himself a former air force general) and never came under opposition or media criticism. Furthermore, the armed forces—like most other defense-security organizations in the Arab world—are an extraordinarily secretive organization that most people know very little about. As an opposition activist noted, "The military is a black box, and no one knows what happens inside."[26]

The generals were able to make up for their waning political clout, moreover, with growing economic involvement in everything from housewares and military-gear production to farming and tourism. Solid numbers are virtually impossible to come by; according to a recent account, the military owns about eighty-seven percent of Egypt's land and over one-third of its businesses.[27] The revenue from these enterprises goes straight to the military's coffers and is disbursed entirely without state oversight. We can sense the importance of these business endeavors by noting that Tantawi not only headed the Defense Ministry but also ran the Ministry of Military Production. Military officers directly profit from the army's business endeavors through relatively high salaries, plus preferential treatment in medical care, housing, and transport. These resources increase the military's institutional autonomy within the country's political system. And, of course, the armed forces also reap $1.3 billion every year in military aid from the United States.

So why did the Egyptian army decline to save Mubarak's regime? First, military elites despised Gamal Mubarak, the president's son and putative successor. A businessman, Gamal headed a faction of what might be called "state entrepreneurs" who, like him, were dedicated to exploiting his family's status and his ruling-party post in order to profit from the liberal economic reforms of the past decade.[28] Second, the top brass were growing anxious about youth alienation and spreading Islamist radicalism, as well as economic malaise and stagnation. Third, Egypt's soldiers, like Tunisia's, were not pleased to see the regime leaning on—and sluicing ever more privileges to—a large police and security apparatus, which, in Egypt, is thought to have employed as many as 1.4 million people. Finally, Egypt's conscript army has so many ties to society at large that, even had the generals been willing to shoot demonstrators, many officers and enlisted men might well have refused to obey such an order. Unfortunately, however, the last point is somewhat mitigated by the fact that CSF troops, also conscripts, had killed numerous demonstrators. One might argue that CSF draftees who usually come from poor and rural backgrounds with inferior education—the better educated conscripts usually end up in one of the branches of the military—might be more susceptible to indoctrination and thus willing to obey orders to turn their guns against protesters.[29]

SOCIETAL FACTORS

In Egypt, as in Tunisia, the combined use of social media and satellite television broadcasts managed to turn initially small protests into massive demonstrations, expressing mounting displeasure with the Mubarak regime. Hundreds of thousands of people representing all segments of society showed up day after day, and as the army's neutrality turned into tacit, and later explicit, support, protesters gave the soldiers flowers and clambered on their tanks to have their photos taken. Cries of "The people and the army are one hand!" spread through the crowds, and most demonstrators were willing to trust the SCAF.[30] The growing fraternization between the soldiers and the protesters, it is worth noting, "drove a potential wedge between the men on the front lines and those calling the shots at headquarters."[31]

In a society where few institutions command much respect, the military—prior to the Arab Spring—had been held in high regard. The head of the opposition movement, *Kefaya* ("enough"), George Ishak, said during the early-February demonstrations on Tahrir Square, "I believe the military will protect us," and then added, "We trust in our military a lot because we don't have anyone else to trust."[32] And, as in Tunisia, the military was respected in large segments of Egyptian society because it was not part of the domestic security apparatus that repressed the population.

EXTERNAL FACTORS

Although apparently no foreign state seriously considered intervening in Egypt, revolutionary diffusion made a strong impact on the country. The generals in Cairo were certainly influenced by their ties to foreign states, more specifically, to one foreign country—the United States. There is evidence that when President Obama's cabinet decided during the course of the uprising that Mubarak was no longer a strategic asset, it communicated its concerns directly to the Egyptian generals, in particular, "the need not to fire at the protestors."[33] As one of the key organizers of Egypt's early protests recalled, the developments in Tunisia were discussed extensively on social media sites, one survey reported that eighty-six percent of its respondents supported covering the protests in the mainstream media—even if the latter was reluctant to do so.[34] The generals in Cairo were shaken by Ben Ali's fall and the scale of the protests.[35] Some Egyptian officers did receive education in Western countries, but the cadres who were selected for such an assignment were controlled far more closely by the regime than in Tunisia. In fact, there is no Arab military that is more closed to the outside world than the Egyptian; for instance, officers are allowed no e-mail contact with fellow officers being trained in the United States, and the Cairo Ministry of Defense (MoD) does not employ a single civilian in a position of consequence.[36] The overall level of professionalism is far lower in the Egyptian military, and it is likely that exposure to foreign training has made a more modest impact on Egyptian officers than on their Tunisian colleagues.

SUMMARY

The background and modern history of the Tunisian army could hardly have been more different from its Egyptian counterpart. The Tunisian military was relatively small, poor, politically marginalized, and was never involved in politics, precisely the opposite of the Egyptian armed forces. Nonetheless, they reached the same decision regarding the uprising in early 2011, even if via different ways. Internal cohesion (I.1.) was not a key source of anxiety to generals in either country, though splits between the army and interior ministry troops (I.1.D.) were important in both contexts, particularly so in Tunisia. The fact that both armies were primarily composed of conscripts (I.2.) was a key consideration, as well as the generals' perceptions of the low and eroding legitimacy of the Ben Ali and Mubarak regimes (I.1.3.). The regime's treatment of the military (II.1.) was an important aggregate factor that influenced the generals in Tunis and Cairo, though somewhat more so in the former than the latter, particularly regarding the relatively poor remuneration of the officer corps. Egyptian generals were more concerned about their diminishing political influence (II.1.B.)—particularly when contrasted with that of the MoI—and being asked to bring the demonstrations under control (II.1.C.), a mission they believed was the professional responsibility of the CSF. The massive popular participation in the demonstration made an impact on generals in both countries (III.1.), the potential for foreign intervention was an issue in neither (IV.1.), and the Egyptian top brass were clearly sensitive to foreign—reactions to the events (IV.2.)—especially that of the United States.[37]

DIVIDED LOYALTIES: LIBYA AND YEMEN

Although Yemen is far poorer than oil-rich Libya, the two states shared many similarities, including low levels of institutional development (independent public institutions were not to be found in either country) and towering corruption. According to one source, the government in Sana'a "makes even the Karzai regime, in Afghanistan, seem like a model of propriety."[38] Libya had not had a constitution since 1951, it had no formal head of state (Qadhafi was nominally the "supreme guide" of what he saw as a large clan), its parliament was symbolic, and Qadhafi had had decades to sap its governmental institutions (the military included) in order to bolster his highly personalized brand of rule.[39] Tribal affiliations—of relatively little consequence in Tunisia and Egypt—and regionalism were—and still are—of foremost importance in Yemen and Libya. Saleh and Qadhafi gave most positions of trust, including key military and security commands, to their own tribesmen and close relatives: both named sons and nephews to head various security agencies and choice military units. In Libya, oil revenues were crucial to allowing Qadhafi "to use distributive largesse to keep Libya politically immobile";[40] in Yemen, Saleh tried to cement loyalties with the selective dispensation of privileges, including business licenses.

Soon after the protests began, President Saleh cut taxes, hiked food subsidies, and vowed to raise civil-service pay. More important, he promised not to extend his rule beyond 2013 nor to permit his son Ahmed Ali—the commander of the elite Republican Guard—to succeed him. The crowds, initially dominated by students, were not satisfied with these concessions and demanded that Saleh immediately resign. The ensuing violence—in particular the killing of fifty-two protesters by security forces on March 18—galvanized the opposition and divided the armed forces. Qadhafi's first response to the revolt against him was to unleash his half dozen or so paramilitary organizations against his opponents, although his administration offered some minor concessions—such as easing housing credit—in order to prevent the spread of the unrest.[41]

In both countries, the military was split in its attitude toward the regime. Parts of the regular army, as well as the special forces, paramilitary groups, and other units that were attached to the ruling family, clan, and tribe, tended to stay with the regime. The rest of the military either turned against the regime or deserted. By mid-2011, both countries were in a state of civil war, with their militaries still split, and the outcome of the fighting uncertain. The situation in Yemen was made more complicated by the presence of four extant armed conflicts: (1) the Houthi rebellion in the north; (2) the separatist movement in the south—rooted in the surviving antagonism between the governorates of the former People's Democratic Republic of Yemen that felt short-changed by the 1990 unification; (3) the government's struggle against extremists in al-Qaeda in the Arabian Peninsula (AQAP), also primarily in the south; and (4) the sectarian conflict that pitted extremist Salafists against moderate Shia and Sunni Muslims.

In both Yemen and Libya, as in most civil wars, outside forces helped determine the outcome. In Libya, a NATO bombing campaign tilted the balance toward the protesters. In Yemen, mediators from the Gulf Cooperation Council (GCC)—an organization of the six oil-rich monarchies of the Persian Gulf—managed to convince Saleh to resign the presidency (after numerous ups and downs) and allow preparations for new elections. In both cases, divisions within the armed forces could be easily anticipated by those who were familiar with contemporary Libyan and Yemeni politics, society, and military affairs.

Military Factors

In both countries, the defense establishment was divided into two parts: the regular army vs. a set of several paramilitary organizations.[42] These institutions had little contact with one another. The regular military was ostensibly charged with the external defense of the country, while the security forces were supposed to protect the regime, though in practice ensuring regime survival was the main mission of all these forces. Unlike the Tunisian and Egyptian armies, the militaries of Libya and Yemen were underinstitutionalized, largely lacking professionalism, and entirely dependent on the dictator's whims. In other words, since both Saleh and Qadhafi came to power by overthrowing their predecessors, "coup-proofing,"—which involved relying on tribal loyalties, creating new paramilitary organizations, and making sure that all entities entrusted with security functions were spying on one another—was indispensable to their survival.[43] Consequently, it is clear that creating a unified defense establishment—or even a cohesive regular army—was not at all what they wanted; their key objective was regime survival, which worked best with a fragmented and heavily supervised force. This intentional breaking up of the defense establishment and the ubiquitous spying on their components also served to isolate military leaders and diminish their decision-making authority.

The biggest loss for the Saleh regime was the defection of General Ali Mohsen al-Ahmar, Saleh's tribesman and longtime ally who had distinguished himself over the past decade by fighting Houthi separatists in the north. A dozen regular army generals joined Ahmar. They included the southerner, Abdallah al-Qahdi, who had recently been cashiered for refusing to use force against peaceful demonstrators.[44] Although the defense minister insisted that the military was still faithful to Saleh, many ordinary soldiers either went over to General Ahmar and the opposition or simply deserted. To keep his hold on power, Saleh relied on the better equipped and better trained Republican Guard, Central Security Organization, and elite army units, whose loyalty he retained. The army itself was deeply divided. During the unrest, a virtual proxy war took place between different Yemeni army units and their commanders. According to rumors, General Ahmar was at increasingly bitter odds with Saleh's eldest son, Ahmed Ali, who headed the elite Republican Guard.[45]

Qadhafi's endgame was also affected by deep divisions within his forces. Suspecting disloyalty, he dismissed his brother-in-law, Abdallah Senoussi, from his post at the head of the secret service and put top army general Abu-Bakr Yunis Jabr under house arrest once the revolt commenced.[46] Even so, the army and air force units based in and near Benghazi and Tobruk (in eastern Libya) defected more or less in their entirety, while large segments of units stationed in Kufra, Misrata, the Western Mountains, and Zawiya deserted as well.[47] In many cases retired military personnel were the first to join the revolutionaries. In order to compensate for the resulting shortage of loyal troops, Qadhafi allegedly brought in thousands of mercenaries from Sahel states, Europe, and Latin America.[48] Soldiers who continued to fight against the rebels reported that their officers lied by telling them that they were being sent to put down not domestic rebels, but foreign-inspired terrorists.[49]

The divisions in the Yemeni and Libyan armed forces reflected the many and deep-seated cleavages in their respective societies. Although the bonds of tribe and kinship do not override every discord, as General Ahmar's example shows, they are tremendously important in determining military attitudes. Several experts note the imperative in both countries to constantly revise the tribal balance because loyalties were uncertain and often shifted unpredictably.[50] Regionalism has also played a major role in shaping people's identities: whether one was from Tripoli or Benghazi, has traditionally been an important marker of one's affinity toward the regime. In addition, coercion and bribery were essential in persuading some segments of the Libyan and Yemeni armed forces to stay with the regime. The threats and bribes were necessary because, as the many defections and desertions show, major segments of the armed forces entertained profound doubts about the legitimacy of these regimes.

Neither the Libyan nor the Yemeni armed forces implemented the sort of regularized draft of institutionalized armies. In 1978, Qadhafi's large-scale expansion of the Libyan military necessitated the introduction of conscription, and it survived until the end of the 1980s; nonetheless, one of the top Western experts on the subject was uncertain if there was a draft in the last few years of the regime.[51] During Saleh's long reign, conscription was introduced, abolished, and then reinstated (in the late 2000s), but one suspects that it was not consistently or fairly applied.[52] In this context, the import of the conscript-versus-enlisted dichotomy is dwarfed by divisions based on tribal and regional identity as well as the split between the regular army and the various paramilitary forces.

State Factors

After Lieutenant Colonel Qadhafi seized power in a bloodless 1969 coup, his fellow army officers attempted to remove him from power four times (most recently in October 1993). Not surprisingly, Qadhafi deliberately marginalized and underfunded the military from the early 1990s, particularly after suspecting it of involvement in a coup attempt and following its debacle in the Chadian-Libyan conflict (1989–87).[53] He gave priority treatment, instead, to parallel elite and paramilitary forces, most of them newly established and commanded by his relatives. According to a senior internal affairs officer in the Libyan Army, "There was no real interest in the state of the Army itself but if I reported about someone being critical of Muammar Qadhafi all hell would break loose."[54] Libya's army was the most heavily politicized Arab army—and quite possibly the most demoralized—with the frequent rotation of commanders, over-lapping chains of command, and the absence of merit-based personnel evaluation. Nevertheless, some senior army officers were able to use their positions to skim funds through arms deals and other ventures related to weapons acquisition.[55] In Saleh's Yemen, the army's top brass were treated well and paid off by the regime in several ways. Perhaps the most important of these was the Military Economic Corporation that emerged in the mid-1980s and was renamed Yemeni Economic Corporation in 1999. It has become an increasingly prosperous conglomerate overseen by military officers and was a main source of revenue for both Saleh and senior army commanders.[56]

Military elites' views of the ruling regimes were primarily colored by their tribal affiliations and, only secondarily, by their leadership posi-tions, which were heavily dependent upon whether or not they belonged to groups favored by the dictator and his clan. In these deeply divided societies, in which there are few if any robust political institutions, one's identity as a soldier or a member of one or the other component of the defense-security establishment is far less consequential than one's mem-bership in one's tribe or clan. Although both sides had done their best to cultivate tribal loyalties, there appears to be some doubt as to their suc-cess in doing so.[57]

Societal Factors

Members of the regular armed forces were not held in high regard ei-ther in Yemen or in Libya, even if they were seldom used as tools of do-mestic suppression. The people understood that, on a professional level, armed forces personnel were undistinguished, not just in terms of vague generalities but in terms of specific failures.[58] The Yemeni military has not been able to master the challenges posed by the Houthi insurgents or to bring the other conflicts under control. The country's notorious corruption affects soldiers, too, who often sell their supposed enemies their weapons and even change sides.[59] The professional incompetence of the Libyan army was clearly revealed by the humiliation it repeatedly received at the hands of rag-tag Chadian forces in the 1980s.[60] There is no reason to believe that its performance would have improved since then (although during the civil war many elite units fought well, according to reports, albeit against mostly undisciplined, untrained, and poorly equipped opponents).[61]

Another reason for the modest public esteem of these two armies is that, not infrequently, soldiers—often entire units—choose desertion rather than fighting. Desertion has been a serious problem in Yemen's conflicts and, to a lesser extent, in Libya's war with Chad. It became a major factor in the civil wars in the wake of the 2011 uprisings. The defection of senior generals—often together with all those under their command—demoralized the remaining soldiers and diminished their fighting capabilities.[62]

External Variables

The revolutionary fervor spread quickly to Libya and Yemen in early 2011. The eruption of increasingly large-scale demonstrations was far less surprising in Yemen, where stability and calm had been absent for a while. In contrast, most experts expected that Libya—seemingly so firmly under the thumb of its mentally unstable dictator—would be the last place to follow Tunisia and Egypt.[63] Some Yemeni officers, unlike their Libyan colleagues, had been exposed to their Western, especially American and British, counterparts both through educational programs abroad and in-country counterterrorism training. Most of these officers sided with Saleh's regime, believing that his rule was more conducive to stability and the continuation of the antiterrorist campaign than any of the hazy alternatives.[64]

After months of fighting, the poorly organized rebels were still unable to take Tripoli and other Qadhafi strongholds in western Libya, despite continuing combat support from NATO. On 15 July 2011, the United States joined more than thirty countries in officially recognizing the rebel leadership, the Transitional National Council, as Libya's legitimate government. Nevertheless, Qadhafi appeared as determined as ever to fight on and held out until late August, although the bombing campaign certainly raised his troops' desertion rate.[65] Owing to his decades-long erratic behavior and his singular talent to antagonize fellow leaders—even those in the Arab League—Qadhafi could garner no support.[66]

The situation in Yemen, meanwhile, remained inconclusive. In June, President Saleh was flown to Saudi Arabia to receive medical treatment after being severely wounded in a rocket attack during clashes between his troops and tribal fighters. In his absence, skirmishes—though not outright combat—between government and opposition forces continued until Saleh's reluctant resignation in November. Antiregime forces were composed not only of army defectors and tribal soldiers but also, most worryingly, al-Qaeda fighters. In Libya, forces supporting the regime and the revolution tended to act

> on parochial logics and historical narratives, which determined their desire to co-opt, support, or oppose the transitional authorities or Qadhafi's state. The result was a revolution disconnected beyond the shared goal of Qadhafi's defeat, resulting in unique political and military structures and relationships in every major city and sub-region.[67]

This meant that Yemeni soldiers, unlike their Libyan counterparts, did not need to worry about a potential foreign intervention. Western governments threw money at Saleh to help him crush the al-Qaeda franchise. Additionally, the number of opposing groups and conflicting loyalties made the situation even more complex and murky than that in Libya. Nevertheless, it is worth reiterating that without the GCC's consistent pressure on Saleh to agree to a peace deal, he would have almost certainly held out considerably longer.

Summary

In both Libya and Yemen, our top six factors had a major impact on the regular armies' leaders as they formulated their responses to the uprisings. The army's internal cohesion (I.1.) was of paramount importance in these settings, where tribal and regional identity (I.1.A.) tended to override every other group affiliation. Divisions between the army and the numerous other security sector entities (I.1.D. and I.1.E.) were also critical. As I noted, the conscription-versus-enlistment issue (I.2.) was somewhat fuzzy in both countries—irregularities, bribes, and overall corruption permeated the draft, even when it was officially implemented—but the generals' views of regime legitimacy (I.3.) were extremely important, even if usually (though not always) predictable, based on tribal and regional affiliations. The regime's marginalization of the regular army (II.1.) was a key factor in Libya, but less so in Yemen, where Saleh did his best to cement the loyalty of his soldiers with a variety of perquisites. Confronting a large demonstration (III.1.) was especially significant in Libya, where public protests were extremely rare, far less so in Yemen. And, of course, the potential for foreign intervention (IV.1.) was also a more critical factor for the Libyan generals, since for them it meant military intervention, as opposed to in Yemen, where it was manifested in intensive diplomatic negotiations targeting Saleh's exit from the political scene.

Sticking with the Status Quo

Although Bahrain and Syria are widely differing countries with widely differing military establishments and widely different initial responses to the upheavals in 2011, both states' officer corps supported their commanders-in-chief, although in Syria's case this support was not nearly as unanimous and unequivocal as in Bahrain. At first, Sheikh Hamad bin Isa al-Khalifa, Bahrain's monarch, offered a mix of financial concessions and reform vows to the demonstrators, while President Bashar al-Assad, Syria's dictator, immediately resorted to a heavy-handed retaliation against peaceful protesters. Their militaries backed them both—albeit for different reasons. The two countries are also similar to the extent that neither of their conflicts ended in 2011: Syria has been torn asunder by an ongoing and ever more complicated civil war, while far more low-key and sporadic disturbances have continued in Bahrain.

Exhibit A: Bahrain

In the Bahraini capital of Manama, a major uprising with a decidedly sectarian character began on February 14, three days after Mubarak's resignation in Cairo. The overwhelmingly Shia protesters converged on Pearl Square in Manama, though the unrest later spread throughout the city center and into the mostly Shia neighborhoods.[68] The royal family responded with a $2,700 grant to every Bahraini family, but this gesture did not stifle the demonstrators' pent-up frustrations. On February 17, the government changed tactics and resorted to violence: security forces used rubber bullets and tear gas on peaceful demonstrators—many of them asleep at what had become something like a street fair—killing at least four and injuring many.[69] The regime's violent actions served to escalate the uprising, which now took on a decidedly antimonarchical character, in spite of King Hamad's offers of dialogue and the government's release of some political prisoners.

The protests continued and occasionally turned into violent riots with groups of demonstrators blocking the entrance to the parliament building and blockading the city's financial district. Some of the demonstrations were quite large, with over 100,000 people (from a citizenry of about 600,000) participating.[70] On March 15, King Hamad issued Royal Decree #18, declaring a "State of National Safety" (i.e., martial law) and tasked the Bahrain Defense Force (BDF), the National Guard, the MoI (i.e., police), and the National Security Agency (NSA) with its enforcement. At least forty-six people died in the conflict, including some police officers. Approximately three thousand people were arrested; seven hundred of them were still behind bars at the end of 2011; over four thousand lost their jobs as a result of their participation in the uprising.[71]

No revolutionary outcome was easier to predict than the one in Bahrain. The Bahrain Defense Force is firmly rooted in the regime, and the opposition's demands for substantive political reforms so contrary to their basic interests, that for Bahraini officers to support the rebels would have been, for a number of reasons, entirely unthinkable. The key thing to understand about the Bahraini military is that it is *not* a national army.[72] Rather, it is a fighting force of Sunni Muslims who are charged with protecting a Sunni ruling family and Sunni political and business elites in a country where about three of every four or five people are Shia. Bahrain's Sunnis dwell in constant fear of Iranian influence among local Shias, who are barred from sensitive jobs and live under suspicion of wanting to seize power at the first opportunity. Put a bit more dramatically: for the country's Sunni minority, the uprising of the Shia community manifested an existential threat. It is hardly surprising, then, that Bahrain's Sunni army speedily confirmed its allegiance to Bahrain's Sunni monarchy by suppressing the overwhelmingly Shia.

Bahrain's military is certainly unified in their loyalty to the Sunni Muslim monarchy but this is not to say that divisions in the military are absent. Political elites, including the top brass, are divided in their support between conservative and reformist members of the royal family.[73] Additionally, junior officers tend to be more progressive than their more senior superiors; furthermore, members of the large Al-Khalifa ruling family and, to a lesser extent, the main Sunni tribes enjoy preferential treatment in the military and security apparatus. It needs to be underscored, though, that there is no question about the firm allegiance of the *entire* officer corps to the regime.

The approximately 8,200-strong BDF must contend with three main institutional rivals: the aforementioned paramilitary National Guard, the MoI's police, and the NSA. The functions of all of these entities include—to varying degrees—the protection of the regime in domestic contingencies, such as the 2011 uprising. This sort of overlapping authority has diminished accord and coherence within the security establishment. All four organizations were involved in defeating the uprising, but only the police and the NSA were faulted by a subsequent independent international inquiry into the excessive use of force and human rights violations.[74]

Many oil monarchies keep their armies small and build up competing security agencies, in part out of mistrust but also in order to satisfy the ambitions of various ruling family members and to keep different family factions in balance.[75] Like other Arab militaries, the Bahraini, too, is overcentralized and decision-making authority is concentrated in the hands of the senior royal family, who hold all consequential command and combat positions in the defense-security establishment.[76] Bahrain has never instituted the draft precisely because its ruling elites do not want Shias bearing arms and receiving military training.[77] Although Shia Muslims do have a token representation in the BDF, they work in administration, logistics, and other fields require no armed service.[78] In the spring of 2011, many Shia "military personnel"—most were actually employed by the MoI—were sacked, presumably for their halfhearted suppression of the demonstrators.[79] Many Bahraini Shia consider the BDF to be the Al-Khalifa monarchy's last line of defense from its *internal* enemies. They believe that the BDF's role in defending the island kingdom is secondary to that of the much larger and better equipped Saudi forces.[80] (It is important to note that, since the 1979 Iranian revolution there have been numerous internal crises in Bahrain, starting with an unsuccessful coup attempt in 1981 and including the 1994–99 uprising.)

Bahrain's soldiers are well taken care of: they enjoy good pay, up-to-date weapons, and, according to some accounts, solid training.[81] Still, given the more lucrative career alternatives available, the relatively low prestige of the military occupation in the kingdom, and the practical necessity to close the military-security realm from the Shia community, the monarchy—like most other GCC members—has resorted to hiring qualified officers and sergeants of the Sunni Muslim faith from abroad—particularly from Pakistan, Jordan, Syria, Yemen, and, since 2003, Iraq—to keep the forces adequately staffed.[82] During the uprising, people knew that many of the security personnel facing them were Pakistanis who did not understand Arabic, so they chanted, "The police are crazy!" in Urdu.[83] The protests that began on 14 February 2011 quickly grew into massive demonstrations. Many marchers did not leave but turned some of downtown Manama into squatter camps, thereby paralyzing traffic and commercial activities, and further angering the authorities. Initially, there were a small number of Sunnis demanding political reforms, but as the crowd was radicalized—in large part owing to the unnecessarily violent police response—it assumed an entirely Shia character.[84]

In Bahrain, the conflict took on a regional quality when King Hamad's appeal (on March 14) to the GCC resulted in the arrival of five hundred policemen from the United Arab Emirates (UAE), plus a thousand Saudi troops, who came rumbling over the fifteen-mile-long King Fahd Causeway in armored vehicles.[85] The turmoil in Bahrain has also been viewed as a proxy conflict between Saudi Arabia and Iran,[86] primarily because the Saudi state has a tremendous political and economic influence on Bahrain. Second, the Saudis were understandably worried about the effect of Bahrain's Shia uprising on their own Shia minority, concentrated in their Eastern Province—where, incidentally, the bulk of the country's oil deposits are. Third, not only has Shia-majority Iran been keenly interested in the fate of its religious brethren in Bahrain, but Iranian officials have claimed Bahrain as a province since 1957 and ayatollahs in Tehran enjoy a strong influence over Bahrain's Shia population.[87] Therefore, the outcome in Bahrain was, as one would expect, of critical importance for Saudi Arabia and the rest of the Gulf kingdoms, all of them—with the exception of Oman[88]—ruled by Sunni Muslim ruling families. The Saudi soldiers did not engage the Bahraini rebels but proceeded to position themselves in the south of the country, whereas the policemen from the UAE guarded strategic facilities so that Bahraini forces would be free to concentrate on suppressing the uprising. Bahraini officers have long participated in training courses abroad in the United States, the United Kingdom, as well as in GCC-member countries. Additionally, since 1995, when the US Fifth Fleet was reactivated after a 48-year hiatus, it has been based in Bahrain, further expanding the opportunities for joint exercises and programs. (The United States has maintained a permanent naval presence in Bahrain since 1947.[89])

Exhibit B: Syria

The conditions of the armed forces are different in Syria but, there too, sectarian identity was the critical factor affecting the military leadership's decision to stand firmly behind Assad's Ba'ath Party dictatorship and to inflict massive violence in its defense. Perhaps more than any other single case in this book—with the possible exception of Romania—this regime's response to the peaceful demonstrators, who were protesting the incarceration of children who spray-painted antiregime graffiti in the provincial city of Dara'a, was swift and extraordinarily brutal. Unlike other Arab leaders, Bashar Assad reckoned that an uncompromising and forceful reaction, rather than conciliatory gestures, was going to nip the uprising in the bud.

This was a miscalculation. The demonstrations spread, the opposition quickly became radicalized, and by summer 2011, Syria was engulfed in a civil war that, at the time of this writing (mid-June 2015) continues to rage unabated with at least 210,000 dead, innumerable casualties, millions forced into exile and refugee camps, and much of the country destroyed.[90] Even though thousands of soldiers and mostly lower-level officers have deserted or joined the uprising, the army's leadership—with a few exceptions—and most of the officer corps have continued to side with the regime. How do we explain the army's response?[91]

The Syrian leadership, perhaps more than that of any other Arab republic, was keenly aware of threats to topple it. Between 1949 and 1970, at least ten coups d'état were mounted in Syria, often with various military factions fighting one another. Bashar's father, President Hafez Assad (1971–2000), a former air force general, was a participant in at least three of them (1962, 1966, 1970) and realized the grave necessity of coup-proofing. Once in power, Assad put his own stamp on the military, unified the different factions of the officer corps, and created a number of internal security organizations—subordinated directly to himself—that spied on each other and on the regular armed forces, all in an attempt to guarantee the military's loyalty.[92] As a number of experts have noted, the Assads were preparing for a popular insurrection all their political lives.[93]

Although ethnically the vast majority of Syrians are Arab with the exception of the Kurdish minority (7–8 percent), the country's twenty-three million citizens are deeply divided along sectarian lines (10–11 percent Alawis, 10–11 percent Christians, perhaps 5 percent other minorities, and the 60–65 percent Sunni Muslim Arab majority).[94] The Assad family—Bashar succeeded his father as president after the latter's death from natural causes in 2000—also hails from the Alawite community. Tensions between majority Sunnis and Alawites, a traditionally disadvantaged group of hill-country origin, are long standing. Nevertheless, Hafez had managed to co-opt a large proportion of the Sunni business elites, granting them various opportunities to enrich themselves.[95] To the extent that there was sectarian peace prior to 2011, it was uneasy, and the threat of coercion was never far from the surface. In February 1982, the Assad regime met the establishment of a Muslim Brotherhood stronghold among Sunnis in the city of Hama with a fierce heavy-weapons assault that lasted for more than three weeks and is believed to have killed tens of thousands.[96]

Why have Syrian officers overwhelmingly sided with Bashar's regime? The Syrian officer corps has been dominated by the Alawites, at least since 1955, when they began to control the military section of the Ba'ath Party.[97] As the uprising began, the question of regime loyalty essentially came down to sectarian affiliation. Roughly four-fifths of the officer corps, as well as the commanders of the numerous intelligence agencies, are Alawites; the rest are Shia and, to a lesser extent, Sunni Muslims of known allegiances.[98] Although the Alawite sect does not staff the entire officer corps, Alawites hold virtually all sensitive and important positions in the armed forces. For instance, while most Syrian air force pilots were Sunni, the air defense force that controlled logistics and communication was mainly Alawite, preventing the pilots from making a play for power.

There are nearly a dozen paramilitary forces in the country, all of them are led by Assad-family confidants and consist of highly motivated fighters who are loyal to the regime. Bashar's brother, Maher, a brigadier general, is the commander of the Republican Guard as well as the army's elite Fourth Armored Division; these two special units, along with Syria's secret police, form the core of the country's security forces. His brother-in-law, Asaf Shawkat, was the head of military intelligence and later became the deputy minister of defense.[99] He died, along with the defense minister and several top defense officials, in a bomb attack in July 2012.

At the beginning of the conflict, the Syrian military numbered approximately 300,000: perhaps two-thirds of these were draftees, a large proportion of whom was drawn from the majority Sunni community. With the onset of the civil war, Sunni conscripts—repelled by the level of violence their Alawite officers were willing to inflict on protesters—started to defect and were joined by Sunni civilians.[100] In fact, a large majority of the Free Syrian Army are made up of these soldiers and their officers, few of whom are Alawites. Many divisions that consist mainly of drafted Sunni soldiers have not been deployed to quell the uprising; instead, the regime has increasingly turned to special forces and irregulars, often called *shabiha*, which are heavily Alawi or Sunnis of known loyalty.[101]

Syrian officers are unlikely to turn against a regime that has treated them well. Notwithstanding the presence of numerous elite and paramilitary forces, regular army officers did not have to accept second-place status behind other security formations, as was the case in Libya or Tunisia.[102] To help keep them loyal, the Damascus regime has permitted them a degree of economic involvement. As is common among armies of authoritarian states, the Syrian military is heavily indoctrinated—some consider it the most politicized Arab army[103]—and loyalty to the regime often outweighs professional merit in determining promotions and rewards. In addition, the Assads integrated numerous influential officers into the Ba'ath Party structures to cement their allegiance to the regime.

The leading military officials consider the rule of Assad and the Ba'ath Party to be entirely legitimate, and they are well aware that they can expect the worst should the opposition eventually come out on top. Since the outbreak of the uprising, Assad and his ruling political elites have managed to convince the Alawites and some of the smaller religious minority communities that the regime's survival was synonymous with their physical survival. The army's involvement in past episodes of brutality, such as the Hama massacre, also counsels against trying to switch sides. Moreover, the military may be confident that the insurrection does not represent the popular will. According to some analysts, the overwhelming majority of Syrians are ambivalent or opposed to the rebellion.[104] In other words, Alawites—and other supporters of Assad's rule—would have nothing to gain but everything to lose if the government were toppled. Consequently, they are in the fight to the bitter end, as they have declared, repeatedly.

Although Syria has plenty of enemies in the region, some of whom have helped the rebels, it is by no means a pariah state like Qadhafi's Libya. Its close relationship with Hezbollah's military arm in Lebanon has yielded significant military assistance. Syria's alliance with Iran may be the most enduring in the Middle East. Iran's Revolutionary Guard and its elite Quds Force has not only trained Syrian soldiers but have fought with them.[105] Both Hezbollah and the Revolutionary Guard have vowed to continue to fight against the rebels, even if Assad is overthrown.[106] The Assads's regime has had a decades-long friendship with the Soviet Union/Russia which, along with Iran, has continued to supply it with armaments including sophisticated new missile systems.[107] Both countries have continued to assist Damascus during the civil war in various ways, including training and the delivery of weapons.[108] Thus, unlike the regime's opponents, whose permanent complaint is "not enough weapons and ammunition," the Syrian government seems not to suffer from a shortage of either.

In short, the Alawite-dominated officer corps has every reason to stick with Assad's regime. Given the treatment they could expect from their enemies if they were to switch sides after more than four years of brutal fighting, that option seems harder and harder to choose; in fact, according to some analysts "military defections have virtually ceased."[109] Those who know Syria are hardly surprised by the officers' loyalty to the regime.

Summary

Notwithstanding the rather similar response of the top brass to the upheavals in Bahrain and Syria, the factors that affected their decision-making process were quite different. For starters, while the armed forces' internal cohesion (I.1.)—particularly insofar as ethnoreligious splits were concerned (I.1.A.)—assumed critical importance in Syria but was essentially a nonissue in Bahrain, with its super-unified security sector (including the military and all other armed services). The fact that Bahrain did not institute a draft (I.2.) was very important there, since non-Sunni soldiers were perceived as inherently unreliable, certainly in a situation of domestic unrest. In Syria, too, the conscription issue was important; however, at the end of the day, conscripted soldiers could be largely expected to side with their coethnics and coreligionists. In both states, the generals' perception of the regime's legitimacy (I.3.) was crucial. In Bahrain, of course, this was obvious, given the Sunni military's support of the Sunni monarchy in a Shia-majority country. In Syria, however, ethnoreligious divisions are more complex, and the chiefly Alawite officer corps' backing of the regime was a crucial variable.

The regime's treatment of the military (II.1.) was not a major issue in Bahrain, mainly because the shared sectarian identity of the regime and its armed forces was, by far, the key decisive variable in the generals' decisions to stick with the state. In other words, even if the monarchy had marginalized its coercive apparatus—which it certainly had not—the soldiers, national guardsmen, and policemen still would have supported the monarchy. Owing to the more multifaceted ethnoreligious makeup and more complicated political setting, the generals' views of the Assad regime as fundamentally legitimate (and, in all likelihood, their perception that it was better than any other potential alternative[110]) made an important difference. In Syria, the outbreak of large demonstrations was likely to be a far weightier variable in the soldiers' minds than in Bahrain, where peaceful public protests had occurred and were mostly tolerated by the authorities in the past.[111] The popularity of the uprising (III.2.) probably was considered a more worrisome factor for Syrian officers than for their Bahraini colleagues.

In terms of the external context, foreign intervention (IV.1.) for Bahraini Sunnis meant a helping hand, if needed, from their GCC allies, whereas the situation was somewhat more murky for the generals in Damascus, although they also had their staunch allies (Iran, Hezbollah, Russia, etc.).[112] Both officer corps had to be keenly aware of foreign relations (IV.2.). The Bahraini generals had maintained a close nexus with the United States and particularly to American personnel stationed on the naval base a few miles away from them (IV.2. and IV.4.). For the Syrian top brass, the alliance with Tehran and Moscow, as well as the continued delivery of military equipment from the latter, were important considerations. In neither country could the generals be unaffected by the diffusion of uprisings (IV.3.) in the region.

THE ARAB MONARCHIES

The Arab world's eight monarchies—Bahrain, Jordan, Kuwait, Morocco, Oman, Qatar, Saudi Arabia, and the UAE—with the notable exception of the first, have escaped the brunt of the upheaval. Demonstrations in these countries were generally small and did not include overnight occupations, protesters demanded reform not revolution, governments reacted to events with a measure of flexibility, and their security forces typically avoided disproportionate retaliation.[113] To be sure, there were significant differences between the individual kingdoms in terms of the unrest: virtually nothing happened in Qatar and the UAE, minor demonstrations took place in Oman and Saudi Arabia, serious protests were organized in Kuwait, and, in Morocco and especially Jordan, there were coordinated political upheavals that elicited some concessions from the monarchs. Nevertheless, the armies' actions did not come into question in any monarchy; they were all fully expected to stand by the regimes. Why?

All Arab kingdoms are absolute monarchies. Several of them faced coups, coup attempts, or other challenges that threatened to topple them: Jordan (1970–71, Morocco (1971, 1972), Oman (1971), and Saudi Arabia (1966, 1969). Not surprisingly, all of the monarchies, including Bahrain, have done their best to ensure the loyalty of their forces. Aside from Bahrain, the regular armed forces were not involved in any other Arab kingdom's response to the challenges the limited upheavals posed— with the exception of Oman, where their role was limited to supporting domestic security organizations.[114] In the Omani port city of Sohar, small army units, along with their tanks and armored personnel careers were tasked with helping the police to disperse protesters. The soldiers reportedly fired live rounds in the air, but not at the demonstrators, as some policemen did.[115]

Let us take a quick look at two of these armies and how the monarchs ensure their loyalty. Until the early 1980s, British personnel held most of the sensitive positions in the Sultan of Oman's armed forces. Since then, the military has undergone a well-conceived program of Omanization, although there are still about ninety British officers in advisory roles throughout the armed forces.[116] The Sultan, who graduated from Sandhurst and served with the British Army in Germany during the Cold War, is the commander-in-chief who coordinates military activities in the country. Nevertheless, members of the royal family do not monopolize key positions in the armed forces, as in some other Gulf monarchies. The regular army is under the supervision of a Ministry of Defense but several elite units are directly subordinated to the Royal Office, that is, to Sultan Qaboos. These include the Royal Guard—a brigade-strength force in charge of protecting the Sultan, the royal family, and their property—as well as the Sultan's Special Forces.[117]

Many of the NCOs and enlisted soldiers are Baluchis from Pakistan, although virtually all officers are Omanis from key tribes. The presence of foreign soldiers is likely to raise the army's willingness for intervention in a potential domestic emergency. Military personnel are well looked after by the Sultanate. They receive good pay and excellent benefit packages, and once they retire, they are assisted with grants for study, business start-up loans, and land to build their homes on. The military is unusual in the Gulf region to the extent that it is highly esteemed by Omani society for their professionalism and demanding training. Like most Arab armies, however, the Omani army is also not immune to the problems of overcentralization (everything must be cleared with the Sultan) and the relative lack of decision-making authority even for high-ranking officers. Omani officers have been studying in the West in significant numbers; for instance, two hundred Omani officers study in the United States every year.[118]

The defense establishment of Morocco, the least prosperous Arab monarchy, largely follows the French model of organizational structure. As elsewhere in the Arab world, the control and direction of the army is directly linked to the king. The two military coup attempts in the early 1970s constituted a formative moment for the Moroccan Royal Armed Forces. After the coup attempts, King Hassan II abolished the defense ministry and the position of defense minister, depoliticized the military, removed its commanders from centers of power, and subordinated it to the Royal Gendarmerie. The Gendarmerie—Morocco's top security institution—is a national paramilitary/police force with its own small but well-equipped navy and air force and is in many ways similar to its French namesake. Even four decades after the coup attempts, political debates within the military and "unsupervised" meetings among high-ranking officers are not allowed.[119] The army's accountability to the Gendarmerie is so complete that, for instance, if military commanders intend to move a convoy of vehicles, they need to secure the permission of the head of the Gendarmerie.[120] Since 1972, the commander-in-chief of the Royal Gendarmerie has been General Housni Benslimane (born in 1935), a close confidant of the royal family.[121]

The first large-scale demonstrations, mainly organized via Facebook, mobilized 150,000–200,000 people across fifty-three Moroccan cities and towns on 20 February 2011. Morocco is considered by many as one of the most liberal of all of the authoritarian systems in the Middle East and North Africa.[122] The response of the authorities—which included the Gendarmerie, the police, and the Forces-Auxiliaire (a lowly paid, not very professional, often ridiculed, but ubiquitous paramilitary contingent)—to the continuing protests was well managed and fairly restrained, though there were beatings, and three protesters were killed.[123] The military was not involved in any capacity. In fact, much of the Moroccan army has been kept busy for decades in the Western Sahara, a Britain-sized territory Morocco annexed in 1975 that is also claimed by Algeria and, less credibly, by Mauritania and Senegal. One of the most obvious signs of coup-proofing in Morocco that even tourists can appreciate is that major public buildings and the royal palace are guarded by soldiers wearing three distinctive uniforms: those of the police, the Royal Gendarmerie, and the regular armed forces.

Military personnel, particularly high-ranking officers, are well paid. There is a consensus among experts that political elites compensated the officer corps for their loss of political influence—active-duty soldiers do not even enjoy the right to vote—after the early 1970s by not just *allowing* them but actually *encouraging* them to be involved in the Moroccan economy.[124] One specific way the regime pays off military elites, as well as high-ranking members of other government agencies, is by granting various often extremely lucrative licenses (fisheries, transportation, sand extraction, etc.). Even though the army is widely considered to be a corrupt institution, its social prestige remains high for several reasons: it is not involved in domestic security operations, it offers steady work in a state with high unemployment, it provides excellent medical and social benefits, and most Moroccans believe that without the army they might have lost the Western Sahara, which remains an important and extremely sensitive issue in the country. Most officers are recruited from middle- or lower-middle-class families. The army is a highly cohesive organization, although, reportedly, there were divisions between senior and junior officers in the early 2000s owing to the latter's perception of inadequate promotion opportunities. King Mohammed VI intervened, however, opening up various avenues to more speedy and equitable advancement in the ranks.[125] Following the 2011 upheaval, the king further improved the conditions for retired and active-duty personnel, in part, as a response to the on-going protests of veterans.[126]

CONCLUSION

Events in the Arab world during 2011 are consistent with the contention that the manner in which a military force responds to a revolution is the most reliable predictor of that revolution's outcome. When the army decides not to back the regime (Tunisia, Egypt), the regime is most likely doomed. Where the armed forces are divided (Libya, Yemen), the result is determined by other factors, such as foreign intervention, the strength of the opposition forces, and the old regime's resolve to persevere. Where the soldiers opt to stick with the status quo (Bahrain, Syria), the regime survives. Syria, of course is a special case, given the on-going civil war.

Three big differences, and several smaller disparities, set Syria apart from a case like Bahrain. First, it was entirely foreseeable that the Alawite-dominated officer corps would side with Bashar Assad's regime (just as the Sunni army would side with the Bahraini monarchy). Moreover, the desertion of a large proportion of Sunni officers, NCOs, and conscripts upon seeing the uncompromising and brutal approach of the regime to the uprising should not have surprised us either. There were no ethnoreligious splits in Bahrain's army, and it, unlike the Syrian forces, was not affected by intramilitary splits between elite and regular units, different security sector entities, or sociopolitical divisions among military elites. Second, Bahrain's army is composed entirely of volunteers—virtually all belonging to the Sunni Muslim creed—whose loyalty to the regime was never in doubt. Third, the army's history with society was a nonissue for Bahraini generals, but it must have given pause to their Syrian colleagues, who have brutally suppressed earlier peaceful unrests and would not have fared well in a post-Assad regime.

Table 4. The Arab upheavals, 2011: Factors affecting the army's response to revolutions

	Tunisia	Egypt	Libya	Yemen	Bahrain	Syria
I. MILITARY FACTORS						
I.1. Armed Forces' Internal Cohesion	2	2	5	5	0	5
I.1.A. ethnic, religious, tribal, and regional splits	0	0	6	6	0	6
I.1.B. generational divisions: senior vs. junior officers	1	3	1	1	0	1
I.1.C. divisions between officers and NCOs/privates	0	1	2	2	0	0
I.1.D. divisions between elite vs. regular units	0	2	4	4	0	3
I.1.E. splits between the army, other branches, and security services	5	3	4	4	0	4
I.1.F. sociopolitical divisions between military elites	0	0	3	3	0	4
I.2. Professional Soldiers vs. Conscripts	5	5	2	2	5	3
I.3. The Generals' Perception of Regime Legitimacy	5	4	3	4	6	5
I.4. The Army's Past Conduct toward Society	2	2	1	1	0	5
II. STATE FACTORS						
II.1. Regime's Treatment of the Military	4	3	5	2	3	5
II.1.A. taking care of the personnel's material welfare	3	2	3	2	3	4
II.1.B. taking care of the army	2	3	4	2	3	3
II.1.C. appropriateness of missions	3	4	0	0	0	2
II.1.D. the generals' professional autonomy and decision-making authority	2	2	4	3	2	3
II.1.E. fairness in top appointments	1	1	2	2	0	1
II.1.F. the military's prestige and public esteem	3	3	0	2	0	0
II.2. Regime Directions to the Military	1	2	1	3	1	3
III. SOCIETAL FACTORS						
III.1. The Size, Composition, and Nature of the Protests	5	5	4	2	3	5
III.2. The Popularity of the Uprising	3	3	2	2	2	4
III.3. Fraternization	2	4	3	3	0	3

IV. EXTERNAL FACTORS

IV.1. The Potential for Foreign Intervention	4	2	2	4	0	0
IV.2. Foreign Affairs	3	4	3	1	3	3
IV.3. Revolutionary Diffusion	4	4	4	3	3	3
IV.4. Foreign Exposure of Military Officers	0	2	2	0	1	2

Top six factors are in bold.
Scale (0–6):
0 = irrelevant, not a factor
1 = of trivial importance
2 = of little importance
3 = somewhat important
4 = quite important
5 = very important
6 = critical, decisive

This chapter featured the most easily predictable outcome in the entire book: Bahrain. No one who was even vaguely aware of Bahrain's politics, society, military, and external affairs should have been surprised in the least that the country's security establishment sided with the regime. Although not nearly so obvious, the Tunisian army's stance also seemed quite logical, given some familiarity with the country. The deep divisions by tribal and regional identities in the Libyan and Yemeni military-security establishments reflected the cleavages in their societies and largely explained their progress toward civil war.

Of the six cases where the military did have a role to play in the region, it was perhaps Egypt where the outcome was the least easily predictable. In hindsight, of course, the decision made by the army's leadership appears entirely reasonable and consistent with the many factors that influenced it: the loss of their political influence, their dissatisfaction with Mubarak's regime, the good chance that their conscripts would not shoot at the crowds, and the tremendous popularity of the uprising and the size and representativeness of the demonstrations. Still, even immediately prior to the outbreak of the revolution, analysts had to take into consideration numerous variables that were just that, *variable*, and what policy makers could expect from them were, at best, educated guesses rather than confident predictions.

Conclusion

As we have seen in this book, predicting how an army responds to a revolution can be easy, and occasionally it is. More often than not, however, it is at least somewhat challenging. And, once in a while, we tackle a case that is affected by so many variables—some of which we know, and some we do not—that interact in such complex ways that causality is dauntingly difficult to confidently identify, let alone state that a specific variable accounted for X proportion of the outcome. Clearly, the more we know about an army, the state and society that form its environment, and the international setting in which it exists, the more self-assured we can be of the accuracy of our forecasts.

Our remaining task is to evaluate how the explanatory factors I identified in chapter 1 stand up to the scrutiny of the empirical analysis. Do they satisfactorily explain the three basic outcomes of a military response to a revolution: support or suppression of the uprising, or division within the institution about how to react to it? Are the six top variables, as I have hypothesized, really the most powerful in explaining the generals' decisions? Are there variables that are trivial or unhelpful in every case we looked at? More generally, how useful have we found the analytical framework I laid out in chapter 1 to help us explain the decisions taken by the armed forces facing the demonstrators? And how easy or difficult was it to predict the various armies' reactions to the upheavals they faced? These are the questions I want to answer here. For easy reference, I have compiled two comprehensive tables to demonstrate the comparative weight of each independent variable as they relate to the eleven case studies, and the relative difficulty of predicting the generals' responses to revolutions. The values assigned to the individual factors are the inductive result of the case studies. Obviously, the deeper our knowledge about a particular case, the less arbitrary these values will be, but, ultimately, they remain debatable or, put differently, falsifiable.

THE USEFULNESS OF EXPLANATORY FACTORS

Let us go through the explanatory variables I listed in the four spheres, one by one, while paying special attention to the six I presented in the introduction as the most useful.

Table 5. Factors affecting the army's response to revolutions

	Iran	Burma 1988	Burma 2007	China	Romania	Tunisia	Egypt	Libya	Yemen	Bahrain	Syria
I. MILITARY FACTORS											
I.1. Armed Forces' Internal Cohesion	5	6	4	3	4	2	2	5	5	0	5
I.1.A. ethnic, religious, tribal, and regional splits	2	0	0	0	1	0	0	6	6	0	6
I.1.B. generational divisions: senior vs. junior officers	3	1	1	2	1	1	3	1	1	0	1
I.1.C. divisions between officers and NCOs/privates	4	2	2	1	1	0	1	2	2	0	0
I.1.D. divisions between elite vs. regular units	1	0	0	0	0	0	2	4	4	0	3
I.1.E. splits between the army, other branches, and security services	1	2	2	0	5	5	3	4	4	0	4
(I.1.F.) sociopolitical divisions between military elites	0	2	2	0	0	0	0	3	3	0	4
I.2. Professional Soldiers vs. Conscripts	6	4	2	3	3	5	5	2	2	5	3
I.3. The Generals' Perception of Regime Legitimacy	1	0	0	6	5	5	4	3	4	6	5
I.4. The Army's Past Conduct toward Society	1	1	1	0	0	2	2	1	1	0	5
II. STATE FACTORS											
II.1. Regime's Treatment of the Military	3	0	0	2	5	4	3	5	2	3	5
II.1.A. taking care of the personnel's material welfare	2	0	0	2	4	3	2	3	2	3	4
II.1.B. taking care of the army	1	0	0	3	4	2	3	4	2	3	3

Factor											
II.1.C. appropriateness of missions	2	0	0	0	4	3	4	3	2	0	2
II.1.D. the generals' professional autonomy and decision-making authority	5	0	0	0	2	2	4	3	3	2	3
(II.1.E.) fairness in top appointments	2	0	0	0	3	2	1	2	2	0	1
II.1.F. the military's prestige and public esteem	1	0	2	0	3	3	3	0	2	0	0
II.2. Regime Directions to the Military	6	0	0	3	1	1	1	2	3	1	3
III. SOCIETAL FACTORS											
III.1. The Size, Composition, and Nature of the Protests	**6**	**6**	**5**	**5**	**5**	**5**	**5**	**4**	**2**	**3**	**5**
(III.2.) The Popularity of the Uprising	4	4	3	3	3	3	3	2	2	2	4
III.3. Fraternization	3	3	3	2	3	2	4	3	3	0	3
IV. EXTERNAL FACTORS											
IV.1. The Potential for Foreign Intervention	1	3	0	0	1	1	0	0	2	2	4
IV.2. Foreign Affairs	4	0	1	1	1	0	0	3	3	4	3
IV.3. Revolutionary Diffusion	0	0	3	4	4	0	0	3	4	4	4
(IV.4.) Foreign Exposure of Military Officers	2	0	0	0	1	1	2	1	2	2	0

Top six factors are in bold.
Scale (0–6):
0 = irrelevant, not a factor
1 = of trivial importance
2 = of little importance
3 = somewhat important
4 = quite important
5 = very important
6 = critical, decisive

I. Military Variables

As I suggested, the army's internal cohesion (I.1.) turned out to be a "decisive" (Burma, 1988) or "very important" (Iran, Libya, Yemen, Syria) factor in five of the eleven case studies, and "quite important" (Burma, 2007; and Romania) in another two. In Burma (1988) the generals' utmost concern was making sure that the army would not be split. In Iran, the deepest cleavage was between officers and NCOs/conscripts (I.1.C.). That coupled with the fact that the soldiers did not remain passive but, in many cases, joined the opposition, fostered the army's disintegration. In Libya and Yemen, the most important split was tribal/regional, while in Syria it was ethnoreligious (I.1.A.). In Burma (2007), keeping the army unified was not so troubling, since the *Tatmadaw* had been ruling for the two decades since the 1988 upheaval, and the opposition was weaker and even less adapt at getting the soldiers to switch sides. Romanian army commanders did not have to worry much about defecting conscripts: when the time came, officers, who generally shared the soldiers' attitudes toward the regime, went over to the revolution with their men. The main concern there, as in all the Arab armies, aside from Bahrain, was the division between the army and other security sector entities (I.1.E.) and, in the latter, between the regular army and elite military detachments (I.1.D.). For Tunisian and Egyptian generals, their armies' cohesion was not a serious issue. In Bahrain, the military's unity was not a factor at all: the entire army was made up of Sunni Muslims, and they were facing the Shia Muslim community, who composed 60–70 percent of the population and who—many Sunnis believed—aspired to establish an Iranian-style Shi'ite theocracy.[1]

It is noteworthy that ethnoreligious, tribal, and regional divisions (I.1.A.) were entirely irrelevant in six of the eleven cases, of trivial importance in one (Romania) and of little importance in another (Iran, where officers tended to be far less devout than their soldiers), but where they did matter (Libya, Yemen, and Syria), they tended to be decisive. Generational splits within the officer corps (I.1.B.) were "somewhat important" (3) in Iran and Egypt but tended to be less significant elsewhere, suggesting that most armies are pretty capable in raising their esprit de corps. Sociopolitical divisions (I.1.F.) were unimportant in most cases, save for Libya, Yemen, and Syria, but in those three settings, the ethnoreligious, tribal, and regional split (I.1.A.) might well pick up the same disparity. For the sake of a more parsimonious analytical framework, therefore, I.1.F. might be eliminated as an explanatory variable. Consequently, I placed it, and the others I found to lack sufficient explanatory strength, in parentheses on Table 5.

I conjectured that the disparity between a professional army made up of volunteers as opposed to one that is composed of conscripts (I.2.) will be a major factor for the generals as they choose their response to an uprising. Indeed, this was a decisive issue in Iran and a "very important" one in Tunisia, Egypt, and Bahrain—the latter composed entirely of Sunni Muslim volunteers. In five other settings (China, Romania, Syria, Libya, and Yemen), this was a "somewhat important" concern. The first three were conscript armies where the soldiers' responses to fraternization—particularly in China during the army's first deployment—was a source of some evident apprehension to generals. In Libya and Yemen, however, conscription was introduced and then abolished more than once in the past few decades and the soldiers' reactions to the uprisings seemed predictable to the extent that they were likely to follow their commanders, based on their shared tribal membership and/or regional identity.

The third military factor, the generals' perceptions of the regime's legitimacy (I.3.) appeared to be an important issue in most cases. It was irrelevant only in Burma, since the generals there *were* the rulers of the state, and was of trivial importance in Iran, where the military constituted the backbone of the regime. The top military leaders' high opinion of the regime, however, was the decisive issue for their actions in China and Bahrain—and, only to a somewhat lesser extent, in Syria. And, the Romanian and Tunisian military elites' negative assessment of regime legitimacy was a crucial reason for choosing not to side with the protesters.

Finally, the army's past conduct toward society (I.4.) appears not to have made too much of a difference in most cases. In Iran, it did not spur generals to suppress the demonstrations, even though they had a history of crushing unrests and they must have known that a post-Shah regime could doom not only their careers but threaten their physical safety. In Syria, however, the brutal crackdown of pre-2011 upheavals is likely to have further steeled the Alawite military leadership's resolve to hitch its wagon to the Assad regime's star.

II. State Variables

The state's treatment of the armed forces (II.1.) appears to have been a distinctly less important class of variables—and, by my reckoning, in no case, a "critical" one—although in some cases it played a "very important" role. These variables were largely irrelevant to the Burmese military regime—with the slight exception that in the 2007 upheaval, the army's relative restraint might have been to some degree influenced by its desire to retain or increase its public esteem (II.1.F.). Although Deng Xiaoping's reforms had made the lives of most army officers more difficult, the deterioration of their conditions did not play an important role in deciding their response to the revolt. The regime's treatment of the military was most important in Romania, Libya, and, to a lesser extent, Tunisia (where the army was neglected) and Syria (where, as the backbone of the regime, it was indulged). Iran would have received a far higher mark except for the armed forces' very limited professional autonomy (II.1.D.), which acted as a veritable straightjacket on the generals when independent decisions had to be made. Only Qadhafi's control over his regular army approximated that of the Shah among our case studies. In this sphere of variables, too, I find one that we might consider superfluous: II.1.E., the regime's fairness in top appointments in the armed forces seemed not to rate above "of little importance" in any of the cases, and I think it could be folded into II.1.D. without losing much analytical nuance.

Regime directions to the military (II.2.) seems to be a pretty uncomplicated factor, as we would generally expect self-preservation to be the key imperative of the ruling regime's leaders who would, consequently, order the army to suppress the demonstrators. As it turns out, this is not necessarily so. The ambiguous messages emanating from the Shah's quarters was one of the critical reasons for the paralysis that gripped the top generals as they tried to find an approach to the revolution in Iran. But this was not the only case where this factor was also at least somewhat important. In the early stages of the crisis in China, the CCP leadership was neither entirely united nor unambiguous in their decisions about dealing with the demonstrations. In Yemen, on the other hand, military units received contradictory messages from their superior officers, who seemed to be unsure of what the divided leadership expected of them. And, the brief analyses of regime change in East Germany and Czechoslovakia revealed that the communist party leaders there, too, were at odds with one another regard instructions to the generals.

III. Societal Variables

I hypothesized in chapter 1 that the size, personnel composition, and nature of the demonstrations (III.1.) would be the fifth most important factor affecting the generals' responses to the revolutions. According to my coding, however, it might possibly be the most important. It is worth our while to think for a moment why this might be so. In all of the eleven case studies, the uprisings took place against deeply embedded authoritarian systems. Prior to the upheavals in question, large-scale demonstrations were either rare occurrences (e.g., Iran, Burma, Tunisia, etc.), or they virtually never happened (China, Romania). Thus, the very fact that tens or hundreds of thousands of citizens took to the streets had undoubtedly stunned political and military elites from Tehran to Beijing and from Rangoon to Prague.

The composition of the demonstrations—a broad cross section of society in Iran, Romania, Tunisia, Egypt, Libya, and Yemen; student-led movements of a narrower societal basis in Burma and China; and protesters primarily based on ethnoreligious identity in Bahrain and Syria—was an important source of information generals could use to decide how to respond to them. And, as I suggested, the manner in which demonstrations progressed—peacefully in all of our cases except until the civil wars started in Libya, Yemen, and Syria—certainly entered into their decision-making process. It is worth noting that in numerous cases—Iran, China, and Romania—there seemed to be no contingency plans that would address large-scale demonstrations, and the armies were utterly unprepared for the task.[2] The Shah of Iran appeared to be just as bewildered by what was happening to his regime as Ceaușescu was eleven years later.

The second societal factor, the popularity of the revolution (III.2.), is an explanatory variable that turned out not to be tremendously useful. Quite likely, this factor is not the source of a distinctive impulse for military elites, perhaps because III.1. (the size, personnel composition, and nature of the protests) seems to cover much the same ground. Thus, for the sake of a more economical framework we could do without it. Finally, although the fraternization factor (III.3.) did not prove to be "decisive" in any of the cases, it was at least a "somewhat important" additional piece of information for commanders in places like Iran, China, Romania, and Egypt. In the first three uprisings, the spreading fraternization between protesters and soldiers persuaded commanders to withdraw their troops to the barracks to maintain control over them and prevent them from possibly handing over their weapons to the demonstrators. On Cairo's Tahrir Square, it was just another reason for officers to doubt the obedience of their soldiers, even if they did order them to shoot civilians.

IV. External Variables

Generally speaking, it was correct to place this class of factors as having the least important impact on military elites' decisions on their responses to the revolutions. The potential of foreign intervention (IV.1.)

seemed "quite important" only in Libya, where army officers were right to anticipate it—owing to Libya's quasi-pariah state status and foreign interest in getting rid of Qadhafi's regime and stopping the bloodshed. As we know, no one seriously considered invading Burma in 1988, but the superstitious and paranoid generals had different views of the issue. Some factions in the Yemeni army leadership expected a GCC military intervention, but the GCC wisely adopted a mediating role instead of inserting its troops into the quagmire.[3] And, in Bahrain, the hoped-for GCC contingent did arrive, but not to help suppress the protests, rather to present a tangible security guarantee to the island monarchy.

Relations with a foreign state(s) or alliance (IV.2.) can be occasionally quite influential, as we saw in the cases of Iran, Egypt, Yemen, Bahrain, and Syria. Similarly, although revolutionary diffusion (IV.3.) is seldom a major factor, when revolutions do occur in one country after another, military leaderships do tend to take note as the fall of a dictator or an oppressive regime elsewhere tends to strengthen the revolutionaries' determination. This was the case in China and Romania, as well as the Middle East and North Africa. Finally, having educational or training experiences in foreign states (IV.4.) was a factor of minor consequence, and it did not override more substantial variables such as the regime's treatment of the armed forces or divisions within military elites. I had the opportunity to interview Tunisian and Bahraini army officers who had received professional training in the United States,[4] and both groups said that their interactions with American colleagues and courses on democratic civil-military relations did affect how they viewed the uprisings in their countries; nevertheless, other factors were far more important in influencing their decision-making. Consequently, this might be a fourth variable that could be discarded without negatively altering the predictive power of our analytical framework.

In sum, I hypothesized in chapter 1 that the most important six factors that help explain the generals' responses to revolutionary uprisings are the armies' internal cohesion, whether their soldiers are volunteers or conscripts, the regimes' treatment of the military, the generals' views of their regime's legitimacy, the size and nature of the demonstrations, and the potential for foreign invasion. Although the ranking of these six factors relative to one another might be debatable, I believe that the empirical case studies I selected largely confirm their explanatory power. The one modification I might suggest is to add "regime directions to the military" (II.2.) to the six factors I considered most influential, as it turned out to be rather more significant than I initially anticipated. Additionally, based on the evidence gathered from our case studies, it looks as though discarding four factors—sociopolitical divisions between military elites (I.1.F.), regime fairness in top appointments (II.1.E.), the popularity of the revolution (III.3.), and foreign exposure of military officers (IV.4.)—will make the framework more parsimonious without sacrificing much analytical richness.

Making Predictions

Let us now return briefly to the individual cases and see if we could have anticipated the generals' decisions with the aid of the analytical framework. In terms of difficulty of prediction, the case studies ran the gamut from very difficult to easy. Here I am going to proceed from the most to the least difficult case. As I noted in chapter 1, the temporal element—that is, *when* a prediction is made—is very important. In general, the farther along we are in the revolutionary process, the more accurate a prediction we can make. Nevertheless, it is quite possible to think of a scenario when the interaction of factors remains so complex and the number of unknowns does not diminish, such that making a prediction does not get any easier. In the discussion that follows I will isolate three separate points in time—T1: three months before the first major mobilizational event (protest); T2: one week after the day of the first major event; and T3: three weeks into the crisis—to gauge our ability to anticipate the generals' decision changes.

The outcome in Iran was clearly the most challenging to correctly predict. In early October 1977, three months before the 9 January 1978 protest in Qom, practically no one could have confidently suggested that the Imperial Armed Forces would not easily suppress the unarmed demonstrators. One week into the upheaval, the only clue to the eventual outcome was that the army did not suppress the protests with its full force. Even three weeks into the upheaval, in late January, most observers expected the regime to easily prevail. It was only in the late summer and early fall of 1978 that the pattern of the Shah's vacillation, oscillating between ordering repression and appeasement, had become clear. Bueno de Mesquita and Smith are wrong to say that the Iranian "army was no longer willing to fight to preserve the regime because they knew that the shah was dying." First, not only did the generals not know about the Shah's disease, even his wife, Queen Farah, did not know.[5] Second, the army would have been willing to fight, certainly as late as the fall of 1978, *if* the generals had received a clear order to suppress the revolution using

Table 6. Ease/difficulty of predicting the army's response

	Iran	Burma 1988	Burma 2007	China	Romania	Tunisia	Egypt	Libya	Yemen	Bahrain	Syria
T1	4	1	0	1	2	2	3	2	2	0	2
T2	3	1	0	1	0	1	1	1	1	0	1
T3	3	0	0	0	—	0	—	0	0	0	0

Scale: 0-4
0 = "no-brainer"
1 = relatively easy
2 = somewhat challenging
3 = challenging
4 = difficult
Time points:
T1 = three months before the first mobilizational event of the crisis
T2 = one week after the first important demonstration
T3 = three weeks into the crisis
— = revolution completed (regime/ruler fell)

all means under their control—the order many of them were clamoring for—instead of the Shah's conflicting, confused, and/or lack of directions.

Perhaps the next most challenging outcome to predict would have been the Egyptian generals' eventual decision to side with the revolution. Three months before the "January 25 Revolution," as it is known in Egypt, it would have been difficult to anticipate that result although, notwithstanding the officer corps' privileged status, their grievances vis-à-vis Mubarak's regime were widely known. A week into the uprising, just prior to regime loyalists' February 2 attack on the demonstrators, it would have been reasonable to anticipate the commanders' decision not to order their conscript soldiers to shoot at the demonstrators—owing to, in particular, the size, nature, and composition of the protests; the top brass's diminishing opinion of the regime and its approach to the uprising as well as their doubts regarding soldiers' willingness to obey the command. And at T3, the Supreme Council of the Armed Forces had already taken control of the country, and Mubarak's regime had fallen.

In hindsight, the choice of Romanian military elites seemed relatively easy for analysts to foresee, but in September 1989—before the collapse of the East German, Bulgarian, and Czechoslovak communist regimes—it was not. The Bucharest leadership appeared to be very much in charge of the country, and there were no clear signs of Romania having been infected with the virus that brought down state socialism in Poland and Hungary and jolted the communist government in China. Predicting generals' decisions at T2, however, was truly a "no-brainer," since it was on that day, precisely a week after the first revolutionary event—the December 15 overnight vigil in front of the Hungarian pastor's house in Timişoara—that all military units joined the revolution, and the Ceauşescus took their hasty flight from the capital. Many observers have noticed how it took a shorter and shorter time for East European regimes to fall as the year 1989 progressed.

Predicting that, in a revolutionary situation, the Tunisian military would not support the Ben Ali regime would have been somewhat challenging but not all that difficult. Even three months before the late-December protests, analysts knew of the marginalized status of the military in the state's coercive apparatus, its institutional conflict with the security forces, the regime's grave legitimacy problems, and the fact that the Tunisian army had no history of political involvement. To be sure, it requires some courage to go out on the limb and predict that the army will take the opposition's side, but in this case, it might have been worth the risk. At T2, it certainly looked highly likely, and by three weeks into the crisis, Ben Ali had already fled to Saudi Arabia (on 14 January 2011).

For the levelheaded analyst, it should not have been difficult to foresee that the regular armies in Libya and Yemen would be split. Both of these organizations were characterized by deep divisions within their officer corps and among their troops, based on tribal membership and regional identity, and it would have been very surprising indeed if they had acted in unison. Therefore, it was also quite reasonable to anticipate that something like a civil war was going to be the outcome of the uprisings against Qadhafi's and Saleh's regimes. Similarly, it was not terribly shocking that the Alawite portion of the Syrian military would stick with Bashar Assad's regime through thick and thin, while Sunni contingents of the officer corps and Sunni troops would sooner or later defect to the opposition, generating another internecine conflict.

The student-led movement in China inspired many democracy activists around the world, but no realistic analyst should have thought that the People's Liberation Army would for a moment hesitate to suppress it when it was directed to do so. Even if, during the period in question, the PLA was arguably treated shabbily by the Chinese Communist Party leadership, and even if there were a small number of officers and soldiers (though well under one percent) who might have hesitated in obeying orders, the outcome was never in doubt. Virtually all PLA officers were communist party members who, along with the vast majority of the population—including the vast majority of conscripted soldiers—considered the regime legitimate and saw no alternative to its continued rule.

Similarly, even those with a superficial understanding of Burmese politics could be certain that the generals would maintain their own regime rather than capitulate to students, monks, or any other social group.[6] The *Tatmadaw*'s officers were adept at controlling their troops and successfully ensured that most of the soldiers obeyed their orders. The decision of Bahrain's military elites—all Sunni Muslims and many related to the ruling royal family by blood—to suppress the mostly Shia protesters was even easier to anticipate.

In the early summer of 2013, the editors of *Foreign Affairs* asked me to apply my initial framework, published in the *Journal of Democracy* earlier in the year, to the situation in Syria. At the time I was quite up-to-date with what was going on there and asked only for a couple of weeks to complete the short piece.[7] In retrospect, it is easy to see that the framework worked well, and it accurately anticipated the unfolding situation, namely that the forces supporting the government would continue to prevail and would not defect. In early 2014, a US intelligence agency contacted me, requesting that I use the framework to study the growing crisis in Ukraine and speculate about the armed forces' likely stance. Since I knew little about the state, its army, or Ukrainian society and was short on time—I was drafting the Iran chapter of this book—I could not in good conscience tackle this assignment. I suggested instead that the agency ask its Ukraine specialist to use my framework as she was drafting her position paper. A few weeks later, I heard back that my framework had correctly anticipated the civil war that was slowly taking shape.

At the end of this book, the main point I want to reiterate is that it *is* quite possible, and in some cases not all that challenging, to confidently predict an army's response to a revolution. Once we do that, it is not hard to see the outcome of the revolution itself, given the massive impact the armed forces' reaction has on that outcome. In other settings, making a prediction may be far more difficult, and a prudent analyst would probably settle for offering the proverbial educated guess. Whatever the case, the analytical framework I set forth in this study should make coming up with that forecast an easier, more straightforward, and more rewarding enterprise.

Notes

INTRODUCTION

1. Mark Mazzetti, "Obama Said to Fault Spy Agencies' Mideast Forecasting," *New York Times*, 4 February 2011.

2. Noueihed and Warren, *Battle for the Arab Spring*, 8.

3. Kamrava, "Military Professionalization," 92.

4. Confidential interviews in Washington, DC, in November 2012 and January 2013.

5. Cambanis, *Once Upon a Revolution*, 9.

6. Gause, "Why Middle East Studies," 83.

7. E-mail message from Robert Springborg (17 March 2011).

8. Barak and David, "Arab Security Sector," 804.

9. See Goldstone, *Revolution and Rebellion*, xxii; and Gerges, *New Middle East*, 18–24; and more generally, Jones and Silberzahn, *Constructing Cassandra*.

10. The literature is rich in scholars' reflections and explanations of the reasons. See, for instance, Gause, "Why Middle East Studies," 81–90; Hirschman, "Is the End of the Cold War," 189; Kuran, "East European Revolutions," 121–25; idem, "Now out of Never," 7–48; Kurzman, *Unthinkable Revolution*; and Jervis, *Why Intelligence Fails*.

11. For a recent analysis on the psychological characteristics of good intelligence analysts, see Tetlock et al., "Psychology of Intelligence Analysis," 1–14.

12. Lipset and Bence, "Anticipations of the Failure of Communism," 202.

13. Pipes, "The Fall of the Soviet Union," 47.

14. For an interesting theoretical approach to this issue, see Kuran, "Sparks and Prairie Fires," 41–74.

15. Cited by Russell, *Rebellion*, 3.

16. Andrzejewski, *Military Organization and Society*, 71.

17. Mills, *Listen Yankee!*, 114.

18. Russell, *Rebellion,* 14; and Tilly and Rule, *Measuring Political Upheaval*, 28.

19. Chorley, *Armies and the Art of Revolution*, 243, my emphasis.

20. Russell, *Rebellion,* 57. See also Hatto, "'Revolution,' 495–517; Hopper, "Revolutionary Process," 270–79; Amann, "Revolution: A Redefinition," 36–53; and Kraminick, "Reflections on Revolution," 26–63.

21. Stone, "Theories of Revolution," 159.

22. Huntington, *Political Order*, 265.

23. Skocpol, *States and Social Revolutions*, 4. See also Himmelstein and Kimmel, "States and Revolutions," 1145–54.

24. Walt, *Revolution and War*, 12.

25. For some classic articles, aside from those cited above, see Marcuse, "Re-Examination of the Concept of Revolution," 27–34; Gurr, " Revolution—Social-Change Nexus," 359–92; Zagorin, "Theories of Revolution," 23–52; Goldfrank, "Theories of Revolution," 135–65; Aya, "Theories of Revolution Reconsidered," 39–99; and Goldstone, "Theories of Revolution," 425–53. For some recent

book-length contributions, see Zimmermann, *Political Violence, Crises and Revolutions*; DeFronzo, *Revolutions and Revolutionary Movements*; and Goldstone, *Revolutions: A Very Short Introduction*.

26. This is even true for some of the classic works on the subject. See, for instance, Brinton, *Anatomy of Revolution*.

27. Those who pointed out this anomaly, nearly three decades apart, include Adelman, *Revolution, Armies, and War*, 5; and Lehrke, "Cohesion Model," 146.

28. Hamilton, *Who Voted for Hitler?*, vi.

29. See Engels and Marx, *On the Paris Commune*. See also Tombs, *War against Paris 1871*; and Merriman, *Massacre*.

30. A partial exception is Chenoweth and Stephan, *Why Civil Resistance Works*.

31. See, for instance, Russell, *Rebellion*, 9.

32. Walt, *Revolution and War*, 6.

33. Cuoco, *Historical Essay*, see especially 64–74, 98–104, 135–41, 164–66.

34. See, for instance, Tilly, "Analysis of a Counter-Revolution," 30-30–58; idem, *From Mobilization to Revolution*; and idem, *European Revolutions*.

35. See Goodwin, *No Other Way Out*.

36. See, for instance, Goldstone, "Understanding the Revolutions of 2011," 8–16; and idem, "Cross-class Coalitions," 457–62.

37. New York: Columbia University Press, 2011.

38. Ithaca, NY: Cornell University Press, 1996, 1.

39. Boulder, CO: Lynne Rienner, 1985.

40. New York: Oxford University Press, 1974.

41. London: Faber & Faber, 1943 (reissued in 1973).

42. New York: Academic Press, 1974.

43. Russell, *Rebellion*, 81–82.

44. See George and Bennett, *Case Studies*, 205–20; and Gerring, *Case Study Research*, 178–85.

45. George and Bennett, *Case Studies*, 67–69.

46. I prefer to use "Burma" rather than "Myanmar" for reasons I explain in endnote 1, chapter 3.

47. Virtually every expert agrees that the uprising in Iran that ended with the replacement of the Shah's authoritarian regime with Ayatollah Khomeini's Islamic dictatorship was an "authentic" revolution. There is less consensus on the revolutionary bona fides of some of my other cases, but all of them have been endowed with "revolution" status by some scholars and researchers. See, for instance, Nakanishi, *Strong Soldiers*; Selth, "Burma's 'Saffron Revolution,'" 281–97; Calhoun, "Revolution and Repression," 21–38; Siani-Davies, *Romanian Revolution*; Zunes, "Bahrain's Arrested Revolution," 149–64; Korany and El-Mahdi, *Arab Spring in Egypt*; Cole and McQuinn, *Libyan Revolution*; Pierret, *Religion and State*; Gana, *Making*; and Yadav, "Antecedents of the Revolution," 550–63.

48. For discussions of this issue, see, for instance, a group of articles from the *New York Times*: Fred M. Hechinger, "Political Scientists Seeking Policy Role," 31 August 1968; "Political Scientists Are in a Revolution Instead of Watching," 4 November 2000; Patricia Cohen, "Field Study: Just How Relevant

Is Political Science?," 20 October 2009; Jacqueline Stevens, "Political Scientists Are Lousy Forecasters," 23 June 2012; Nicholas Kristof, "Professors, We Need You!" 15 February 2014; and "The Decline of the Public Intellectual?," 18 February 2014. See also Scott Jaschik, "Should Political Science Be Relevant," *Inside Higher Ed*, 7 September 2010, http://www.insidehighered.com/news/2010/09/07/polisci#sthash.eIG1HrrK.dpbs; Greg Ferenstein, "Former Political Scientist to Congress: Please Defund Political Science," *The Atlantic*, 12 February 2013, http://www.theatlantic.com/politics/archive/2013/02/former-political-scientist-to-congress-please-defund-political-science/273060/; and James Fearon, "Data on the Relevance of Political Scientists to the *NYT*," *Monkey Cage*, 23 February 2014, http://www.washingtonpost.com/blogs/monkey-cage/wp/2014/02/23/data-on-the-relevance-of-political-scientists-to-the-nyt/, all three last accessed on 6 June 2014.

49. Malcolm Gladwell, "The Gift of Doubt," *The New Yorker*, 24 June 2013, 75.

50. Ibid. See also Adelman, *Worldly Philosopher*, especially 115–16, 145–46, and 647.

CHAPTER 1: WHAT DETERMINES THE ARMY'S REACTION TO AN UPRISING?

1. Lenin, "Lecture on the 1905 Revolution," 253.

2. There are notable exceptions, such as Bueno de Mesquita, *Predictioneer's Game*; and Silver, *Signal and the Noise*.

3. See, for instance, Chorley, *Armies and the Art of Revolution*; Russell, *Rebellion*; and, more recently, Bellin, "Robustness of Authoritarianism,", 145–46; an "Reconsidering the Robustness of Authoritarianism in the Middle East: Lessons from the Arab Spring," *Comparative Politics* 44:2 (January 2012): 130–35; Barany, "Comparing the Arab Revolts," 25–26; and Lutterbeck, "Arab Uprisings and Armed Forces," 15–17.

4. Russell, *Rebellion*, 81–82.

5. "Comparing the Arab Revolts," 24–35, but particularly 25–26; and "Armies and Revolutions," 62–76, respectively.

6. Bellin, "Robustness of Authoritarianism," 145–46.

7. In a more recent article, Bellin adds more nuance to her analysis, in particular introducing the behavior and number of "civilian troublemakers" as important variables. See idem, "Reconsidering the Robustness," 130–35.

8. Lutterbeck, "Arab Uprisings and Armed Forces" 15–17.

9. Chorley, *Armies and the Art of Revolution*, 164.

10. Tilly, "Does Modernization Breed Revolution?," 443.

11. See, for instance, Shils and Janowitz, "Cohesion and Disintegration," 280–315; Siebold, "Essence of Military Group Cohesion," 286–95; and Lehrke, "Cohesion Model," 146–67.

12. Owens, *U.S. Civil-Military Relations*, 142–44.

13. Castillo, *Endurance and War*.

14. Lee, "Military Cohesion," 84–85. See also Siebold, "Misconceived Construct of Task Cohesion," 163–67.

15. See McLauchlin, "Loyalty Strategies," 333.

16. Ibid.

17. Ibid.

18. Pion-Berlin, Esparza, and Grisham, "Staying Quartered," 230–59.

19. For instance, in contrast to the article (Ibid.), the Chinese military followed orders in 1989 even though it was losing funding at the time (234); "legality" usually has a discounted value in the authoritarian states that most revolutions intend to overthrow (235); armies, like Romania's, that in the end side with the uprising, often shoot civilians in the beginning of the conflict (247); and it is hugely important to consider the ratio of conscripted soldiers to enlisted soldiers, as well as which units were used to repress protesters (249).

20. See, for instance, Rihoux and Ragin, *Configurational Comparative Methods*; and Marx, Rihoux, and Ragin, "Origins, Development, and Application," 115–42.

21. In particular, assigning only two possible values (e.g., 0 = low, 1 = high) is not helpful in cases when one must consider an entire spectrum of outcomes. For other criticisms of QCA, see, for instance, Collier and Mahoney, "Insights and Pitfalls," 56–91.

22. Notwithstanding his detractors who made fun of what they considered Rumsfeld's tortured language, according to the eminent linguist Geoffrey K. Pullum, Rumsfeld was "completely straightforward," and "the quotation is impeccable, syntactically, semantically, logically, and rhetorically." See Pullum, "Not Foot in Mouth," submitted to "Language Log," posted on 2 December 2003. Accessed on 28 July 2014 at http://itre.cis.upenn.edu/~myl/languagelog/archives/000182.html.

23. "U.S. Department of Defense News Briefing: Secretary Donald H. Rumsfeld and Chairman, Joint Chiefs of Staff General Richard Myers, 12 February 2002." Accessed on 28 July 2014 at http://www.defense.gov/transcripts/transcript.aspx?transcriptid=2636.

24. Lee, "Military Cohesion," 85.

25. For an excellent discussion of this issue, see Peled, *Question of Loyalty*.

26. See Ball, "Ethnic Conflict," 239–58.

27. See, for instance, Shils and Janowitz, "Cohesion and Disintegration"; Lee, "Military Cohesion"; as well as Pion-Berlin, Esparza, and Grisham, "Staying Quartered."

28. Baynham, *Military and Politics*, 139.

29. Al-Marashi, "Iraq's Security."

30. Lefever, *Spear and Scepter*, 146.

31. Barany, *Soldier and the Changing State*, 131–32.

32. See Lutterbeck, "Arab Uprisings and Armed Forces," 16–17.

33. See, for instance, Cook, *Struggle for Egypt*, 282–84; Mel Frykberg, "Egypt's Brutal Security Forces Also Victims of State Brutality," Interpress Service News Agency (Cairo), 27 November 2012, available at http://www.ipsnews.net/2012/11/egypts-brutal-security-forces-also-victims-of-state-brutality/; and "Six Military Conscripts Shot Dead Near Cairo," *Ahram Online*, 15 March 2014, http://english.ahram.org.eg/NewsContent/1/64/96693/Egypt/Politics-/Six-military-conscripts-shot-dead-near-Cairo.aspx, both accessed on 1 August 2014.

34. For various approaches to the concept of legitimacy, see Lipset, "Some Social Requisites of Democracy," 69–105; Dahl, *Polyarchy*, 122–66; Nagel, "Moral Conflict," 215–40; Weatherford, "Measuring Political Legitimacy," 149–66; and Buchanan, "Political Legitimacy and Democracy," 689–719.

35. Janos, "Authority and Violence," 132.

36. Ibid.

37. See, for instance, Pereira, *Authoritarianism and the Rule of Law in Brazil, Chile, and Argentina* (Pittsburgh, PA: University of Pittsburgh Press, 2005); and Sikkink, *Justice Cascade.*

38. See, for instance, Misol, *Unkept Promise*; and e-mail message from former Indonesian Defense Minister Juwano Sudarsono to the author (28 March 2010).

39. See, for instance, Tilly, "Does Modernization Breed Revolution?," 443–46.

40. See, for instance, Chorley, *Armies and the Art of Revolution*, ix; and Skocpol, *States and Social Revolutions*, 96.

41. Gurr, *Why Men Rebel*, 254.

42. Huntington, *Soldier and the State*, 79–83.

43. Pion-Berlin, Esparza, and Grisham, "Staying Quartered," especially 233–34 and 238–41.

44. Skocpol, *States and Social Revolutions*, 95–99.

45. McFaul, "Transitions from Postcommunism," 15.

46. See, for instance, Clark, *Mito y Realidad*53–70; and Guerra, *Visions of Power*, 47–48.

47. See, for instance, Ketchley, "'Army and the People," 155–86.

48. See, for instance, Borghard and Pischedda, "Allies and Airpower in Libya," 63–74.

49. See, for instance, Lukowski and Zawadzki, *History of Poland.*

50. See, for instance, Michael R. Gordon and Mark Landler, "In Crackdown Response, U.S. Temporarily Freezes Some Military Aid to Egypt," *New York Times*, 9 October 2013; and Hroub, "Qatar and the Arab Spring."

51. See Mitchell, *Color Revolutions.*

52. See Weyland, "Diffusion of Revolution," 391-423; and, more broadly, idem, *Making Waves.*

53. Fink, "Moment of the Monks," 361.

54. See Shifaw, *Diary of Terror.*

55. Bunbongkarn, *Military in Thai Politics*, 9–34.

56. Handley, *King Never Smiles*, 126, 233. See also McCargo, "Network Monarchy," 499–519.

57. Chalk, *Malay-Muslim Insurgency.*

58. See, for instance, Montesano and Jory, *Thai South.*

59. It bears underscoring that the chief difficulty in studying the North Korean army is less about a lack of information than about the reliability of the data. There is actually sufficient information related to North Korea, but a researcher should be careful about the quality and contextual meaning of the information.

60. For a few recent additions to the literature, see Michishita, *North Korea's Military-Diplomatic*; Cha, *Impossible State*; Bechtol, *North Korea and Regional Security*; French, *North Korea*; Woo, "Kim Jong-il's Military-First Politics," 117–25; and Harden, *Great Leader.*

CHAPTER 2: IRAN, 1979

1. Kurzman, *Unthinkable Revolution in Iran*, vii. Very different numbers are offered by Abbas Milani (*The Shah*, 394). According to him eleven percent of

Iran's thirty-eight million people participated in the uprising as opposed to seven percent in France and nine percent in the Bolshevik Revolution. I find particularly the last figure highly improbable. See also McDaniel, *Autocracy*.

2. Cited in Ward, *Immortal*, 150.

3. Kapuściński, *Shah of Shahs*, 25.

4. See de Bellaigue, *Patriot of Persia*. Roosevelt's *Countercoup* is an interesting, though deeply biased, account. For a recent scholarly exchange featuring different interpretations, see Takeyh, "What Really Happened in Iran," 2–13; and de Bellaigue and Takeyh, "Coupdunnit," 163–67.

5. Ramazani, "Who Lost America?," 10.

6. Lucas, "Monarchical Authoritarianism," 110.

7. Rubin, *Paved with Good Intentions*, 177–78.

8. Ramazani, "Who Lost America?," 18.

9. See Kamrava, *Revolution in Iran*, 121–25.

10. See Mackey, *Iranians*, 263–67.

11. The Shah in an interview with the West German weekly, *Der Spiegel*, quoted in Kapuściński, *Shah of Shahs*, 52. For an excellent examination of the Shah's modernization campaign, see McDaniel, *Autocracy*, 78–87. For his exploitation of the 1973 oil embargo, see Cooper, *Oil Kings*, especially 139–42, 144–47.

12. Bayne, *Persian Kingship*, 435.

13. Buchan, *Days of God*, 246.

14. Goldstone, *Revolutions: Theoretical, Comparative, and Historical*, 123.

15. Litwak, *Détente and the Nixon Doctrine*, 141.

16. See, for instance, Bill and Leiden, *Politics in the Middle East*, 253–54.

17. Ward, *Immortal*, 237. See also Zabih, *Iranian Military*.

18. John Stempel, *Inside the Iranian Revolution*, 149.

19. Bayne, *Persian Kingship*, 186.

20. Halpern, *Politics of Social Change in the Middle East and North Africa*, 251.

21. Owen, *State, Power, and Politics*, 81.

22. Ward, *Immortal*, 195.

23. Huyser, *Mission to Tehran*, 27.

24. I thank Mehran Kamrava for these insights.

25. Mirfakhraei, *Imperial Iranian Armed Forces*, 330.

26. Kurzman, *Unthinkable Revolution*, 114.

27. Afkhami, *Iranian Revolution*, 121.

28. Interview with Iranian exiles (Paris, December 2011).

29. Entessar, "Military and Politics," 58; and Graham, *Iran*, 143.

30. Entessar, "Military and Politics," 57–58; and Eisenstadt, "Iran's Islamic Revolution," 2.

31. Mirfakhraei, *Imperial Iranian Armed Forces*, 237.

32. This paragraph draws on Mirfakhraei, *Imperial Iranian Armed Forces*, 276–77.

33. Hashim, "Iranian Armed Forces," 67.

34. Mackey, *Iranians*, 244.

35. Sullivan, *Mission to Iran*, 79.

36. Ward, *Immortal*, 193.

37. Klare, *American Arms Supermarket*, 108.

38. Sullivan, *Mission to Iran*, 80; and Abrahamian, *Iran between Two Revolutions*, 435.

39. Kurzman, *Unthinkable Revolution*, 90.

40. Ward, *Immortal*, 208.

41. Entessar, "Military and Politics," 59; and Huyser, *Mission to Tehran*, 178.

42. Interviews with former Iranian military officers (New York, March 2009).

43. Interviews with Omani military personnel (Muscat, December 2012). See also Allen and Rigsbee, *Oman under Qaboos*, 72–73; and Peterson, *Oman's Insurgencies*, 329–31.

44. Parsons, *Pride and the Fall*, 144.

45. De Tocqueville, *Old Regime and the Revolution*, 214.

46. Mirfakhraei, *Imperial Iranian Armed Forces*, 289–90.

47. See Abrahamian, *History of Modern Iran*, 158.

48. Mirfakhraei, *Imperial Iranian Armed Forces*, 293.

49. Accounts of this incident as well as the number of the dead vary considerably. See, for instance, Ward, *Immortal*, 214; Axworthy, *History of Iran*, 257; and Buchan, *Days of God*, 210–26.

50. Fischer, *Iran*, 201.

51. See, for instance, Afkhami, *Life and Times of the Shah*, 463–66; and Nahavandi, *Carnets Secrets*, 139.

52. Michel Foucault, an oft-cited French journalist, initially reported 2,000–3,000 dead and then raised his figure to 4,000. His "evidence," if any, remains unclear. See Cyrus Kadivar, "A Question of Numbers," *Iranian Voice*, 8 August 2003. Accessed on 5 August 2014 at http://www.emadbaghi.com/en/archives/000592 .php#more; and Bar-Joseph, "Forecasting a Hurricane," 733.

53. Fischer, *Iran*, 198.

54. Abrahamian, *History of Modern Iran*, 160–61.

55. Mirfakhraei, *Imperial Iranian Armed Forces*, 304.

56. See, for instance, Kurzman, *Unthinkable Revolution*, 62.

57. Ward, *Immortal*, 218–19.

58. Mirfakhraei, *Imperial Iranian Armed Forces*, 306–7.

59. Axworthy, *History of Iran*, 258.

60. This paragraph draws on Ward, *Immortal*, 219. Just a few days prior to installing him as prime minister, the Shah assessed Bakhtiar as "one of those worms" that always crawls out of the woodwork in times of trouble. See Sullivan, *Mission to Iran*, 213.

61. Abrahamian, *Iran between Two Revolutions*, 524.

62. Ibid., 525.

63. Ward, *Immortal*, 219.

64. "1979: Exiled Ayatollah Khomeini Returns to Iran," *BBC On This Day, 1950-2005*. Accessed on 8 January 2014 at http://news.bbc.co.uk/onthisday/hi /dates/stories/february/1/newsid_2521000/2521003.stm.

65. Keddie, *Modern Iran*, 238.

66. Mirfakhraei, *Imperial Iranian Armed Forces*, 343.

67. See, for instance, Keddie, *Modern Iran*, 159–60.

68. See the accounts of Axworthy, *Revolutionary Iran*, 8–10; and Ward, *Immortal*, 224.

69. Bill, *Eagle and the Lion*, 227.

70. Mirfakhraei, *Imperial Iranian Armed Forces*, 325, 326; Sullivan, *Mission to Iran*, 151, 156–57; and Jervis, *Why Intelligence Fails*, 32.

71. The Shah's first post-ouster interview was entitled "How America Overthrew Me," *Now*, 7 December 1979; cited in Mirfakhraei, *Imperial Iranian Armed Forces*, 346. See also the Shah's memoirs in Pahlavi, *Answer to History*, 155.

72. Milani, *Shah*, 391; and Jervis, *Why Intelligence Fails*, 32. References to conspiracies, some more far-fetched than others, permeated my interviews with Iranian exiles (New York, April 2009; and Paris, December 2011).

73. Jervis, *Why Intelligence Fails*, 32.

74. See, for instance, Huyser, *Mission to Tehran*, 50, 58; and Buchan, *Days of God*, 251.

75. See the appropriate sections in Brzezinski, *Power and Principle*; Carter, *Keeping Faith*; Sullivan, *Mission to Iran*; Huyser, *Mission to Tehran*; and Vance, *Hard Choices*.

76. Carter, "Tehran, Iran Toasts." See also Eric Pace, "Shah, Seeking Modern Society, Built Police State and Offended Moslem Faithful," *New York Times*, 28 July 1980.

77. See, for instance, Ramazani, "Who Lost America?," 6.

78. Bill, *Eagle and the Lion*, 257.

79. Sullivan, *Mission to Iran*, 204; Huyser, *Mission to Tehran*, 18; and phone interview with Professor Peter Chelkowski of New York University (4 November 2011).

80. Bill, *Eagle and the Lion*, 257, 410.

81. Ibid. See also more generally, Kamrava, *Revolution in Iran*, 40–50.

82. Sullivan chose not to accept a new post because he "did not have the confidence in the judgment of the president in time of crisis." See Carter, *Keeping Faith*, 443–49; Brzezinski, *Power and Principle*; 359, 381; Sullivan, *Mission to Iran*, 287.

83. Bill, *Eagle and the Lion*, 254. See also Huyser, *Mission to Tehran*.

84. Carter, *Keeping Faith*, 449.

85. This paragraph draws on Jervis, *Why Intelligence Fails*, 21–25.

86. Kamrava, *Revolution in Iran*, 42. See also Barry Rubin, *Paved with Good Intentions*, 209.

87. See Bar-Joseph, "Forecasting a Hurricane," 718–42.

88. Mirfakhraei, *Imperial Iranian Armed Forces*, 310.

89. Kurzman, *Unthinkable Revolution*, 108.

90. Entessar, "Military and Politics," 60.

91. Ward, *Immortal*, 216–17. See also Mirfakhraei, *Imperial Iranian Armed Forces*, 329–30.

92. Kurzman, *Unthinkable Revolution*, 63, 114.

93. Afkhami, *Iranian Revolution*, 121.

94. Kurzman, "Structural Opportunity," 153–70.

95. Sick, *All Fall Down*, 140.

96. Eisenstadt, "Iran's Islamic Revolution," 3.

97. See, for instance, R. W. Apple, Jr., "Shah's Army is Showing Stresses," *New York Times*, 19 December 1978.

98. In one well-known case 800 *homafars* defected together to the revolution in the second half of January. See Axworthy, *Revolutionary Iran*, 6.

99. R. W. Apple, Jr., "A Lull in the Battle for Iran," *New York Times*, 3 February 1979.

100. Afkhami, *Iranian Revolution*, 126.

101. I thank Mehran Kamrava for this general point, which was also echoed by my Iranian exile interviewees in our conversations (Paris, December 2011).

102. Entessar, "Military and Politics," 60.

103. See Arjomand, *Turban for the Crown*, 126-128.

104. Ward, *Immortal*, 220.

105. See, for instance, Entessar, "Military and Politics," 60.

106. Ward, *Immortal*, 219.

107. Ganji, *Defying the Iranian Revolution*, 29.

108. See Afkhami, *Iranian Revolution*, 115; Gharabaghi, *Verites sur la crise iranienne*; and author's interviews with prominent Iranian exiles (Paris, December 2011).

109. Zabih, *Iranian Military*, 31, 35.

110. Huyser, *Mission to Tehran*, 281-282; and Axworthy, *Revolutionary Iran*, 7–8.

111. Buchan, *Days of God*, 293.

112. The source for the figures in this paragraph is Ward, *Immortal*, 225.

113. Mirfakhraei, *Imperial Iranian Armed Forces*, 398–99.

114. Eisenstadt, "Iran's Islamic Revolution," 3.

115. Entessar, "Military and Politics," 61.

116. Interview with Iranian exiles (Paris, December 2011).

117. All of them were dealt with harshly with the exception of Gharabaghi. See Rose, "Post-Revolutionary Purge," 153–94.

118. Kurzman, *Unthinkable Revolution*, 108.

119. Ibid., 1.

120. Ramazani, "Who Lost America?," 19.

121. Mirfakhraei, *Imperial Iranian Armed Forces*, 360.

122. Milani, *Shah*, 3.

123. Huyser, *Mission to Tehran*, 78. In his memoir, the Shah wrote, "A sovereign may not save his throne by shedding his countrymen's blood." See Pahlavi, *Answer to History*, 167.

124. See Mirfakhraei, *Imperial Iranian Armed Forces*; Kamrava, *Revolution in Iran*; and author's interviews with Iranian exiles (Paris, December 2011).

125. Sullivan, *Mission to Iran*, 212.

126. Kapuściński, *Shah of Shahs*, 61.

127. Interviews with an associate of the Shah who was in weekly personal contact with him in his last years. (Paris, December 2011). According to Mirfakhraei, even the Shah's wife was unaware that her husband was suffering from lymphomatous cancer (*Imperial Iranian Armed Forces*, 310). Jervis claims that the CIA knew nothing of the Shah's illness (*Why Intelligence Fails*, 31).

128. Mirfakhraei, *Imperial Iranian Armed Forces*, 320; and author's interview with a close confidant of the Shah's wife, Queen Farah (Paris, December 2011).

CHAPTER 3: BURMA, 1988 AND 2007

1. I refer to the country as "Burma" and not "Myanmar" which is what the unelected generals decided to call the country in 1989 without asking the population and because the country's democracy movement prefers "Burma," even if internationally both names are recognized. For a discussion of the name issue, see Dittmer, "Burma vs. Myanmar" 885–88.

2. See Smith, *Burma*, 1; and Steinberg, *Burma/Myanmar*, 1–3.

3. Selth, "Known Knowns," 272–95; and Marshall, *Trouser People*, 155.

4. For the importance of color in the Buddhist monks' robes, see Nietupski, "Clothing," 307–9.

5. As Fenichel and Khan explained in their article, "Burmese Way to 'Socialism,'" Burma did not have a socialist economy, and neither did its leaders have the will, or, indeed, the ability, to build a socialist society (813–24).

6. See Charney, *History of Modern Burma*. For three equally excellent nonacademic books that are very helpful to understand the country one could do worse than to read Orwell, *Burmese Days*; Larkin, *Finding George Orwell*; and Thant Myint-U, *River of Lost Footsteps*.

7. Nakanishi, *Strong Soldiers*, 45.

8. Steinberg, *Burma/Myanmar*, 102.

9. Nakanishi, *Strong Soldiers*, 217.

10. I am grateful for this point to Andrew Selth.

11. For issues of authoritarian regime survival, see Gandhi, *Political Institutions under Dictatorship*, 163–77.

12. See Tin Maung Maung Than, "Tatmadaw in Transition," in Raghavan, *Internal Conflicts in Myanmar*, 17.

13. Lasswell, "Garrison State," 455–68.

14. See McGowan, "Burmese Hell," 47–56; and Wakeman and San Tin, *No Time for Dreams*, xviii.

15. Boudreau, *Resisting Dictatorship*, 152–53.

16. Selth, *Transforming the Tatmadaw*, 129.

17. On this subject, see Gombrich, *Theravāda Buddhism*; and Tilakaratne, *Theravāda Buddhism*.

18. See U Min Naing, *National Ethnic Groups*; Farrelly, "Discipline without Democracy," 313–14.

19. Larkin, *Everything Is Broken*, 120.

20. Rogers, "Saffron Revolution," 115.

21. McCarthy, "Overturning the Alms Bowl," 301.

22. Smith, *Burma*, 7.

23. Taylor, "Stifling Change," 6–7; and Egreteau and Jagan, *Back to Old Habits*, 13–17.

24. Nakanishi, *Strong Soldiers*, 270.

25. Fink, *Living in Silence*, 47. See also Wakeman and San Tin, *No Time for Dreams*, 115–48.

26. Boudreau, *Resisting Dictatorship*, 195.

27. Schock, *Unarmed Insurrections*, 94.

28. Mya Maung, *Burma Road*, 217.

29. Some controversy remains about precisely who ordered the military to step in. See Nakanishi, *Strong Soldiers*, 14; Taylor, *State in Myanmar*, 387; and Maung Maung, *1988 Uprising*, the former president's rather self-serving post-humously published recollections, and its insightful review by Myint Zan, sug-gestively titled "Misremembrance of an Uprising," available at http://www.burma library.org/docs6/Myintzan-Maungmaung.pdf accessed on 6 August 2014. Ac-cording to Min Zin's research, Ne Win asked ex-spy chief Khin Nyunt and Saw Maung, then Commander-in-Chief of the *Tatmadaw*, to stage the coup. E-mail from Min Zin (24 July 2014).

30. Lintner, *Outrage*, 132; and Farrelly," Discipline without Democracy," 317.

31. Steinberg, *Burma/Myanmar*, 80.

32. See, for instance, Jagan, "Myanmar's Military Mindset," in Raghavan, *In-ternal Conflicts in Myanmar*, 223; and Farrelly, "Discipline without Democracy," 312–26.

33. Selth, *Burma's Armed Forces*, 266–67.

34. Callahan, "Endurance of Military Rule," in Levenstein, *Finding Dollars*, 63.

35. Steinberg, *Burma/Myanmar*, 139.

36. Win Min, "Looking Inside," 161.

37. This paragraph draws on Andrew Selth's comments e-mailed to the au-thor on 5 June 2014.

38. Smith, *Burma*, 15.

39. Taylor, "Stifling Change," 8–9; and author's interview with Ko Ko Gyi (Rangoon, 4 October 2014).

40. Taylor, "Stifling Change," 8–9; and Lintner, *Outrage*, 139.

41. Author's interviews with participants of the1988 uprising (Rangoon, 1-4 October 2014); and e-mail message from Andrew Selth (2 October 2014).

42. I thank Andrew Selth for this insight, which was confirmed by numerous Burmese politicians and democracy activists in my interviews (Rangoon, 1–5 Oc-tober 2014).

43. Finer, *Man on Horseback*, 190–97.

44. See Schock, *Unarmed Insurrections*, 96; Nakanishi, *Strong Soldiers*, 273; and Boudreau, *Resisting Dictatorship*, 201 (see especially footnote #46 on this page) and 205.

45. Author's interviews with 1988 student leaders (Rangoon, 1 and 3 October 2014).

46. Aung San Suu Kyi, "Speech to a Mass Rally," 195. See also Silverstein, "Aung San Suu Kyi," 1007–19.

47. Fink, *Living in Silence*, 59.

48. Fink, "Moment of the Monks," 361–62. See also Nakanishi, *Strong Sol-diers*, 293.

49. Williams, "Cracks in the Firmament," 1208.

50. Egretau and Jagan, *Back to Old Habits*, 35–36.

51. Min, "Looking Inside," 158.

52. See McCarthy, "Overturning the Alms Bowl," 302; and Taylor, "Stifling Change," 10. Burmese political elites could be so "astonished" at the electoral outcome only because they were entirely unaware of the depth of the people's disapproval of and dissatisfaction with their regime. Their opacity reminds one of the Polish communist party leaders' incredulity at the trouncing they received at the polls in June 1989.

53. See Callahan, "Myanmar's Perpetual Junta," 40; and Daniel Pepper, "Aftermath of a Revolt: Myanmar's Lost Year," *New York Times*, 5 October 2008.

54. Cited in Kaufman, Kraay, and Mastruzzi, "Governance Matters IV."

55. Selth, *Transforming the Tatmadaw*, 11.

56. Author's interview with retired generals (Rangoon, 4 September 2015).

57. Selth, *Transforming the Tatmadaw*, 50.

58. See Prager Nyein, "Expanding Military," 638–48; and e-mail letter from Andrew Selth (1 October 2014).

59. See Selth, "Myanmar's Police Forces," 53–79.

60. Steinberg, *Burma/Myanmar*, 103–4.

61. Callahan, "Myanmar's Perpetual Junta," 42.

62. Maung Aung Myoe, *Building the Tatmadaw*, 176. Of the fifty-one companies, UMEHL fully owned thirty-five, including nine subsidiaries and seven affiliations. Author's interview with a retired general (Rangoon, 28 August 2015).

63. Steinberg, "Aung San Suu Kyi," 35–59.

64. Farrelly, "Discipline without Democracy," 323.

65. I am grateful to Min Zin for this point.

66. Chirot, *Modern Tyrants*, 309. On King Kyanzittha, see Harvey, *History of Burma*, 23–44.

67. McCarthy, "Overturning the Alms Bowl," 304.

68. Callahan, "Myanmar's Perpetual Junta," 42.

69. For depictions of everyday life in Burma, see Seekins, "Myanmar in 2008," 166–73; and Lemere and West, *Nowhere to Be Home*.

70. Selth, "Burma's 'Saffron Revolution,'" 282.

71. McCarthy, "Overturning the Alms Bowl," 308.

72. Fink, *Living in Silence*, 102–3.

73. McCarthy, "Overturning the Alms Bowl," 308.

74. Selth, "Burma's 'Saffron Revolution,'" 283.

75. Rogers, "Saffron Revolution," 116.

76. McCarthy, "Overturning the Alms Bowl," 309.

77. Fink, "Moment of the Monks," 366.

78. "Myanmar: Monk Receives 68 Years in Prison," Amnesty International, 3 October 2008, http://www.amnestyusa.org/pdfs/UGambiraCaseSheet.pdf, retrieved on 28 May 2014.

79. See Coclanis, "Myanmar Moment?," 91; Boudreau, *Resisting Dictatorship*, 210; and Wakeman and San Tin, *No Time for Dreams*, xviii.

80. Selth, "Burma's 'Saffron Revolution,'" 283.

81. Barany, "Armies and Revolutions," 74; and interviews with participants of the uprising (Rangoon, 3 October 2014).

82. McCarthy, "Overturning the Alms Bowl," 309.

83. See also Steinberg, *Burma/Myanmar*, 138; and Shaazka Beyerle and Cynthia Boaz, "Saffron Revolution: The Power of Nonviolence," *New York Times*, 18 October 2007.

84. Lower estimate from Rogers, "Saffron Revolution," 116; the higher from Callahan, "Myanmar's Perpetual Junta," 32.

85. For analyses of the opposition's shortcomings, see Min Zin, "Opposition Movements," in Levenstein, *Finding Dollars*, 77–94; and Shen and Chi-yuen Chan, "Failure of the Saffron Revolution," 31–57.

86. See Chowdhury, "Role of the Internet."

87. Selth, "Burma's 'Saffron Revolution,'" 284.

88. See "Faced with Myanmar Protests, China Reaffirms Nonintervention," *Inquirer.net*, 25 September 2007; and "World Urges Restraint amid Myanmar Protests," *Agence France-Presse*, of the same day.

89. Callahan, "Endurance of Military Rule," 67; and Selth, "Burma's 'Saffron Revolution,'" 289, respectively.

90. Goodwin and Skocpol, "Explaining Revolutions," 489–509.

CHAPTER 4: CHINA AND EASTERN EUROPE, 1989

1. Established in 1955, the Warsaw Pact was the Communist Bloc's response to NATO. In addition to the Soviet Union and the six East European states discussed in this chapter, Albania was also a member until its formal withdrawal in 1968.

2. See Verona, *Military Occupation*, 122–41.

3. See, for instance, Johnson, Dean, and Alexiev, *East European Military Establishments*; Völgyes, *Political Reliability*; and Rakowska-Harmstone, et al., *Warsaw Pact*.

4. Polish Central Committee member Mieczysław Rakowski cited in Pryce-Jones, *War that Never Was*, 211. See also Kramer, "Beyond the Brezhnev Doctrine," 25–67.

5. See also Charles Powers, "Gorbachev Visit Sparks Hopes for 'Renewal' in Poland," *Los Angeles Times*, 11 July 1988.

6. Barany and Vinton, "Breakthrough to Democracy," 191–212.

7. Interview with Professor Jerzy Wiatr (Warsaw, 3 September 2012). For the political involvement of the Polish armed forces, see Wiatr, *Soldier and the Nation*; and Michta, *Red Eagle*.

8. Interviews with Jerzy Wiatr, General Stanisław Koziej (Warsaw, 4 September 2012), and Professor Jerzy Eisner (Warsaw, 5 September 2012).

9. Gierek cited in the interview volume by Rolicki, *Edward Gierek*, 187.

10. Interviews with General Koziej and with two other senior officers who asked to remain anonymous.

11. Interviews with Wiatr, Koziej, and Col. (Ret.) Sławomir Szczepanski (Warsaw, 4–5 September 2012).

12. Interview with former Polish Defense Minister Jan Parys (Austin, 21 August 1992).

13. For a detailed account, see Tőkés, *Hungary's Negotiated Revolution*. For a brief consideration, see Barany, "The Bankruptcy of Hungarian Socialism," 191–213.

14. Tőkés, *Hungary's Negotiated Revolution*, 362.
15. Interview with Col. Péter Deák (Budapest, 28 December 1990).
16. Cited in Pryce-Jones, *War that Never Was*, 228.
17. Vogel, *Deng*, 604.
18. Lieberthal, *Governing China*, 141.
19. Brook, *Quelling the People*, 39.
20. Scobell, "Why the People's Army," 197.
21. Brook, *Quelling the People*, 29.
22. Schock, *Unarmed Insurrections*, 214.
23. Zhao died in 2005. For more on his views, see Zhao, *Prisoner of the State*.
24. See Nathan and Link, *Tiananmen Papers*, 264–65; Scobell, "Why the People's Army," 200; and Shambaugh, *Modernizing*, 24.
25. Zhao, *Power of Tiananmen*, 171; and Nathan and Link, *Tiananmen Papers*.
26. Vogel, *Deng*, 621. See also Walder and Xiaoxia, "Workers in the Tiananmen Protests," 1–29.
27. Walder, "Political Sociology," 30–40.
28. Vogel, *Deng*, 619.
29. Brook, *Quelling the People*, 7.
30. Nathan and Link, *Tiananmen Papers*, xxxviii–xxxix.
31. Zhao, *Power of Tiananmen*, 201; Andrew Jacobs, "Q & A: Chen Guang on the Soldiers Who Retook Tiananmen Square," *New York Times*, 2 June 2014.
32. Cunningham, *Tiananmen Moon*, 245.
33. Han, *Cries for Democracy*, 261–62.
34. Scobell, *China's Use of Military*, 158.
35. Scobell, "Why the People's Army," 202.
36. Lieberthal, *Governing China*, 142. The source of the three thousand figure—corroborated by the Swiss Ambassador—is the Chinese Red Cross. See Brook, *Quelling the People*, 155.
37. Mulvenon, "China," 323. See also Joffe, "Party-Army Relations," 299–314.
38. Kou, "Why the Military Obeys," 48–49.
39. Scobell, "Why the People's Army," 199. See also Wong, "Tiananmen," 79–95.
40. Nathan and Link, *Tiananmen Papers*, 213. See also John Garnaut, "How Top Generals Refused to March on Tiananmen Square," *Sydney Morning Herald*, 4 June 2010. Garnaut mentions two other recalcitrant generals, Qin Jiwei and He Yanran, but his account has yet to be corroborated.
41. Shambaugh, *Modernizing*, 24–25.
42. Reported in Brook, *Quelling the People*, 41.
43. Deng's military reforms reduced the socioeconomic status of servicemen, some of whom were complaining by 1988 that they had difficulties finding a wife. See *Far Eastern Economic Review*, 18 August 1988, cited in Kou, "Why the Military," 43. See also Dreyer, "Deng Xiaoping," 215–31.
44. Dreyer, "China after Tiananmen," 649.
45. Ibid., 648.
46. Shambaugh, *Modernizing*, 16.
47. Dreyer, "China after Tiananmen, 647.

48. See, for instance, Segal and Phipps, "Why Communist Armies," 962; and Andrew Jacobs and Chris Buckley, "25 Years Later, Details Emerge of Army's Chaos before Tiananmen Square," *New York Times*, 2 June 2014.

49. Vogel, *Deng*, 620; Brook, *Quelling the People*, 7; and Lim, *People's Republic*, 10–28.

50. Nathan and Link, *Tiananmen Papers*, 149.

51. Lim, *People's Republic*, 12–13.

52. Wu, "China," 126.

53. Sarotte, "China's Fear," 161.

54. Idem, *1989: The Struggle*, 17. This hypothesis is contradicted by Gorbachev's acquiescence to Soviet security and military personnel murdering freedom fighters in Lithuania, Latvia, and elsewhere in 1991, only a few months after he received the Nobel Peace Prize. See also Lieven, *Baltic Revolution*.

55. Feigon, *China Rising*, 221.

56. Segal and Phipps, "Why Communist Armies," 960-961.

57. Zhang Liang in Nathan and Link, *Tiananmen Papers*, xi.

58. Orville Schell on the Charlie Rose (PBS) program on Tiananmen's twenty-fifth anniversary (4 June 2014).

59. See Hirschman, "Exit, Voice, and the Fate," 173–202.

60. See Gedmin, *Hidden Hand*; and McCauley, "Gorbachev," 172–91.

61. Maier, *Dissolution*, 148.

62. Dale, *East German Revolution*, 21.

63. See Kuhn, *Der Tag der Entscheidung*; and Lohmann, "Dynamics of Informational Cascades," 42–101, especially 57–84.

64. Sarotte, *Collapse*, 53.

65. Pfaff, *Exit-Voice Dynamics*, 183.

66. Ross, *East German Dictatorship*, 130. For a detailed exposition, on the Leipzig events, see Sarotte, *Collapse*, 46–82.

67. Dale, *East German Revolution*, 16.

68. Interview with General (Ret.) Jörg Schönbohm (Kleinmachnow, Germany, 13 December 2011).

69. See Sarotte, *Collapse*.

70. Kenney, *Carnival of Revolution*, 257–58.

71. Cited by Segal and Phipps, "Why Communist Armies," 964.

72. Interview with General (Ret.) Werner von Scheven (Geltow-Schwielowsee, Germany, 14 December 2011); and Dale, *East German Revolution*, 21–22.

73. Dale, *East German Revolution*, 178.

74. Interview with Col. Dr. Gerhard P. Groß and Dr. Rüdiger Wenzke at the Bundeswehr's Militärgeschichtliches Forschungsamt (Potsdam, 14 December 2011).

75. Cited in Pryce-Jones, *War that Never Was*, 275. See also Schönbohm, *Two Armies*, 17–19.

76. See Barany, *Soldiers and Politics*, 156–57; and interview with Velizar Shalamanov, Ministry of Defense (Sofia, 18 November 1999).

77. Interview with Col. Valeri Ratchev (Sofia, 13 November 1999).

78. Dimitrov, *Bulgaria*, 37; and interview with Lubomir Ivanov (Sofia, 19 November 1999).

79. Sebestyen, *Revolution 1989*, 364–65.

80. Wydra, "Revolution and Democracy," 37.

81. Ibid.; and Petersen, *Resistance and Rebellion*, 249–53.

82. Interview with Vasil Hudak (Prague, 25 August 1999).

83. Simon, *NATO*, 10.

84. Interview with Czechoslovak Prime Minister Marián Čalfa (Austin, TX, 13 April 1992).

85. Petersen, *Resistance and Rebellion*, 254.

86. Interview with Dr. Prokop Tomek, Institute of Military History (Prague, 6 September 2012).

87. See Johnson, Dean, and Alexiev, *East European Military Establishments*, 134–77; and Barany, *Soldiers and Politics*, 140–66.

88. Interview with Prokop Tomek. See also Rice, *Soviet Union*, 157–217.

89. Interview with Marián Čalfa.

90. Ithaca, NY: Cornell University Press, 2005. For theoretical discussions, see Roper, "Romanian Revolution," 401–10; and Hall, "Theories of Collective Action," 1069–93.

91. Ratesh, *Romania*, 7.

92. See Chirot, *Modern Tyrants*, especially 236–58; and Gabányi, *Ceausescu Cult*.

93. Gilberg, *Nationalism and Communism*, 270.

94. This was admitted by former Interior Minister Tudor Postelnicu while under arrest in March 1990. See Suciu, *Reportaj cu sufletul* and documents last accessed on 10 August 2014 at www.dosarelerevolutiei.ro.

95. See the 1992 documentary film, directed by Farocki and Ujică, *Videograms of a Revolution* for some of the original film footage of this and other events of the revolution.

96. Milea's retort was widely reported in the Romanian media, for instance in *Adevarul*, 14 January and 6 February 1990; and *Romania Libera*, 16 and 20 January 1990. I am thankful to Larry Watts for this point (e-mail communication [19 September 2013]).

97. Sebestyen, *Revolution 1989*, 389.

98. Siani-Davies, *Romanian Revolution*, 149–65; and Ratesh, *Romania*, 58–61. On Brucan's credibility, see Pryce-Jones, *War that Never Was*, 340.

99. See Ioan, *Teroriştii din '89*.

100. Siani-Davies, *Romanian Revolution*, 119. See also *Videograms of a Revolution*.

101. Watts, "Civil-Military Relations," 523.

102. Siani-Davies, *Romanian Revolution*, 36.

103. Ibid., 40.

104. See Crowther, "'Ceausescuism,'" 207–25.

105. Interviews with former Romanian conscripts (Munich, December 1981; Bucharest, March 1995; Cluj and Sibiu, October 1999).

106. Siani-Davies, *Romanian Revolution*, 39. See also Deletant, *Ceauşescu and the Securitate*.

107. The poet Mircea Dinescu cited in Rady, *Romania in Turmoil*, 106.

108. Ratesh, *Romania*, 93; and Siani-Davies, *Romanian Revolution*, 40.

109. See "Crimele Revoluţiei: Masacrul de la Otopeni," *Aciduzzul*, 17 December 2009. Accessed on 25 September 2013 at http://www.badpolitics.ro /crimele-revolutiei-masacrul-de-la-otopeni-adevarul/; and accessed on 25 September 2013 at http://www.waymarking.com/waymarks/WMEPC5_Otopeni_Airport _Massacre_Otopeni_RO.

110. Cited in Sebestyen, *Revolution 1989*, 394–95.

111. Interviews with Teodor Repciuc and Cristian Mureşanu of the Institute of Political Studies and Defense and Military History (Bucharest, 4 November 1999); and Andrea Bartosin of *Adevarul* (Austin, TX, 29 August 2000).

112. Watts, "Romanian Army," 106.

113. See, for instance, Codrescu, *Hole in the Flag*, 195; Rady, *Romania in Turmoil*, 95; and Sebestyen, *Revolution 1989*, 388 and 394.

114. See, for instance, Galloway and Wylie, *Downfall*, 151.

115. Tismaneanu, *Stalinism for All Seasons*, 227.

116. See Kramer, "Collapse of East European Communism," 197–98; and Tismaneanu, *Stalinism for All Seasons*, 229.

117. See, for instance, Siani-Davies, *Romanian Revolution*, 188; Sava and Monac, *Revoluţia română*, 337–40; Scurtu, *Romanian Revolution*; Savranskaya, Blanton, and Zubok, *Peaceful End*, 90–91.

118. E-mail communication from Ambassador Matlock (12 January 2014) and author's conversation with Matlock (Austin, TX, 22 September 2014).

119. See, for instance, Bucur, "Possible Soviet Intervention."

120. Stănculescu, a key figure in the escape of Ceauşescu from the Central Committee building on 22 December 1989, was thoroughly "debriefed": Săraru, *Generalul Revoluţiei*.

121. According to Stănculescu "both the post mortem and coroner's report gave a suicide verdict." See Galloway and Wylie, *Downfall*, 144.

122. See Hall, "Theories of Collective Action."

123. See, for instance, Chen, Zhong, and Hillard, "Level and Sources," 45–64; and Chen, "Institutional Legitimacy," 3–13.

124. Chirot, "What Happened in Eastern Europe," 20.

125. Pacepa, *Red Horizons*, 427–38.

126. Greenfield, *Washington*, xiii.

127. Zuo and Benford, "Mobilization Processes," 131–56; and Yang, "Achieving Emotions," 593–614.

CHAPTER 5: THE MIDDLE EAST AND NORTH AFRICA, 2011

1. Phillips, *Yemen's Democracy*, 69–71.

2. See Owen, "Arab 'Demonstration' Effect," 372–81; and Weyland, "Arab Spring," 917–34.

3. See, for instance, Brownlee, Masoud, and Reynolds, *Arab Spring*, 40–63.

4. See, for instance, Simon Sebag Montefiore, "Every Revolution Is Revolutionary in Its Own Way," *New York Times*, 26 March 2011.

5. According to some analysts, the critical factor that convinced the general to take the course of action he did was the defection of Ammar's own security

detail. I am grateful for this point to Yezid Sayigh (e-mail communication, 21 February 2014). I find the contrarian view, outlined in Pachon, "Loyalty and Defection," 508–31, unpersuasive.

6. See Ware, "Role of the Tunisian Military," 27–47.

7. Within a month of becoming Tunisia's leader, Ben Ali fired twenty-seven of his military academy classmates—who presumably knew too much about him—and appointed four others as ambassadors so as to remove them from the country. Author's interviews with retired senior army officers (Tunis, 6 December 2011).

8. Ware, "Role of the Tunisian Military," 39. For the interior ministry figures, I am grateful to Yezid Sayigh (e-mail communication, 21 February 2014).

9. Ware, "Role of the Tunisian Military," 38–39.

10. Clement Henry and Robert Springborg, "The Tunisian Army: Defending the Beachhead of Democracy in the Arab World," *Huffington Post*, 26 January 2011.

11. Steve Coll, "The Casbah Coalition: Tunisia's Second Revolution," *The New Yorker*, 4 April 2011, 38.

12. See "Tunisie: L'armée qui a lâché Ben Ali," *Le Monde*, 16 January 2011.

13. Lutterbeck, "Arab Uprisings, Armed Forces," 34.

14. Brooks, "Abandoned at the Palace," 214.

15. Author's interviews with retired army colonels (Tunis, 6 December 2011). See also Brooks, "Abandoned at the Palace," 214–15.

16. Elisabeth Bumiller, "Egypt Stability Hinges on a Divided Military," *New York Times*, 5 February 2011; and Scott Shane and David D. Kirkpatrick, "Military Caught Between Mubarak and Protesters," *New York Times*, 11 February 2011.

17. Cook, *Struggle for Egypt*, 285.

18. David E. Sanger, "When Armies Decide," *New York Times*, 19 February 2011. See also Albrecht and Bishara, "Back on Horseback," 19–20.

19. Confidential interview with Coptic Christian activists (Cairo, October 2014).

20. Confidential interviews with military personnel (Cairo, October 2014).

21. Droz-Vincent, "Military amidst Uprisings," in Gerges, *New Middle East*, 189–190.

22. Harb, "Egyptian Military," 269–90.

23. Kandil, *Soldiers, Spies, and Statesmen*, 234.

24. Clement Henry and Robert Springborg, "A Tunisian Solution for Egypt's Military: Why Egypt's Military Will Not Be Able to Govern," *Foreign Affairs*, 21 February 2011, www.foreignaffairs.com/print/67290. See also Sayigh, "Above the State"; and Kandil, *Soldiers, Spies, and Statesmen*.

25. Elisabeth Bumiller, "Egypt's Stability Hinges on a Divided Military," *New York Times*, 5 February 2011; and e-mail communication from Yezid Sayigh (21 February 2014).

26. Wendell Steavenson, "On the Square: Were the Egyptian Protesters Right To Trust the Military?," *New Yorker*, 28 February 2011, 38.

27. Maikel Nabil Sanad, "How Egypt's Conscription Generates Unemployment and Refugees," *Huffington Post*, 15 September 2014. Accessed on 22 October 2014 at www.huffingtonpost.ca/maikel-nabil-sanad/egypt-refugees_b_5818444 .html#es_share_ended.

28. Steavenson, "On the Square," 43.

29. See Mohamad Adam and Sarah Carr, "Brute force: Inside the Central Security Forces," *Egypt Independent*, 11 November 2012. Accessed on 11 August 2014 at http://www.egyptindependent.com/news/brute-force-inside-central-security-forces.

30. Noueihed and Warren, *Battle for the Arab Spring*, 109; and Ghonim, *Revolution 2.0*, 215. It is worth noting that by November/December 2011, when the army and the police brutally suppressed demonstrations, those who chanted "The people and the military are one hand!" began now to cry furiously "The military and the police are one hand!" See Kandil, *Soldiers, Spies, and Statesmen*, 234.

31. Cook, *Struggle for Egypt*, 287.

32. Steavenson, "On the Square," 38. See also author's interviews with 2011 protesters (Cairo, 12 October 2014).

33. See Gerges, *New Middle East*, 17. See also Helene Cooper and Mark Landler, "White House and Egypt Discuss Plan for Mubarak," *New York Times*, 3 February 2011; and Ryan Lizza, "The Consequentialist: How the Arab Spring Remade Obama's Foreign Policy," *New Yorker*, 2 May 2011, 44–55.

34. Ghonim, *Revolution 2.0*, 131–32.

35. Marfleet, "Never 'One Hand,'" 166.

36. E-mail communication from Robert Springborg (November 2012); and interviews with Egyptian military officers at the Naval Postgraduate School (Monterey, CA, July 2008) and at National Defense University (Washington, DC, January 2013).

37. Sharp, "Egypt," ii and 11.

38. Dexter Filkins, "After the Uprising: Can the Protestors Find a Path between Dictatorship and Anarchy?," *New Yorker*, 11 April 2011, 42.

39. Lacher, "Libya after Qadhafi."

40. Vandewalle, "Libya's Uncertain Revolution," in Cole and McQuinn, *Libyan Revolution*, 23.

41. Lacher and Labnouj, "Factionalism Resurgent," in Cole and McQuinn, *Libyan Revolution*, 262.

42. For a concise examination of the Libyan case, see Vandewalle, *History of Modern Libya*, 147–49.

43. On coup-proofing, see Quinlivan, "Coup-proofing," 131–65; and Albrecht, "Myth of Coup-Proofing."

44. Tom Finn, "Yemen Showdown Looms as Army Loyalties Divide," *Guardian*, 21 March 2011.

45. Noueihed and Warren, *Battle for the Arab Spring*, 198–99.

46. Lacher, "Libya after Qadhafi," 4.

47. E-mail message to author from Wolfram Lacher, North Africa expert at the German Institute for International and Security Affairs, Berlin, (25 May 2011). A fascinating account of how the revolution actually proceeded and how the opposing forces coalesced is in Lacher and Labnouj, "Factionalism Resurgent," 262–72.

48. Ashish Kumar Sen, "Libyan Rebels: Colombian Female Snipers Fighting for Gadhafi," *Washington Times*, 12 April 2011; and Lacher, "Regional Repercussion," in Asseburg, *Protest, Revolt, and Regime Change*, 47.

49. C.J. Chivers, "Captive Soldiers Tell of Discord in Libyan Army," *New York Times*, 13 May 2011.

50. See, for instance, Martínez, *Libyan Paradox*, 98–101; Gaub, "Libyan Armed Forces," 232; and Knights, "Military Role," 273.

51. See Pollack, *Arabs at War*; and interview with Wolfram Lacher (Berlin, 13 December 2011).

52. Barany, *Soldier and the Changing State*, 328.

53. See Wright, *Libya, Chad, and the Central Sahara*.

54. Jon Lee Anderson, "King of Kings: The Last Days of Muammar Qaddafi," *New Yorker*, 7 November 2011, 52.

55. Sorenson, "Civil-Military Relations," 109–10.

56. Clark, *Yemen*, 122–23; and Paul Dresch, *History*, 208.

57. Vandewalle, "Libya's Uncertain Revolution," in Cole and McQuinn, *Libyan Revolution*, 19.

58. See Seitz, "Ties that Bind," in Lackner, *Why Yemen Matters*, 50–67; and Brandt, "Irregulars of the Sa'ada War," 105–22, both in Lackner, *Why Yemen Matters*; and Dunne and Gifkins, "Libya," 515–29.

59. See, for instance, Carapico, *Civil Society in Yemen*, 78; and Phillips, *Yemen's Democracy*, 70.

60. Nolutshungu, *Limits of Anarchy*, 218–23; and Dresch, *History*, 147–48.

61. Gaub, "Libyan Armed Forces," 221.

62. Knights, "Military Role," 18; and Gaub, "Libyan Armed Forces," 279.

63. Author's interview with Wolfram Lacher (Berlin, 13 December 2011).

64. Author's confidential interviews with Western military officers in Manama, Bahrain, Muscat, Oman, and Doha, Qatar (December 2012).

65. Sebnem Arsu and Steven Erlanger, "Libya Rebels Get Formal Backing, and $30 Billion," *New York Times*, 15 July 2011.

66. Interview with Elsadig B. Elfaqih, Secretary General of the Arab Thought Forum (Amman, 26 April 2012).

67. Cole and McQuinn, *Libyan Revolution*, 2. McQuinn gives an account of how now fewer than 236 separate armed groups emerged from Misrata alone. See his chapter, "History's Warriors," in Cole and McQuinn, *Libyan Revolution*, 229–56.

68. Katzman, "Bahrain," 5.

69. Ibid.

70. Niethammer, "Calm and Squalls," in Asseburg, *Protest, Revolt, and Regime Change*, 15.

71. "Arab Spring? That's the Business of Other Countries: Interview with King Hamad of Bahrain," *Der Spiegel*, 13 February 2012, available at www.spiegel.de/international/world/0,1518,druck-814915,00.html, last accessed on 21 August 2014.

72. Barany, "Comparing the Arab Revolts," 31.

73. Author's interviews in Bahrain (December 2012 and October 2014). See also Louër, "Sectarianism," 245–60; and, especially, Gengler, "Royal Factionalism," 53–79.

74. See the over-five-hundred-page report of the Bahrain Independent Commission Inquiry at http://www.bici.org.bh/BICIreportEN.pdf.

75. Hertog, "Rentier Militaries," 400–402.

76. Interviews in Manama (December 2012 and October 2014). See also Lutterbeck, "Arab Uprisings, Armed Forces," 42.

77. Of the six Gulf monarchies, only Kuwait ever tried to enforce mandatory conscription—it was not a successful experiment and was abandoned in 2001—yet it is once again under consideration. See "Kuwait Plans Compulsory Military Conscription," *Al Defaiya*, 23 August 2011.

78. Author's interviews with Bahraini military experts in (Manama and Cairo, October 2014).

79. A list of 115 of these individuals—some worked in "grey areas" such as civil defense and traffic police—was published (in Arabic) on the Internet. Accessed on 29 October 2014 at http://www.castancafe.com/forum/showthread .php?t=110267. I am grateful to Amy Austin Holmes for bringing this point, and the source, to my attention.

80. Author's interviews with Shia Muslim Bahraini opposition leaders and military experts (Manama, October 2014).

81. Author's interviews with Bahraini military personnel in Manama and Washington, DC (December 2012).

82. See, for instance, Louër, "Sectarianism," 249–52; Abdulhadi Khalaf, "Bahrain's Military Is Closely Tied to the Monarch," *New York Times* "Room for Debate," 28 August 2012; and "Breaking News: Pakistan army exports new mercenaries to kill Bahraini protesters." Accessed on 11 December 2012 at http://criticalppp.com/archives/42347.

83. Mujib Mashal, "Pakistani Troops Aid Bahrain's Crackdown," *Al-Jazeera*, 30 July 2011. Accessed on 16 October 2014 at http://www.aljazeera.com /indepth/features/2011/07/2011725145048574888.html.

84. E-mail from Prof. Abdulhadi Khalaf (1 October 2012).

85. Katzman, "Bahrain," 7. Owing to its delicate sectarian balance and the Bahraini monarch's spurning Kuwaiti attempts to mediate between the opposition and the regime in Manama, Kuwait sent only a symbolic naval detachment that could not be used against Bahraini protesters. Oman was also reluctant but, owing to Saudi pressure, it eventually supported Bahrain's invasion. See Matthiesen, *Sectarian Gulf*, 96, 111.

86. See Kamrava, "Arab Spring," 96–104; and Steinberg, "Leading the Counter-Revolution."

87. See Margaret Coker and Farnaz Fassihi, "Iran, Saudi Arabia Tensions Spur Fears of a Proxy War," *Wall Street Journal*, 17 March 2011; and, more broadly, "GCC Protests at Iranian Cleric's 'False' Bahrain Claims," *Agence France-Presse* (Riyadh), 19 July 2011.

88. In the Sultanate of Oman, the state religion is Ibadism, a form of Islam distinct from Sunni and Shia denominations. See Wilkinson, *Ibadism*.

89. See Holmes, "Base that Replaced the British Empire," 20–37.

90. This figure was reported by the Syrian Observatory for Human Rights, noting that "nearly half of them [the dead] were civilians" and that the real figure was "probably much higher." See "Syria Death Toll Now Exceeds 210,000, Says Rights Group," *Reuters* (Amman), 7 February 2015.

91. This section draws on Zoltan Barany, "General Failure in Syria: Without the Officers' Support, the Insurgents Can't Win," *Foreign Affairs*, 17 July

2013, available at www.foreignaffairs.com/articles/139585/zoltan-barany
/general-failure-in-syria.

92. See, for instance, Zisser, "Syrian Army," 1–12.

93. See, for instance, Landis, "Syrian Uprising," 73.

94. These figures are from Steven Heydemann in Ziadeh et al., "Crisis in
Syria," 15.

95. See, for instance, Droz-Vincent, "'State of Barbary,'" 40–41.

96. See Friedman, "Hama Rules," chapter 4, esp. 77–87.

97. Alawites are often described as a branch of Shia Islam, though the question of their religious categorization is a complicated and somewhat fraught one.
For background, see Kramer, *Shi'ism, Resistance, and Revolution*, 237–54. See
also Batatu, "Some Observations," 331–44.

98. Noueihed and Warren, *Battle for the Arab Spring*, 230. See also Fildis,
"Roots of Alawite-Sunni," 148–56.

99. Roger Owen, *Rise and Fall*, 87. See also Amir Taheri, "The Lonely Dictator," *New York Post*, 15 August 2012.

100. Gelvin, *Arab Uprisings*, 110.

101. Landis, "Syrian Uprising," 73.

102. Author's interviews with US intelligence personnel (Washington, DC,
December 2012 and January 2013).

103. Pollack, *Arabs at War*, 551.

104. al-Gharbi, "Syria Contextualized," 60–61.

105. See Fulton, Holliday, and Wyer, *Iranian Strategy*; and Dexter Filkins,
"Shadow Commander: Qassem Suleimani, the Middle East's Most Powerful Operative," *New Yorker*, 30 September 2013, 63–69.

106. Dexter Filkins, "The Thin Red Line," *New Yorker*, 13 May 2013, 45, 49.

107. Anshel Pfeffer, "Russian Military Aid to Syria: Burning Questions and
Answers," *Haaretz*, 19 May 2013.

108. See "The Battle for Syria," *Frontline*, PBS (September 18, 2012); Pfeffer,
"Russian Military Aid,"; "Why Is Russia Still Arming Syria?," *New York Times*,
21 May 2013.

109. al-Gharbi, "Syria Contextualized," 61.

110. See, for instance, Liz Sly, "On Third Anniversary of Syrian Rebellion,
Assad Is Steadily Winning the War," *Washington Post*, 14 March 2014; and, more
broadly, Hinnebusch, "Syria," 95–113.

111. See, for instance, Bahri, "Socioeconomic Foundations," 129–43; and
Matthiesen, *Sectarian Gulf*, 6–7, 12–13.

112. See, for instance, Dexter Filkins, "The Shadow Commander: Qassem
Suleimani, the Middle East's Most Powerful Operative," *New Yorker*, 30 September 2013, 63–69; Sullivan, *Hezbollah in Syria*; and Allison, "Russia and Syria,"
795–823.

113. See Yom and Gause, "Resilient Royals," 74–88.

114. Barany, "After the Arab Spring," 89–101.

115. Worrall, "Oman," 100–102.

116. Author's confidential interviews with Omani military personnel (Muscat, 9 December 2012).

117. Valeri, "Oman," 155–56.

118. Author's interview with US military personnel (Muscat, 10 December 2012).

119. Author's interview with Professor Abdallah Saaf at Mohamed V University (Rabat, 9 April 2012).

120. Interview with Professor Driss Maghraoui (Ifrane, Morocco, 18 April 2012).

121. "Message de fidélité et de loyalisme à S. M. du général de corps d'armée Housni Benslimane," *Le Matin* (Rabat), 22 April 2009.

122. James N. Sater, "Morocco's 'Arab' Spring," *Middle East Institute*, 1 October 2011.

123. Benchemsi, "Morocco," 58.

124. Author's confidential interviews (Rabat and Ifrane, Morocco, April 2012).

125. Interview with Abdallah Saaf.

126. Karam Souhail, "Moroccan Army Promised Better Deal after Protests," *Reuters* (Rabat), 7 February 2012; and author's interviews with protesting veterans (Rabat, April 2012).

Conclusion

1. Barany, "Unrest and State Response," 20.

2. In Iran, for instance, there was no riot police force in 1978–79. Confidential interview (Paris, December 2011).

3. See Hill and Nonneman, "Yemen, Saudi Arabia."

4. Confidential interviews in Tunis (December 2011), Bahrain (December 2012), and Washington, D.C. (December 2012–January 2013).

5. Bueno de Mesquita and Smith, *Dictator's Handbook*, 27.

6. Even as I write this (March 2015), four years after the tentative and highly reversible democratization process began in Burma, there is ample reason to believe that the generals' will not soon give up their control of Burmese politics. See my "Exits from Military Rule," 86–100.

7. Barany, "General Failure in Syria."

Bibliography

The bibliography includes all cited sources with the exception of daily newspaper articles which appear in the endnotes. All entries appear once, including those with overlapping relevance.

GENERAL, METHODOLOGICAL, AND THEORETICAL

Adelman, Jeremy. *Worldly Philosopher: The Odyssey of Albert O. Hirschman.* Princeton, NJ: Princeton University Press, 2013.

Adelman, Jonathan R. *Revolution, Armies, and War.* Boulder, CO: Lynne Rienner, 1985.

Amann, Peter. "Revolution: A Redefinition." *Political Science Quarterly* 77:1 (March 1962): 36–53.

Andrzejewski, Stanislaw. *Military Organization and Society.* London: Routledge & Kegan Paul, 1954.

Aya, Rod. "Theories of Revolution Reconsidered." *Theory and Society* 8:1 (July 1979): 39–99.

Barany, Zoltan. *The Soldier and the Changing State: Building Democratic Armies in Africa, Asia, Europe, and the Americas.* Princeton, NJ: Princeton University Press, 2012.

———. "Armies and Revolutions." *Journal of Democracy* 24:3 (April 2013): 62–76.

Brinton, Crane. *The Anatomy of Revolution.* New York: Vintage, 1965 [1938].

Buchanan, Allen. "Political Legitimacy and Democracy." *Ethics* 112:4 (July 2002): 689–719.

Bueno de Mesquita, Bruce. *The Predictioneer's Game.* New York: Random House, 2010.

Bueno de Mesquita, Bruce, and Alastair Smith. *The Dictator's Handbook: Why Bad Behavior Is Almost Always Good Politics.* New York: Public Affairs, 2011.

Castillo, Jasen J. *Endurance and War: The National Sources of Military Cohesion.* Stanford, CA: Stanford University Press, 2014.

Chenoweth, Erica, and Maria J. Stephan. *Why Civil Resistance Works: The Strategic Logic of Nonviolent Conflict.* New York: Columbia University Press, 2011.

Chirot, Daniel. *Modern Tyrants: The Power and Prevalence of Evil in Our Age.* Princeton, NJ: Princeton University Press, 1996.

Chorley, Katherine. *Armies and the Art of Revolution.* London: Faber & Faber, 1943.

Collier, David, and James Mahoney. "Insights and Pitfalls: Selection Bias in Qualitative Research." *World Politics* 49:1 (October 1996): 56–91.

Cuoco, Vincenzo. *Historical Essay on the Neapolitan Revolution of 1799* (1801). Translated by David Gibbons. Toronto: University of Toronto Press, 2014.

Dahl, Robert A. *Polyarchy: Participation and Opposition.* New Haven, CT: Yale University Press, 1971.

DeFronzo, James. *Revolutions and Revolutionary Movements*. Boulder, CO: Westview Press, 2014.

de Tocqueville, Alexis. *The Old Regime and the Revolution*. Translated by John Bonner. New York: Harper & Brothers, 1856.

Ellis, John. *Armies in Revolution*. New York: Oxford University Press, 1974.

Engels, Friedrich, and Karl Marx. *On the Paris Commune*. Moscow: Progress Publishers, 1971.

Gandhi, Jennifer. *Political Institutions under Dictatorship*. New York: Cambridge University Press, 2008.

George, Alexander L., and Andrew Bennett. *Case Studies and Theory Development in the Social Sciences*. Cambridge, MA: MIT Press, 2005.

Gerring, John. *Case Study Research: Principles and Practices*. New York: Cambridge University Press, 2007.

Goldfrank, Walter L. "Theories of Revolution and Revolution without Theory." *Theory and Society* 7:1–2 (July–October 1979): 135–65.

Goldstone, Jack A. "Theories of Revolution: The Third Generation." *World Politics* 32:3 (April 1980): 425–53.

———. *Revolutions: Theoretical, Comparative, and Historical Studies*. New York: Harcourt Brace, 1986.

———. *Revolution and Rebellion in the Early Modern World*. Berkeley: University of California Press, 1991.

———. "Understanding the Revolutions of 2011." *Foreign Affairs* 90:3 (May–June 2011): 8–16.

———. "Cross-class Coalitions and the Making of the Arab Revolts of 2011." *Swiss Political Science Review* 17:4 (December 2011): 457–62.

———. *Revolutions: A Very Short Introduction*. New York: Oxford University Press, 2014.

Goodwin, Jeff. *No Other Way Out: States and Revolutionary Movements, 1945–1991*. New York: Cambridge University Press, 2001.

Goodwin, Jeff, and Theda Skocpol. "Explaining Revolutions in the Contemporary Third World." *Politics and Society* 17:4 (December 1989): 488–509.

Gurr, Ted Robert. *Why Men Rebel*. Princeton, NJ: Princeton University Press, 1970.

———. "The Revolution—Social-Change Nexus: Some Old Theories and New Hypotheses." *Comparative Politics* 5:3 (April 1973): 359–92.

Hamilton, Richard. *Who Voted for Hitler?* Princeton, NJ: Princeton University Press, 1982.

Hatto, Arthur. "'Revolution': An Enquiry Into the Usefulness of an Historical Term," *Mind: A Quarterly Review of Philosophy*, n. s., 58:232 (October 1949): 495–517.

Himmelstein, Jerome L., and Michael S. Kimmel. "States and Revolutions: The Implications and Limits of Skocpol's Structural Model." *American Journal of Sociology* 86:5 (March 1981): 1145–54.

Hirschman, Albert O. "Is the End of the Cold War a Disaster for the Third World?" In Albert O. Hirschman, *A Propensity to Self-Subversion*, 189–96. Cambridge, MA: Harvard University Press, 1995.

Hopper, Rex D. "The Revolutionary Process." *Social Forces* 28:3 (March 1950): 270–79.

Huntington, Samuel P. *The Soldier and the State*. Cambridge, MA: Harvard University Press, 1957.

———. *Political Order in Changing Societies*. New Haven, CT: Yale University Press, 1968.

Janos, Andrew C. "Authority and Violence." *Internal War: Problems and Approaches*, edited by Harry Eckstein, 130–41. New York: Free Press, 1964.

Jones, Milo, and Philippe Silberzahn. *Constructing Cassandra: Reframing Intelligence Failure at the CIA, 1947–2001*. Stanford, CA: Stanford University Press, 2013.

Kraminick, Isaac. "Reflections on Revolution: Definition and Explanation in Recent Scholarship." *History and Theory* 11:1 (February 1972): 26–63.

Kuran, Timur. "Sparks and Prairie Fires: A Theory of Unanticipated Political Revolution." *Public Choice* 61:1 (April 1989): 41–74.

———. "The East European Revolutions of 1989: Is It Surprising that We Are Surprised?" *American Economic Review* 81:2 (May 1991): 121–25.

———. "Now out of Never: The Element of Surprise in the East European Revolution of 1989." *World Politics* 44:1 (October 1991): 7–48.

Lasswell, Harold D. "The Garrison State" *American Journal of Sociology* 46:4 (January 1941): 455–68.

Lee, Terence. "Military Cohesion and Regime Maintenance: Explaining the Role of the Military in 1989 China and 1998 Indonesia." *Armed Forces & Society* 32:1(October 2005): 80–104.

Lefever, Ernest W. *Spear and Specter: Army, Police, and Politics in Tropical Africa*. Washington, DC: Brookings Institution Press, 1970.

Lehrke, Jesse Paul. "A Cohesion Model to Assess Military Arbitration of Revolutions." *Armed Forces & Society* 40:1 (January 2014): 146–67.

Lenin, V. I. "Lecture on the 1905 Revolution." Vol. 23, *Collected Works*. Moscow: Progress Publishers, 1964.

Lipset, Seymour Martin. "Some Social Requisites of Democracy: Economic Development and Political Legitimacy." *American Political Science Review* 53:1 (March 1959): 69–105.

Lipset, Seymour Martin, and György Bence. "Anticipations of the Failure of Communism." *Theory and Society* 23:2 (April 1994): 169–210.

Marcuse, Herbert. "Re-Examination of the Concept of Revolution." *New Left Review* 56:1 (July–August 1969): 27–34.

Marx, Axel, Benoît Rihoux, and Charles Ragin. "The Origins, Development, and Application of Qualitative Comparative Analysis: The First 25 Years." *European Political Science Review* 6:1 (February 2014): 115–42.

McFaul, Michael. "Transitions from Postcommunism." *Journal of Democracy* 16:3 (July 2005): 5–19.

McLauchlin, Theodore. "Loyalty Strategies and Military Defection in Rebellion." *Comparative Politics* 42:3 (April 2010): 333–50.

Merriman, John. *Massacre: The Life and Death of the Paris Commune*. New York: Basic Books, 2014).

Nagel, Thomas. "Moral Conflict and Political Legitimacy." *Philosophy and Public Affairs* 16:3 (Summer 1987): 215–40.

Owens, Mackubin Thomas. *U.S. Civil-Military Relations after 9/11: Renegotiating the Civil-Military Bargain*. New York: Continuum, 2011.

Peled, Alon. *A Question of Loyalty: Military Manpower Policy in Multiethnic States.* Ithaca, NY: Cornell University Press, 1998.

Pereira, Anthony W. *Authoritarianism and the Rule of Law in Brazil, Chile, and Argentina.* Pittsburgh, PA: University of Pittsburgh Press, 2005.

Pion-Berlin, David, Diego Esparza, and Kevin Grisham. "Staying Quartered: Civilian Uprisings and Military Disobedience in the Twenty-First Century." *Comparative Political Studies* 47:2 (February 2014): 230–59.

Pipes, Richard. "The Fall of the Soviet Union." In *The Collapse of Communism*, edited by Lee Edwards, 35–49. Stanford, CA: Hoover Institution Press, 1999.

Rihoux, Benoît, and Charles C. Ragin, eds. *Configurational Comparative Methods: Qualitative Comparative Analysis (QCA) and Related Techniques.* Thousand Oaks, CA: Sage, 2009.

Russell, D. E. H. *Rebellion, Revolution, and Armed Force.* New York: Academic Press, 1974.

Schock, Kurt. *Unarmed Insurrections: People Power Movements in Nondemocracies.* Minneapolis: University of Minnesota Press, 2005.

Shils, Edward A., and Morris Janowitz. "Cohesion and Disintegration in the Wehrmacht in World War II." *Public Opinion Quarterly* 12:2 (Summer 1948): 280–315.

Siebold, Guy L. "The Essence of Military Group Cohesion." *Armed Forces & Society* 33:2 (January 2007): 286–95.

———. "The Misconceived Construct of Task Cohesion." *Armed Forces & Society* 41:1 (January 2015): 163–67.

Sikkink, Kathryn. *The Justice Cascade: How Human Rights Prosecutions Are Changing World Politics.* New York: Norton, 2011.

Silver, Nate. *The Signal and the Noise: Why So Many Predictions Fail—But Some Don't.* New York: Penguin, 2012.

Skocpol, Theda. *States and Social Revolutions: A Comparative Analysis of France, Russia and China.* New York: Cambridge University Press, 1979.

Stone, Lawrence. "Theories of Revolution." *World Politics* 18:2 (January 1966): 159–76.

Tetlock, Philip, Barbara Mellers, Eric Stone, Pavel Atanasov, Nick Rohrbaugh, S. Emlen Metz, Lyle Ungar, Michael M. Bishop, Michael Horowitz, and Ed Merkle. "The Psychology of Intelligence Analysis: Drivers of Prediction Accuracy in World Politics." *Journal of Experimental Psychology: Applied* 21:1 (2015): 1–14.

Tilly, Charles. "The Analysis of a Counter-Revolution." *History and Theory* 3:1 (1963): 30–58.

———. "Does Modernization Breed Revolution?" *Comparative Politics* 5:3 (April 1973): 425–47.

———. *From Mobilization to Revolution.* New York: McGraw-Hill, 1978.

———. *European Revolutions, 1492–1992.* New York: Wiley-Blackwell, 1996.

Tilly, Charles, and James Rule. *Measuring Political Upheaval.* Monograph No. 19. Princeton, NJ: Center for International Studies Research, 1965.

Tombs, Robert. *The War against Paris 1871.* Cambridge, UK: Cambridge University Press, 1981.

Walt, Stephen M. *Revolution and War.* Ithaca, NY: Cornell University Press, 1996.

Weatherford, M. Stephen. "Measuring Political Legitimacy." *American Political Science Review* 86:1 (March 1992): 149–66.

Weyland, Kurt. "The Diffusion of Revolution: '1848' in Europe and Latin America." *International Organization* 63:3 (July 2009): 391–23.

———. *Making Waves: Democratic Contention in Europe and Latin America since the Revolutions of 1848*. New York: Cambridge University Press, 2014.

Zagorin, Perez. "Theories of Revolution in Contemporary Historiography." *Political Science Quarterly* 88:1 (March 1973): 23–52.

Zimmermann, Ekkart. *Political Violence, Crises and Revolutions: Theories and Research*. London: Routledge, 2013.

IRAN

Abrahamian, Ervand. *Iran between Two Revolutions*. Princeton, NJ: Princeton University Press, 1982.

———. *A History of Modern Iran*. New York: Cambridge University Press, 2008.

Afkhami, Gholam R. *The Iranian Revolution: Thanatos on a National Scale*. Washington, DC: Middle East Institute, 1985.

———. *The Life and Times of the Shah*. Berkeley: University of California Press, 2009.

Allen, Calvin H., and W. Lynn Rigsbee. *Oman under Qaboos: From Coup to Constitution, 1970–1996*. London: Routledge, 2000.

Arjomand, Said Amir. *The Turban for the Crown: The Islamic Revolution of Iran*. Oxford, UK: Oxford University Press, 1989.

Axworthy, Michael. *A History of Iran: Empire of the Mind*. New York: Basic Books, 2008.

———. *Revolutionary Iran: A History of the Islamic Republic*. Oxford: Oxford University Press, 2013.

Bar-Joseph, Uri. "Forecasting a Hurricane: Israeli and American Estimations of the Khomeini Revolution." *Journal of Strategic Studies* 36:5 (October 2013): 718–42.

Bayne, E. A. *Persian Kingship in Transition*. New York: American Universities Field Staff, 1968.

Bill, James A. *The Eagle and the Lion: The Tragedy of American-Iranian Relations*. New Haven, CT: Yale University Press, 1988.

Bill, James A., and Carl Leiden. *Politics in the Middle East*. Boston, MA: Little, Brown & Co., 1984 [2nd ed].

Brzezinski, Zbigniew. *Power and Principle: Memoirs of the National Security Adviser, 1977–1981*. New York: Farrar, Straus, Giroux, 1983.

Buchan, James. *Days of God: The Revolution in Iran and Its Consequences*. London: John Murray, 2012.

Carter, Jimmy. "Tehran, Iran Toasts of the President and the Shah at a State Dinner." Speech, 31 December 1977. Gerhard Peters and John T. Woolley. *The American Presidency Project*. Accessed on 11 May 2014 at http://www.presidency.ucsb.edu/ws/?pid=7080.

———. *Keeping Faith: Memoirs of a President*. New York: Bantham, 1982.

Cooper, Andrew Scott. *The Oil Kings: How the U.S., Iran, and Saudi Arabia Changed the Balance of Power in the Middle East*. New York: Simon & Schuster, 2011.

de Bellaigue, Christopher. *Patriot of Persia: Muhammad Mossadegh and a Tragic Anglo-American Coup*. New York: Harper Perennial, 2013.

de Bellaigue, Christopher, and Ray Takeyh. "Coupdunnit." *Foreign Affairs* 93:5 (September–October 2014): 163–67.

Eisenstadt, Michael. "Iran's Islamic Revolution: Lessons for the Arab Spring of 2011." *Strategic Forum* 267 (April 2011): 1–11.

Entessar, Nader. "The Military and Politics in the Islamic Republic of Iran." In *Post-Revolutionary Iran*, edited by Hooshang Amirahmadi and Manoucher Parvin, 56–74. Boulder, CO: Westview Press, 1988.

Fischer, Michael M. J. *Iran: From Religious Dispute to Revolution*. Madison: University of Wisconsin Press, 2003.

Ganji, Manouchehr. *Defying the Iranian Revolution*. Westport, CT: Praeger, 2002.

Gharabaghi, Abbas. *Verites sur la crise iranienne*. Paris: La Pensee universelle, 1985.

Graham, Robert. *Iran: The Illusion of Power*. New York: St. Martin's Press, 1979.

Halpern, Manfred. *The Politics of Social Change in the Middle East and North Africa*. Princeton, NJ: Princeton University Press, 1963.

Hashim, Ahmed. "The Iranian Armed Forces in Politics, Revolution, and War: Part Two." *Middle East Policy* 19:3 (Fall 2012): 65–83.

Huyser, Robert E. *Mission to Tehran*. New York: Harper & Row, 1986.

Jervis, Robert L. *Why Intelligence Fails: Lessons from the Iranian Revolution and the Iraq War*. Ithaca, NY: Cornell University Press, 2010.

Kadivar, Cyrus. "A Question of Numbers." *Iranian Voice*. Accessed on 6 January 2014. http://www.emadbaghi.com/en/archives/000592.php#more.

Kamrava, Mehran. *Revolution in Iran: The Roots of Turmoil*. London: Routledge, 1990.

Kapuściński, Ryszard. *Shah of Shahs*. New York: Vintage, 1992.

Keddie, Nikki R. *Modern Iran: Roots and Results of Revolution*. New Haven, CT: Yale University Press, 2003.

Klare, Michael T. *American Arms Supermarket*. Austin: University of Texas Press, 1984.

Kurzman, Charles. "Structural Opportunity and Perceived Opportunity in Social Movement Theory: The Iranian Revolution of 1979." *American Sociological Review* 61 (February 1996): 153–70.

———. *The Unthinkable Revolution in Iran*. Cambridge, MA: Harvard University Press, 2004.

Litwak, Robert. *Détente and the Nixon Doctrine: American Foreign Policy and the Pursuit of Stability*. New York: Cambridge University Press, 1984.

Mackey, Sandra. *The Iranians: Persia, Islam, and the Soul of a Nation*. New York: Dutton, 1996.

McDaniel, Tim. *Autocracy, Modernization, and Revolution in Russia and Iran*. Princeton, NJ: Princeton University Press, 1991.

Milani, Abbas. *The Shah*. New York: Palgrave Macmillan, 2011.

Mirfakhraei, Hooshmand. "The Imperial Iranian Armed Forces and the Revolution of 1978–1979." PhD diss., State University of New York at Buffalo, 1984.

Nahavandi, Houshang. *Carnets Secrets: Chute et mort du Shah*. Paris: Editions Osmondes, 2003.

Owen, Roger. *State, Power, and Politics in the Making of the Modern Middle East*. New York: Routledge, 2004 [3rd ed.].

Pahlavi, Mohamed Reza. *Answer to History*. New York: Stein & Day, 1980.

Parsons, Anthony. *The Pride and the Fall: Iran 1974–1979*. London: Jonathan Cape, 1984.

Peterson, J. E. *Oman's Insurgencies: The Sultanate's Struggle for Supremacy*. Beirut: Saqi, 2007.

Ramazani, R. K. "Who Lost America? The Case of Iran." *Middle East Journal* 36:1 (Winter 1982): 5–21.

Roosevelt, Kermit. *Countercoup: The Struggle for the Control of Iran*. New York: McGraw-Hill, 1971.

Rose, Gregory F. "The Post-Revolutionary Purge of Iran's Armed Forces: A Revisionist Assessment." *Iranian Studies* 17:2–3 (Spring/Summer 1984): 153–94.

Rubin, Barry. *Paved with Good Intentions: The American Experience in Iran*. Oxford: Oxford University Press, 1980.

Sick, Gary. *All Fall Down: America's Tragic Encounter with Iran*. New York: Random House, 1985.

Stempel, John. *Inside the Iranian Revolution*. Bloomington: Indiana University Press, 1981.

Sullivan, William H. *Mission to Iran*. New York: W. W. Norton, 1981.

Takeyh, Ray. "What Really Happened in Iran." *Foreign Affairs* 93:4 (July–August 2014): 2–13.

Vance, Cyrus R. *Hard Choices: Critical Years in America's Foreign Policy*. New York: Simon & Schuster, 1983.

Ward, Steven R. *Immortal: A Military History of Iran and Its Armed Forces*. Washington, DC: Georgetown University Press, 2009.

Zabih, Sepehr. *The Iranian Military in Revolution and War*. London: Routledge, 1985.

BURMA

Aung San Suu Kyi. "Speech to a Mass Rally at the Shwedagon Pagoda, August 26, 1988." In *Freedom from Fear and Other Writings*. New York: Penguin, 1995.

Barany, Zoltan. "Exits from Military Rule: Lessons for Burma." *Journal of Democracy* 26:2 (April 2015): 86–100.

Boudreau, Vincent. *Resisting Dictatorship: Repression and Protest in Southeast Asia*. New York: Cambridge University Press, 2004.

Callahan, Mary P. "Myanmar's Perpetual Junta: Solving the Riddle of the Tatmadaw's Long Reign." *New Left Review* 60 (November–December 2009): 27–63.

———. "The Endurance of Military Rule in Burma: Not Why but Why Not?" In Levenstein, *Finding Dollars*, 54–76.

Charney, Michael W. *A History of Modern Burma*. New York: Cambridge University Press, 2009.

Chowdhury, Mridul. "The Role of the Internet in Burma's Saffron Revolution." Berkman Center for Internet & Society at Harvard University (September 2008): 1–17.

Coclanis, Peter A. "The Myanmar Moment? Why Washington Made Its Move." *World Affairs* 174:5 (January/February 2012): 89–95.

Dittmer, Lowell. "Burma vs. Myanmar: What's in a Name?" *Asian Survey* 48:6 (November–December 2008): 885–88.

Egreteau, Renaud, and Larry Jagan. *Back to Old Habits: Isolationism or the Self-Preservation of Burma's Military Regime.* Occasional Paper #8. Paris: IRASEC, 2008.

Farrelly, Nicholas. "Discipline without Democracy: Military Dominance in Post-Colonial Burma." *Australian Journal of International Affairs* 67:3 (June 2013): 312–26.

Fenichel, Allen, and Azfar Khan. "The Burmese Way to 'Socialism.'" *World Development* 9:9–10 (September–October 1981): 813–24.

Finer, Samuel E. *The Man on Horseback.* London: Pall Mall, 1962.

Fink, Christina. "The Moment of the Monks: Burma, 2007." In *Civil Resistance and Power Politics: The Experience of Non-Violent Action from Gandhi to the Present,* edited by Adam Roberts and Timothy Garton Ash, 354–70. Oxford: Oxford University Press, 2009.

———. *Living in Silence in Burma: Surviving under Military Rule.* London: Zed Books, 2010 [2nd ed.].

Gombrich, Richard F. *Theravāda Buddhism: A Social History from Ancient Benares to Modern Colombo.* London: Routledge, 2006.

Harvey, G. E. *History of Burma: From the Earliest Times to 10 March 1824.* London: Frank Cass & Co., 1925.

Jagan, Larry. "Myanmar's Military Mindset Intensifies Internal Conflicts." In Raghavan, *Internal Conflicts in Myanmar,* 217–44.

Kaufman, Daniel, Aart Kraay, and Massimo Mastruzzi. "Governance Matters IV: Governance Indicators for 1996–2004." Washington, DC: World Bank Policy Research Paper #3630, 2005.

Larkin, Emma. *Finding George Orwell in Burma.* New York: Penguin, 2005.

———. *Everything is Broken: A Tale of Catastrophe in Burma.* New York: Penguin, 2010.

Lemere, Maggie, and Zoe West, eds. *Nowhere to Be Home: Narratives from Survivors of Burma's Military Regime.* San Francisco, CA: McSweeney's, 2011.

Levenstein, Susan L., ed. *Finding Dollars, Sense, and Legitimacy in Burma.* Washington, DC: Woodrow Wilson International Center for Scholars, 2010.

Lintner, Bertil. *Outrage: Burma's Struggle for Democracy.* London: White Lotus, 1990.

Marshall, Andrew. *The Trouser People: A Story of Burma in the Shadow of Empire.* New York: Counterpoint, 2002.

Maung Aung Myoe. *Building the Tatmadaw: Myanmar Armed Forces since 1998.* Singapore: Institute of Southeast Asian Studies, 2009.

Maung Maung. *The 1988 Uprising in Burma.* New Haven, CT: Yale Southeast Asian Studies, 1999.

McCarthy, Stephen. "Overturning the Alms Bowl: The Price of Survival and the Consequences for Political Legitimacy in Burma." *Australian Journal of International Affairs* 62:3 (September 2008): 298–314.

McGowan, William. "Burmese Hell." *World Policy Journal* 10:2 (1993): 47–56.

Min Naing. *National Ethnic Groups in Myanmar*. Translated by Hpone Thant. Yangon: Thein Myint Win Press, 2000.

Min Zin. "Opposition Movements in Burma: The Question of Relevancy." In Levenstein, *Finding Dollars*, 77–94.

Mya Maung. *The Burma Road to Poverty*. New York: Praeger, 1991.

Nakanishi, Yoshihiro. *Strong Soldiers, Failed Revolution: The State and Military in Burma, 1962–88*. Singapore: NUS Press, 2013.

Nietupski, Paul. "Clothing: Buddhist Perspectives." In *Encyclopedia of Monasticism*. Vol. 2, edited by William P. Johnston, 307–9. London: Taylor & Francis, 2000.

Orwell, George. *Burmese Days: A Novel*. London: V. Gollancz, 1935.

Prager Nyein, Susanne. "Expanding Military, Shrinking Citizenry, and the New Constitution in Burma." *Journal of Contemporary Asia* 39:4 (2009): 638–48.

Raghavan, V. R., ed. *Internal Conflicts in Myanmar: Transnational Consequences*. New Delhi: Vij Books India, 2011.

Rogers, Benedict. "The Saffron Revolution: The Role of Religion in Burma's Movement for Peace and Democracy." *Totalitarian Movements and Political Religions* 9:1 (March 2008): 115–18.

Seekins, Donald M. "Myanmar in 2008: Hardship, Compounded." *Asian Survey* 49:1 (2009):166–73.

Selth, Andrew. *Burma's Armed Forces: Power without Glory*. Norwalk, CT: Eastbridge, 2002.

———. *Transforming the Tatmadaw: The Burmese Armed Forces since 1988*. Canberra: Strategic and Defence Studies Centre, Australian National University, 2006.

———. "Burma's 'Saffron Revolution' and the Limits of International Influence." *Australian Journal of International Affairs* 62:3 (September 2008): 281–97.

———. "Known Knowns and Known Unknowns: Measuring Myanmar's Military Capabilities." *Contemporary Southeast Asia* 31:2 (2009): 272–95.

———. "Myanmar's Police Forces: Coercion, Continuity, and Change." *Contemporary Southeast Asia* 34:1 (2012): 53–79.

Shen, Simon, and Paul Chi-yuen Chan. "Failure of the Saffron Revolution and Aftermath: Revisiting the Transitologist Assumption." *The Journal of Comparative Asian Development* 9:1 (2010): 31–57.

Silverstein, Josef. "Aung San Suu Kyi: Is She Burma's Woman of Destiny?" *Asian Survey* 30:10 (October 1990): 1007–19.

Smith, Martin. *Burma: Insurgency and the Politics of Ethnicity*. London: Zed Books, 1999 [rev. and updated ed.].

Steinberg, David I. "Aung San Suu Kyi and U.S. Policy toward Burma/Myanmar." *Journal of Current Southeast Asian Affairs* 29:3 (2010): 35–59.

———. *Burma/Myanmar: What Everyone Needs to Know*. New York: Oxford University Press, 2013 [2nd ed.].

Taylor, Robert H. "Stifling Change: The Army Remains in Command." In *Burma: Political Economy under Military Rule*, edited by Robert H. Taylor, 5–14. London: C. Hurst & Co., 2001.

———. *The State in Myanmar*. London: Hurst & Co., 2009.

Thant Myint-U. *The River of Lost Footsteps: A Personal History of Burma*. New York: Farrar, Straus, & Giroux, 2008.

Tilakaratne, Asanga. *Theravāda Buddhism: The View of the Elders*. Honolulu: University of Hawaii Press, 2012.

Tin Maung Maung Than. "Tatmadaw in Transition: Dealing with Internal Conflict." In Raghavan, *Internal Conflicts in Myanmar*, 13–37.

Wakeman, Carolyn, and San San Tin. *No Time for Dreams: Living in Burma under Military Rule*. Boulder, CO: Rowman & Littlefield, 2009.

Williams, David C. "Cracks in the Firmament of Burma's Military Government: From Unity through Coercion to Buying Support." *Third World Quarterly* 32:7 (2011): 1199–1215.

Win Min. "Looking Inside the Burmese Military." In *Burma or Myanmar? The Struggle for National Identity*, edited by Lowell Dittmer, 155–84. Singapore: World Scientific Publishing, 2010.

China and Eastern Europe

Barany, Zoltan. "The Bankruptcy of Hungarian Socialism." *Südost-Europa* 38:4 (April 1989): 191–213.

———. *Soldiers and Politics in Eastern Europe, 1945–90*. London: Macmillan, 1993.

Barany, Zoltan, and Louisa Vinton. "Breakthrough to Democracy: Elections in Poland and Hungary." *Studies in Comparative Communism* 23:2 (Summer 1990): 191–212.

Brook, Timothy. *Quelling the People: The Military Suppression of the Beijing Democracy Movement*. New York: Oxford University Press, 1992.

Bucur, Ambassador Ion. "The Possible Soviet Intervention in Romania." In *Making the History of 1989*, Item #204. Accessed 23 January 2014 at http://chnm.gmu.edu/1989/items/show/204.

Calhoun, Craig. "Revolution and Repression on Tiananmen Square." *Society* 26:6 (September 1989): 21–38.

Chen, Cheng. "Institutional Legitimacy of an Authoritarian State: China in the Mirror of Eastern Europe." *Problems of Post-Communism* 52:4 (July–August 2005): 3–13.

Chen, Jie, Yang Zhong, and Jan William Hillard. "The Level and Sources of Popular Support for China's Current Political Regime." *Communist and Post-Communist Studies* 30:1 (March 1997): 45–64.

Chirot, Daniel. "What Happened in Eastern Europe in 1989?" In *The Crisis of Leninism and the Decline of the Left: The Revolutions of 1989*, edited by Chirot, 3–32. Seattle: University of Washington Press, 1991.

Codrescu, Andrei. *The Hole in the Flag: A Romanian Exile's Story of Return and Revolution*. New York: Avon Books, 1991.

Crowther, William E. "'Ceausescuism' and Civil-Military Relations in Romania." *Armed Forces & Society* 15:2 (Winter 1989): 207–25.

Cunningham, Philip J. *Tiananmen Moon: Inside the Chinese Student Uprising of 1989*. Lanham, MD: Rowman & Littlefield, 2009.

Dale, Gareth. *The East German Revolution of 1989*. Manchester: Manchester University Press, 2006.

Deletant, Dennis. *Ceauşescu and the Securitate: Coercion and Dissent in Romania, 1965–1989*. London: C. Hurst & Co., 1996.

Dimitrov, Vesselin. *Bulgaria: The Uneven Transition*. London: Routledge, 2002.

Dreyer, June Teufel. "Deng Xiaoping and Modernization of the Chinese Military." *Armed Forces & Society* 14:2 (Winter 1988): 215–31.

———. "China after Tiananmen: The Role of the Military." *World Policy Journal* 6:4 (Fall 1989):647–55.

Farocki, Harun, and Andrei Ujică, dir. *Videograms of a Revolution*. Film. 1992.

Feigon, Lee. *China Rising: The Meaning of Tiananmen*. Chicago: Ivan R. Dee, 1990.

Gabányi, Anneli Ute. *The Ceausescu Cult: Propaganda and Power Policy in Communist Romania*. Bucharest: Romanian Cultural Foundation Publishing House, 2000.

Galloway, George, and Bob Wylie. *Downfall: The Ceauşescus and the Romanian Revolution*. London: Futura, 1991.

Gedmin, Jeffrey. *The Hidden Hand: Gorbachev and the Collapse of East Germany*. Washington, DC: American Enterprise Institute, 1992.

Gilberg, Trond. *Nationalism and Communism in Romania: The Rise and Fall of Ceauşescu's Personal Dictatorship*. Boulder, CO: Westview Press, 1991.

Greenfield, Meg. *Washington*. New York: Public Affairs, 2001.

Hall, Richard Andrew. "Theories of Collective Action and Revolution: Evidence from the Romanian Transition of December 1989." *Europe-Asia Studies* 52:6 (September 2000): 1069–93.

Han, Minzhu, ed. *Cries for Democracy: Writing and Speeches from the 1989 Chinese Democracy Movement*. Princeton, NJ: Princeton University Press, 1990.

Hirschman, Albert O. "Exit, Voice, and the Fate of the German Democratic Republic." *World Politics* 45:2 (January 1993): 173–202.

Ioan, Dan. *Teroriştii din '89: Probe prezentate şi comentate de un fost şef al Procuraturilor Militare*. Bucharest: Lucman, 2012.

Joffe, Ellis. "Party-Army Relations in China: Retrospect and Prospect." *China Quarterly* 146 (June 1996): 299–314.

Johnson, A. Ross, Robert W. Dean, and Alexander Alexiev. *East European Military Establishments: The Warsaw Pact Northern Tier*. Santa Monica, CA: Rand, 1980.

Kenney, Padraic. *A Carnival of Revolution: Central Europe 1989*. Princeton, NJ: Princeton University Press, 2002.

Kou, Chien-wen. "Why the Military Obeys the Party's Orders to Repress Popular Uprisings: The Chinese Military Crackdowns of 1989." *Issues & Studies* 36:6 (November/December 2000): 27–51.

Kramer, Mark. "Beyond the Brezhnev Doctrine: A New Era in Soviet-East European Relations?" *International Security* 14:3 (Winter 1989–90): 25–67.

———. "The Collapse of East European Communism and the Repercussions within the Soviet Union (Part 1)." *Journal of Cold War Studies* 5:4 (Fall 2003): 178–256.

Kuhn, Ekkehard. *Der Tag der Entscheidung: Leipzig, 9. Oktober 1989*. Berlin: Ullstein, 1992.

Lieberthal, Kenneth. *Governing China: From Revolution through Reform*. New York: Norton, 1995.

Lieven, Anatol. *The Baltic Revolution: Estonia, Latvia, Lithuania, and the Path to Independence*. New Haven, CT: Yale University Press, 1994.

Lim, Louisa. *The People's Republic of Amnesia: Tiananmen Revisited*. New York: Oxford University Press, 2014.

Lohmann, Susanne. "The Dynamics of Informational Cascades: The Monday Demonstrations in Leipzig, East Germany, 1989–91." *World Politics* 41:1 (October 1994): 42–101.

Maier, Charles S. *Dissolution: The Crisis of Communism and the End of East Germany*. Princeton, NJ: Princeton University Press, 1997.

McCauley, Martin. "Gorbachev, the GDR, and Germany." In *The German Revolution of 1989*, edited by Gert-Joachim Glaeßner and Ian Wallace, 172–91. Oxford, UK: Berg, 1992.

Michta, Andrew A. *Red Eagle: The Army in Polish Politics, 1944–1988*. Stanford, CA: Hoover Institution Press, 1989.

Mulvenon, James. "China: Conditional Compliance." In *Coercion and Governance: The Declining Political Role of the Military in Asia*, edited by Muthiah Alagappa, 317–35. Stanford, CA: Stanford University Press, 2001.

Nathan, Andrew J., and Perry Link, eds. *The Tiananmen Papers*. Compiled by Zhang Liang. New York: Public Affairs, 2001.

Pacepa, Ion Mihai. *Red Horizons: The True Story of Nicolae and Elena Ceauşescus' Crimes, Lifestyle, and Corruption*. Washington, DC: Regnery, 1990.

Petersen, Roger D. *Resistance and Rebellion: Lessons from Eastern Europe*. New York: Cambridge University Press, 2001.

Pfaff, Steven. *Exit-Voice Dynamics and the Collapse of East Germany: The Crisis of Leninism and the Revolution of 1989*. Durham, NC: Duke University Press, 2006.

Pryce-Jones, David. *The War that Never Was: The Fall of the Soviet Empire, 1985–1991*. London: Weidenfeld & Nicholson, 1995.

Rady, Martin. *Romania in Turmoil: A Contemporary History*. London: I. B. Tauris, 1992.

Rakowska-Harmstone, Teresa, Christopher D. Jones, John Jaworsky, Ivan Sylvain, and Zoltan Barany. *Warsaw Pact: The Question of Cohesion*. Ottawa: Department of National Defence, 1986.

Ratesh, Nestor. *Romania: The Entangled Revolution*. Westport, CT: Praeger, 1991.

Rice, Condoleezza. *The Soviet Union and the Czechoslovak Army, 1948–1983: Uncertain Allegiance*. Princeton, NJ: Princeton University Press, 1984.

Rolicki, Janusz. *Edward Gierek: Przerwana dekada*. Warsaw: BGW, 1990.

Roper, Steven D. "The Romanian Revolution from a Theoretical Perspective." *Communist and Post-Communist Studies* 27:4 (December 1994): 401–10.

Ross, Corey. *The East German Dictatorship: Problems and Perspectives in the Interpretation of the GDR*. New York: Oxford University Press, 2002.

Săraru, Dinu, with Victor Atanasie Stănculescu. *Generalul Revoluţiei cu piciorul în ghips*. Bucharest: Rao, 2005.

Sarotte, M. E. *1989: The Struggle to Create Post-Cold War Europe*. Princeton, NJ: Princeton University Press, 2009.

————. "China's Fear of Contagion: Tiananmen Square and the Power of the European Example." *International Security* 37:2 (Fall 2012): 156–82.

————. *The Collapse: The Accidental Opening of the Berlin Wall*. New York: Basic Books, 2014.

Sava, Constantin, and Constantin Monac. *Revoluția română din Decembrie 1989 retrăită prin documente și mărturii*. Bucharest: Axioma, 2001.

Savranskaya, Svetlana, Thomas S. Blanton, and Vladislav Martinovich Zubok. *The Peaceful End of the Cold War in Eastern Europe, 1989*. Budapest: Central European University Press, 2010.

Schönbohm, Jörg. *Two Armies and One Fatherland: The End of the Nationale Volksarmee*.Translated by Peter and Elfi Johnson. Providence, RI: Berghahn, 1996.

Scobell, Andrew. "Why the People's Army Fired on the People: The Chinese Military and Tiananmen." *Armed Forces & Society* 18:2 (Winter 1992): 193–213.

————. *China's Use of Military Force: Beyond the Great Wall and the Long March*. New York: Cambridge University Press, 2003.

Scurtu, Ioan. *The Romanian Revolution of December 1989 in International Context*. Bucharest: Redacția Publicațiilor pentru Străinătate, 2009.

Sebestyen, Victor. *Revolution 1989: The Fall of the Soviet Empire*. New York: Pantheon, 2008.

Segal, Gerald, and John Phipps. "Why Communist Armies Defend Their Parties." *Asian Survey* 30:10 (October 1990): 959–76.

Shambaugh, David. *Modernizing China's Military: Progress, Problems, and Prospects*. Berkeley: University of California Press, 2002.

Siani-Davies, Peter. *The Romanian Revolution of 1989*. Ithaca, NY: Cornell University Press, 2007.

Simon, Jeffrey. *NATO and the Czech and Slovak Republics: A Comparative Study in Civil-Military Relations*. Boulder, CO: Rowman & Littlefield, 2004.

Suciu, Titus. *Reportaj cu sufletul la gură*. Timișoara: Editura Facla, 1990.

Tismaneanu, Vladimir. *Stalinism for All Seasons: A Political History of Romanian Communism*. Berkeley: University of California Press, 2003.

Tőkés, Rudolf L. *Hungary's Negotiated Revolution: Economic Reform, Social Change, and Political Succession*. New York: Cambridge University Press, 1996.

Verona, Sergiu. *Military Occupation and Diplomacy: Soviet Troops in Romania, 1944–1958*. Durham, NC: Duke University Press, 1991.

Vogel, Ezra F. *Deng Xiaoping and the Transformation of China*. Cambridge, MA: Harvard University Press, 2011.

Völgyes, Iván. *The Political Reliability of the Warsaw Pact Armies: The Southern Tier*. Durham, NC: Duke Press Policy Studies, 1981.

Walder, Andrew G. "The Political Sociology of the Beijing Upheaval of 1989." *Problems of Communism* 38:5 (September–October 1989): 30–40.

Walder, Andrew G., and Gong Xiaoxia. "Workers in the Tiananmen Protests: The Politics of the Beijing Workers' Autonomous Federation." *Australian Journal of Chinese Affairs* 29 (January 1993): 1–29.

Watts, Larry L. "The Romanian Army in the December Revolution and Beyond." In *Romania after Tyranny*, edited by Daniel N. Nelson, 95–126. Boulder, CO: Westview Press, 1993.

———. "Civil-Military Relations: Continuity or Exceptionalism?" In *Romania Since 1989: Politics, Economics, and Society*, edited by Henry F. Carey, 523–51. Lanham, MD: Lexington Books, 2004.

Wiatr, Jerzy. *The Soldier and the Nation: The Role of the Military in Polish Politics, 1918–85*. Boulder, CO: Westview Press, 1988.

Wong, Gerrit W. "Tiananmen: Causes and Consequences." *Washington Quarterly* 13:1 (1990): 79–95.

Wu, Xinbo. "China: Security Practice of a Modernizing and Ascending Power." In *Asian Security Practice*, edited by Muthiah Alagappa, 115–56. Stanford, CA: Stanford University Press, 1998.

Wydra, Harald. "Revolution and Democracy: The European Experience." In *Revolution in the Making of the Modern World*, edited by John Foran, David Lane, and Andreja Zivkovic, 27–44. London: Routledge, 2008.

Yang, Guobin. "Achieving Emotions in Collective Action: Emotional Processes and Movement Mobilization in the 1989 Chinese Student Movement." *Sociological Quarterly* 41:4 (September 2000): 593–614.

Zhao, Dingxin. *The Power of Tiananmen: State-Society Relations and 1989 Beijing Student Movement*. Chicago: University of Chicago Press, 2001.

Zhao, Ziyang. *Prisoner of the State: The Secret Journal of Premier Zhao Ziyang*. New York: Simon & Schuster, 2009.

Zuo, Jiping, and Robert D. Benford. "Mobilization Processes and the 1989 Chinese Democracy Movement." *Sociological Quarterly* 36:1 (January 1995): 131–56.

The Middle East and North Africa

Albrecht, Holger. "The Myth of Coup-Proofing Risk: and Instances of Military Coups d'État in the Middle East and North Africa, 1950–2013." *Armed Forces & Society* 41:4 (October 2015): 659–87.

Albrecht, Holger, and Dina Bishara. "Back on Horseback: The Military and the Political Transformation in Egypt." *Middle East Law and Governance* 3:1–2 (2011): 13–23.

Allison, Roy. "Russia and Syria: Explaining Alignment with a Regime in Crisis." *International Affairs* 89:4 (July 2013): 795–823.

Asseburg, Muriel, ed. *Protest, Revolt, and Regime Change in the Arab World*. Berlin: Stiftung Wissenschaft und Politik, February 2012.

Bahri, Luayy. "The Socioeconomic Foundations of the Shiite Opposition in Bahrain." *Mediterranean Quarterly* 11:3 (Summer 2000): 129–143.

Barak, Oren, and Assaf David. "The Arab Security Sector: A New Research Agenda for a Neglected Topic." *Armed Forces & Society* 36:5 (October 2010): 804–24.

Barany, Zoltan. "Comparing the Arab Revolts: The Role of the Military." *Journal of Democracy* 22:4 (October 2011): 27–39.

———. "Unrest and State Response in Arab Monarchies." *Mediterranean Quarterly* 24:2 (Spring 2013): 5–38.

———. "General Failure in Syria: Without the Officers' Support, the Insurgents Can't Win." *Foreign Affairs*, 17 July 2013. Accessed on 7 June 2014 at www.foreignaffairs.com/articles/139585/zoltan-barany/general-failure-in-syria.

———. "After the Arab Spring: Revolt and Resilience in the Arab Kingdoms." *Parameters: The U.S. Army War College Quarterly* 43:2 (Summer 2013): 89–101.

Batatu, Hanna. "Some Observations on the Social Roots of Syria's Ruling Military Group and the Causes for Its Dominance." *Middle East Journal* 35 (Summer 1981): 331–44.

Bellin, Eva. "The Robustness of Authoritarianism in the Middle East: Exceptionalism in Comparative Perspective." *Comparative Politics* 36:2 (2004), 139–57

———. "Reconsidering the Robustness of Authoritarianism in the Middle East: Lessons from the Arab Spring." *Comparative Politics* 44:2 (January 2012): 127–51.

Benchemsi, Ahmed. "Morocco: Outfoxing the Opposition." *Journal of Democracy* 23:1 (January 2012): 57–69.

Borghard, Erica D., and Constantino Pischedda. "Allies and Airpower in Libya." *Parameters: Journal of the U.S. Army War College* 42:1 (Spring 2012): 63–74.

Brandt, Marieke. "The Irregulars of the Sa'ada War: 'Colonel Sheikhs' and 'Tribal Militias' in Yemen's Huthi Conflict (2004–2010)." In Lackner, ed. *Why Yemen Matters*, 105–22.

Brooks, Risa. "Abandoned at the Palace: Why the Tunisian Military Defected from the Ben Ali Regime in January 2011." *Journal of Strategic Studies* 36:2 (April 2013): 205–20.

Brownlee, Jason, Tarek Masoud, and Andrew Reynolds. *The Arab Spring: Pathways of Repression and Reform*. New York: Oxford University Press, 2015.

Cambanis, Thanassis. *Once Upon a Revolution: An Egyptian Story*. New York: Simon & Schuster, 2015.

Carapico, Sheila. *Civil Society in Yemen*. New York: Cambridge University Press, 1998.

Clark, Victoria. *Yemen: Dancing on the Heads of Snakes*. New Haven, CT: Yale University Press, 2010.

Cole, Peter, and Brian McQuinn, eds. *The Libyan Revolution and Its Aftermath*. New York: Oxford University Press, 2015.

Cook, Steven A. *The Struggle for Egypt: From Nasser to Tahrir Square*. New York: Oxford University Press, 2012.

Dresch, Paul. *A History of Modern Yemen*. New York: Cambridge University Press, 2000.

Droz-Vincent, Philippe. "'State of Barbary' (Take Two): From the Arab Spring to the Return of Violence in Syria." *Middle East Journal* 68:1 (Winter 2014): 33–58.

———. "The Military amidst Uprisings and Transitions in the Arab World." In Gerges, *New Middle East*, 180–208.

Dunne, Tim, and Jeff Gifkins. "Libya and the State of Intervention." *Australian Journal of International Affairs* 65:5 (2011): 515–29.

Fildis, Ayse Tekdal. "Roots of Alawite-Sunni Rivalry in Syria." *Middle East Policy* 19:2 (Summer 2012): 148–56.

Friedman, Thomas L. *From Beirut to Jerusalem*. New York: Farrar, Straus, & Giroux, 1989.

Fulton, Will, Joseph Holliday, and Sam Wyer. *Iranian Strategy in Syria*. Washington, DC: Institute for the Study of War and American Enterprise Institute, May 2013.

Gana, Nouri, ed. *The Making of the Tunisian Revolution: Contexts, Architects, Prospects.* Edinburgh, UK: Edinburgh University Press, 2013.

Gaub, Florence. "The Libyan Armed Forces between Coup-Proofing and Repression." *Journal of Strategic Studies* 36:2 (April 2013): 221–44.

Gause, F. Gregory, III. "Why Middle East Studies Missed the Arab Spring." *Foreign Affairs* 90:4 (July–August 2011): 81–90.

Gelvin, James L. *The Arab Uprisings.* New York: Oxford University Press, 2012.

Gengler, Justin J. "Royal Factionalism, the Khawalid, and the Securitization of the 'Shi'a' Problem' in Bahrain." *Journal of Arabian Studies* 3:1 (June 2013): 53–79.

Gerges, Fawaz A., ed. *The New Middle East: Protest and Revolution in the Arab World.* New York: Cambridge University Press, 2014.

al-Gharbi, Musa. "Syria Contextualized: The Numbers Game." *Middle East Policy* 20:1 (Spring 2013): 56–67.

Ghonim, Wael. *Revolution 2.0: The Power of the People Is Greater than the People in Power: A Memoir.* New York: Houghton Mifflin, 2012.

Harb, Imad. "The Egyptian Military in Politics: Disengagement or Accommodation?" *Middle East Journal* 57:2 (Spring 2003): 269–90.

Hertog, Steffen. "Rentier Militaries in the Gulf: The Price of Coup-Proofing." *International Journal of Middle East Studies* 43:3 (August 2011): 400–402.

Hill, Ginny, and Gerd Nonneman. "Yemen, Saudi Arabia, and the Gulf States: Elite Politics, Street Protests, and Regional Diplomacy." Chatham House (London) Transcript, 12 May 2011. Last accessed on 5 October 2014 at http://www.chathamhouse.org/sites/files/chathamhouse/public/Meetings/Meeting%20Transcripts/120511yemen.pdf.

Hinnebusch, Raymond. "Syria: From 'Authoritarian Upgrading' to Revolution?" *International Affairs* 88:1 (January 2012): 95–113.

Holmes, Amy Austin. "The Base that Replaced the British Empire: De-Democratization and the American Navy in Bahrain." *Journal of Arabian Studies* 4:1 (June 2014): 20–37.

Hroub, Khalid. "Qatar and the Arab Spring—Conflict & International Politics." Berlin: Heinrich Böll Stiftung, 3 March 2014. Accessed on 21 August 2014 at http://lb.boell.org/en/2014/03/03/qatar-and-arab-spring-conflict-intl-politics.

Kamrava, Mehran. "Military Professionalization and Civil-Military Relations in the Middle East." *Political Science Quarterly* 115:1 (Spring 2000): 67–92.

———. "The Arab Spring and the Saudi-Led Counterrevolution." *Orbis* 56:1 (Winter 2012): 96–104.

Kandil, Hazem. *Soldiers, Spies, and Statesmen: Egypt's Road to Revolt.* London: Verso, 2012.

Katzman, Kenneth. "Bahrain: Reform, Security, and U.S. Policy." Washington, DC: Congressional Research Service, 21 March 2011 (7-5700, 95-1013).

Ketchley, Neil. "'The Army and the People are One Hand!' Fraternization and the 25th January Egyptian Revolution." *Comparative Studies in Society and History* 56:1 (January 2014): 155–86.

Knights, Michael. "The Military Role in Yemen's Protests: Civil-Military Relations in the Tribal Republic." *Journal of Strategic Studies* 36:2 (April 2013): 261–88.

Korany, Bahgat, and Rabab El-Mahdi, eds. *The Arab Spring in Egypt: Revolution and Beyond.* Oxford, UK: Oxford University Press, 2012.

Kramer, Martin, ed. *Shi'ism, Resistance, and Revolution.* Boulder, CO: Westview Press, 1987.

Lacher Wolfram. "Libya after Qadhafi: State Formation or State Collapse?" *SWP Comments* #9, March 2011, 1–8; available at www.swp-berlin.org/fileadmin /contents/products/comments/2011C09_lac_ks.pdf.

———. "Regional Repercussion of Revolution and Civil War in Libya." In Asseburg, *Protest, Revolt, and Regime Change,* 47–51.

Lacher, Wolfram, and Ahmed Labnouj. "Factionalism Resurgent: The War in the Jabal Nafusa." In Cole and McQuinn, *Libyan Revolution,* 257–84.

Lackner, Helen, ed. *Why Yemen Matters: A Society in Transition.* London: Saqi Books, 2014.

Landis, Joshua. "The Syrian Uprising of 2011: Why the Assad Regime is Likely to Survive to 2013." *Middle East Policy* 19:1 (Spring 2012): 72–84.

Louër, Laurence. "Sectarianism and Coup-Proofing Strategies in Bahrain." *Journal of Strategic Studies* 36:2 (April 2013): 245–60.

Lucas, Russell E. "Monarchical Authoritarianism: Survival and Political Liberalization in a Middle Eastern Regime Type." *International Journal of Middle East Studies* 36:1 (February 2004): 103–19.

Lutterbeck, Derek. "Arab Uprisings and Armed Forces: Between Openness and Resistance." DCAF (Geneva Centre for the Democratic Control of Armed Forces), SSR Paper 2 (2011), 68 pp.

———. "Arab Uprisings, Armed Forces, and Civil-Military Relations." *Armed Forces & Society* 39:1 (January 2013): 28–52.

al-Marashi, Ibrahim. "Iraq's Security and Intelligence Network: A Guide and Analysis." *Middle East Review of International Affairs* 6:3 (September 2002). Accessed on 21 August 2014 at http://www.gloria-center.org/2002/09 /al-marashi-2002-09-01/.

Marfleet, Philip. "Never 'One Hand': Egypt 2011." In *Arms and the People: Popular Movements from the Paris Commune to the Arab Spring,* edited by Mike Gonzalez and Houman Barekat, 149–72. London: Pluto, 2013.

Martínez, Luis. *The Libyan Paradox.* New York: Columbia University Press, 2007.

Matthiesen, Toby. *Sectarian Gulf: Bahrain, Saudi Arabia, and the Arab Spring that Wasn't.* Stanford, CA: Stanford University Press, 2013.

McQuinn, Brian. "History's Warriors: The Emergence of Revolutionary Battalions in Misrata." In Cole and McQuinn, *Libyan Revolution,* 229–56.

Niethammer, Katja. "Calm and Squalls: The Small Gulf Monarchies in the Arab Spring." In Asseburg, *Protest, Revolt, and Regime Change,* 15–18.

Nolutshungu, Sam C. *Limits of Anarchy: Intervention and State Formation in Chad.* Charlottesville: University of Virginia Press, 1996.

Noueihed, Lin, and Alex Warren. *The Battle for the Arab Spring: Revolution, Counter-revolution and the Making of a New Era.* New Haven, CT: Yale University Press, 2012.

Owen, Roger. *The Rise and Fall of Arab Presidents for Life.* Cambridge, MA: Harvard University Press, 2012.

———. "The Arab 'Demonstration' Effect and the Revival of Arab Unity in the Arab Spring." *Contemporary Arab Affairs* 5:3 (July–September 2012): 372–81.

Pachon, Alejandro. "Loyalty and Defection: Misunderstanding Civil-Military Relations in Tunisia during the 'Arab Spring.'" *Journal of Strategic Studies* 37:4 (August 2014): 508–31.

Phillips, Sarah. *Yemen's Democracy Experiment in Regional Perspective: Patronage and Pluralized Authoritarianism.* New York: Palgrave Macmillan, 2008.

Pierret, Thomas. *Religion and State in Syria: The Sunni Ulama from Coup to Revolution.* New York: Cambridge University Press, 2013.

Pollack, Kenneth M. *Arabs at War: Military Effectiveness, 1948–1991.* Lincoln: University of Nebraska Press, 2002.

Quinlivan, James T. "Coup-Proofing: Its Practice and Consequences in the Middle East." *International Security* 24:2 (Fall 1999): 131–65.

Sater, James N. "Morocco's 'Arab' Spring." *Middle East Institute*, 1 October 2011. Accessed 16 February 2015 at http://www.mei.edu/content/morocco's -"arab"-spring.

Sayigh, Yezid. "Above the State: The Officers' Republic in Egypt." *The Carnegie Papers.* Washington, DC: CEIP, August 2012.

Seitz, Adam C. "Ties That Bind and Divide: The 'Arab Spring' and Yemeni Civil-Military Relations." In Lackner, *Why Yemen Matters*, 50–67.

Sharp, Jeremy M. "Egypt: Background and U.S. Relations." Washington, DC: Congressional Research Service, June 2014 (7-5700, RL33003).

Sorenson, David S. "Civil-Military Relations in North Africa." *Middle East Policy* 14:4 (Winter 2007): 99–114.

Steinberg, Guido. "Leading the Counter-Revolution: Saudi Arabia and the Arab Spring." *SWP Research Paper* #7. Berlin: Stiftung Wissenschaft und Politik, June 2014.

Sullivan, Marisa. *Hezbollah in Syria.* Washington, DC: Middle East Security Report #19, Institute for the Study of War, April 2014.

Valeri, Marc. "Oman." In *Power and Politics in the Persian Gulf Monarchies*, edited by Christopher M. Davidson, 136–60. New York: Columbia University Press, 2011.

Vandewalle, Dirk. *A History of Modern Libya.* New York: Cambridge University Press, 2006.

———. "Libya's Uncertain Revolution." In Cole and McQuinn, *Libyan Revolution*, 17–30.

Ware, L. B. "The Role of the Tunisian Military in the Post-Bourguiba Era." *Middle East Journal* 39 (Winter 1985): 27–47.

Weyland, Kurt. "The Arab Spring: Why the Surprising Similarities with the Revolutionary Wave of 1848?" *Perspectives on Politics* 10:4 (December 2012): 917–34.

Wilkinson, John. *Ibadism: Origins and Early Development in Oman.* New York: Oxford University Press, 2010.

Worrall, James. "Oman: The 'Forgotten' Corner of the Arab Spring." *Middle East Policy* 19:3 (Fall 2012): 98–115.

Wright, John L. *Libya, Chad, and the Central Sahara.* London: C. Hurst, 1989.

Yadav, Stacey Philbrick. "Antecedents of the Revolution: Intersectoral Networks and Post-Partisanship in Yemen." *Studies in Ethnicity and Nationalism* 11:3 (December 2011): 550–63.

Yom, Sean L., and F. Gregory Gause, III. "Resilient Royals: How Arab Monarchies Hang On." *Journal of Democracy* 23:4 (October 2012): 74–88.

Ziadeh, Radwan, Leon Hadar, Mark N. Katz, and Steven Heydemann. "Crisis in Syria: What Are the U.S. Options?" *Middle East Policy* 19:3 (Fall 2012): 1–24.

Zisser, Eyal. "The Syrian Army: Between the Domestic and the External Fronts." *Middle East Review of International Affairs* 5:1 (March 2001): 1–12.

Zunes, Stephen. "Bahrain's Arrested Revolution," *Arab Studies Quarterly* 35:2 (Spring 2013):149–64.

Other Sources

Ball, Deborah Yarsike. "Ethnic Conflict, Unit Performance, and the Soviet Armed Forces." *Armed Forces & Society* 20:2 (Winter 1994): 239–58.

Baynham, Simon. *The Military and Politics in Nkrumah's Ghana*. Boulder, CO: Westview Press, 1988.

Bechtol, Bruce E., Jr. *North Korea and Regional Security in the Kim Jong-un Era*. New York: Palgrave, 2014.

Bunbongkarn, Suchit. *The Military in Thai Politics*. Singapore: Institute of Southeast Asian Studies, 1987.

Cha, Victor. *The Impossible State: North Korea, Past and Future*. New York: Ecco, 2013.

Chalk, Peter. *The Malay-Muslim Insurgency in Southern Thailand*. Santa Monica, CA: Rand, 2008.

Clark, Juan. *Mito y Realidad: Testimonios de un Pueblo*. Miami: Saeta Ediciones, 1990.

French, Paul. *North Korea: State of Paranoia*. London: Zed Books, 2014.

Guerra, Lillian. *Visions of Power in Cuba: Revolution, Redemption, and Resistance, 1959–1971*. Chapel Hill: University of North Carolina Press, 2012.

Handley, Paul M. *The King Never Smiles: A Biography of Thailand's Bhumibol Adulyadej*. New Haven, CT: Yale University Press, 2006.

Harden, Blaine. *The Great Leader and the Fighter Pilot*. New York: Viking, 2015.

Lukowski, Jerzy, and Hubert Zawadzki. *A History of Poland*. New York: Cambridge University Press, 2006 [2nd ed.].

McCargo, Duncan. "Network Monarchy and Legitimacy Crises in Thailand." *Pacific Review* 18:4 (2005): 499–519.

Michishita, Narushige. *North Korea's Military-Diplomatic Campaigns, 1966–2008*. London: Routledge, 2011.

Mills, C. Wright. *Listen Yankee! The Revolution in Cuba*. New York: McGraw-Hill, 1960.

Misol, Lisa. *Unkept Promise: Failure to End Military Business Activity in Indonesia*. New York: Human Rights Watch, 2010.

Mitchell, Lincoln A. *The Color Revolutions*. Philadelphia: University of Pennsylvania Press, 2012.

Montesano, Michael John, and Patrick Jory, eds. *Thai South and Malay North: Ethnic Interactions on the Plural Peninsula*. Singapore: NUS Press, 2008.

Shifaw, Dawit. *The Diary of Terror: Ethiopia 1974–1991*. Bloomington, IN: Trafford, 2012.

Woo, Jongseok. "Kim Jong-il's Military-First Politics and Beyond: Military Control Mechanisms and the Problem of Power Succession." *Communist and Post-Communist Studies* 47:2 (June 2014): 117–25.

Index